Other books by Roger S. Gottlieb

History and Subjectivity: The Transformation of Marxist Theory
Marxism 1844-1990: Origins, Betrayal, Rebirth
A Spirituality of Resistance: Finding a Peaceful Heart and Protecting the Earth
Joining Hands: Politics and Religion Together for Social Change
A Greener Faith: Religious Environmentalism and Our Planet's Future
Engaging Voices: Tales of Morality and Meaning in an Age of Global Warming
Spirituality: What It Is and Why It Matters

Edited by Roger S. Gottlieb

An Anthology of Western Marxism: From Lukacs and Gramsci to Socialist-Feminism
A New Creation: America's Contemporary Spiritual Voices
Thinking the Unthinkable: Meanings of the Holocaust
Radical Philosophy: Tradition, Counter-Tradition, Politics
This Sacred Earth: Religion, Nature, Environment (First and Second editions)
The Ecological Community
Deep Ecology and World Religions: New Essays on Common Ground
(with David L. Barnhill)
Liberating Faith: Religious Voices for Justice, Peace, and Ecological Wisdom
The Oxford Handbook of Religion and Ecology
Religion and the Environment

POLITICAL AND SPIRITUAL

Essays on Religion, Environment, Disability, and Justice

Roger S. Gottlieb

ROWMAN & LITTLEFIELD
Lanham • Boulder • New York • London

Published by Rowman & Littlefield
A wholly owned subsidiary of The Rowman & Littlefield
Publishing Group, Inc.
4501 Forbes Boulevard, Suite 200, Lanham, Maryland 20706
www.rowman.com

Unit A, Whitacre Mews, 26-34 Stannery Street, London SE11 4AB,
United Kingdom

British Library Cataloguing in Publication Information Available

Library of Congress Control Number: 2014952284

∞ ™ The paper used in this publication meets the minimum requirements of
American National Standard for Information Sciences Permanence of Paper
for Printed Library Materials, ANSI/NISO Z39.48-1992.

Printed in the United States of America

Earth's the right place for love: I don't know
where it's likely to go better.
—Robert Frost, "Birches"

CONTENTS

INTRODUCTION

Written over the last three decades, these essays embody a philosophical perspective on our collective struggles for a just, rational, and caring society and our personal strivings for contentment, wisdom, and compassion.

My philosophical writings emerged from the two sides of my personal identity: serious involvement in the New Left political movements of the 1960s and 70s—and search for insights from non-ordinary, more enlightened, forms of consciousness. Or, more concretely: participation in anti-war and other leftist organizations—and psychedelic experiences, meditative practices, and fifteen months on the road in the Far East. As early as the mid-seventies I described the necessary connection between personal enlightenment and movements for social justice in a lecture titled "Why Bodhisattvas Belong on the Barricades." I sensed that these often opposed perspectives shared a common rejection of society's oppressive and unfulfilling values, institutions, and ways of understanding human beings; and it has been a central task of my theoretical life to try to show how they can help compensate for each other's deficiencies and support each other's aims.

Social and political philosophy, particularly Marxism and feminism, had made clear to me that our beliefs, relationships, and institutions are collective products, set in great measure by social structures. These structures are in many ways unjust and irrational; and it is the task of philosophy as I understand it to criticize present reality (capitalism, patriarchy, racism, anthropocentrism, anti-Semitism, and all the rest) and describe a better one; to be the intellectual dimension of a movement for progressive social change.

At the same time, however, human reality also encompasses a psychologically based spiritual dimension. This, while perhaps not timeless, has remained relatively stable for at least two and a half millennia. Plato's central question—is it better to be an unjust man thought just or a just man thought unjust?—is as relevant as statistics about depression in the world's richest country or headlines about relentless greed among Wall Street CEOs. Craving, envy, violence, the lust for power, self-hatred, unnecessary repression of our legitimate needs—all these call for the work of personal as well as social change: for the spiritual virtues of mindfulness, acceptance, gratitude, compassion, and love.

In this perspective politics and spirituality (and versions of institutional religion not dogmatically attached to being the sole metaphysical truth) are not separate, parallel pursuits—one collective and public, the other personal and private. Ideally, they will combine in a manner that enables each tradition, set of insights, and practices to help overcome the deficiencies of the other.

My earliest publications were separate papers on Marxism and Kierkegaard, followed by studies of individual thinkers and problems; a challenge to the left's inability to comprehend Jewish experience and the Arab-Israeli conflict; and a philosophical analysis of Jewish resistance during the Holocaust.[1]

My first book was an attempt to transform Marxist tradition in light of the history of the New Left, socialist, communist, Civil Rights, and feminist movements, the transition from competitive to state managed monopoly capitalism, and my own personal connection to anti-Semitism and Jewish identity.[2] Its conclusions are the starting point for the essays gathered here: Economic structures (*the* source of social change according to traditional historical materialism) are in advanced capitalism joined by socialization processes (especially gender) and degrees of political cooperation among socially differentiated groups (defined by class *and* race, ethnicity, gender, sexual preference, etc.) as socially primary in the creation of a just and liberated society. How we are conditioned as men and women and the degree of solidarity we can generate across lines of social difference had become—I argued—as important as the economic and political consequences of capitalist development. Economic forces might set the possibilities of social change, but which possibilities would be realized depended on these other factors.

Further, the history of radical movements of the late 19th and 20th centuries revealed countless instances in which the pursuit of social transformation devolved into careerism, opportunism, racism and sexism, or tyrannical domination. Clearly, something was missing from the left's analysis of social life and from the moral and emotional development of leftists.

This something had a great deal to do with personal maturity, emotional intelligence, the ability to deal reasonably and responsibly with political differences, masculine attachment to domination, and a failure to realize, as French socialist Andre Gorz observed, that the working class will not make a revolution merely for a ten percent increase in pay.[3] Other goals than state power and a better material standard of living were necessary. And other techniques than theoretical tomes, demands, demonstrations, political parties, verbal violence, and emotional armoring were required. I concluded that despite their enduring importance progressive political movements had theoretical and practical blind spots which required the moral and psychological insights of spiritual traditions.

Within the horizon of political theory itself, I found a theoretical commitment to the importance of psychology, socialization, emotional comportment, gender, and relationality in the work of Western Marxists[4] (Karl Korsch, Georg Lukacs, Max Horkheimer, Theodor Adorno, Wilhelm Reich, Herbert Marcuse) and socialist-feminists (Sheila Rowbotham, Juliet Mitchell, Anne Ferguson). But while I found these thinkers tremendously important, they lacked a detailed understanding of the psychology of attachment, the virtues of compassion, gratitude, and love, and techniques for self-transformation that are the heart of spiritual teachings.

This heart I found both within and outside of formal, organized religions: in sources as diverse as Kierkegaard, Buddhism, Elie Wiesel, Riane Eisler, Gandhi, Thich Nhat Hanh, Chogyam Trungpa, Martin Luther King, Aung San Suu Kyi, Joanna Macy, I. L. Peretz, Michael Lerner, David Steindl-Rast, and Dorothy Day; and in the practices of yoga, meditation, and prayer.[5] Spirituality, as I conceived it, was rooted in the idea that spiritual virtues such as acceptance and compassion were the only sure path to lasting human fulfillment. Thus conceived spirituality is compatible with any and all religious metaphysics (God, Heaven, revelation, etc.) or with none. It is, essentially, moral and psychological.[6] The only faith it requires is the verifiable belief that, for example, living with gratitude will make one happier and a lot more fun to be around than living with envy, greed, or discontent. Also, spiritual traditions possess resources to deal with life's ineluctable realities (for example, birth, aging, death) typically lacked by exclusively political perspectives.

Yet purely spiritual perspectives, uninformed by progressive political insights, tend to concentrate on the psychology of the individual without attending to the social context in which the individual arises; and to ignore how oppressive ideologies and social structures are reproduced within religious or spiritual settings. The task, therefore, was not to replace radical politics with a morally critical spirituality, but to try to find some way for them to enlighten each other: to infuse political movements with spiritual values, and spiritual practices with awareness of social realities. I did not abandon Marxist theory or the broad political goals of the New Left, but sought to expand them with humanity's accumulated spiritual wisdom. Meditating on the barricades would strengthen both the revolutionary tide and the spiritual center.

By 1990 a new theme became central to my writing, teaching, and personal reflection: the comprehensive environmental crisis embodied in climate destabilization, global spread of toxins, elimination of countless other life forms, mass slaughter of animals, destruction of ecosystems, and technological colonization of mental space by media and gadgets. This crisis reflects virtually all aspects of our civilization—capitalism, to be sure, but also patriarchy, racial oppression, speciesism, consumerism, nationalism, the scientistic reduction of nature, and the commodification of all of life.

To the political left the environmental crisis posed new questions: was the universality of the problem the basis of a potentially more inclusive political movement? Did the fact that the vast majority of leftists in developed countries contributed to ecological damage demand a reduction in verbal self-righteousness and aggression? What did the left have to offer to a population addicted to environmentally polluting consumerism? How much could Marxism's critique of capitalism or feminism's of patriarchy help us understand what had happened and what we should do about it—and how much did those perspectives themselves have to shift?[7]

Similarly, spiritual traditions—so rich in resources for physical and psychological health, and teachings of compassion and love—now confronted a planetary emergency in which simply "changing yourself before you change the world" would inevitably be a kind of self-indulgence; and also the psychological truth that it is often impossible to change oneself without trying to live a morally and socially connected life. More starkly, contemporary spirituality's tendencies to narcissism, consumerism, and escapism not only violated the essential principles of the best of spiritual traditions, but tended towards complete irrelevance in the face of a toxic and toxifying environment. The same questions were posed for organized religion—and in a surprising and hopeful turn a multitude of theologians, religious leaders, and lay people have risen to the challenge with deep theological change, profound institutional commitment, and thousands of examples of real world political action. Chronicling global faith's response to environmental crisis became an essential part of my intellectual work.[8]

I had another reason to focus on spirituality and organized religion. It was not only that spiritual traditions held rich resources for social change, but that a vocabulary of religious tradition and spiritual insight might prove at least as motivating as one grounded in class struggle or liberation from oppression. As far as I could see, working class movements had been limited to trade union self-protection; and feminist and racial politics were too often defined by personal enhancement or the interests of one particular group. The vast majority of the population seemed stuck in politically quiescent passivity so different from the raucous and utopian movements of my youth. At the same time, many people remained within the orbit of traditional religions and tens of millions defined themselves as "spiritual but not religious." Therefore, it might be *politically* significant that despoiling the earth and wreaking environmental injustice on racial minorities were violations of traditional religious teachings and that consumerism could not coexist with authentic spirituality. The language and the style of the politics of my youth, though not without important historical effects, had reached their limits. It was necessary to appeal to a wider variety of ideological and personal identities.

Two other themes are represented in these essays, both of intense personal importance. The first is my Jewish identity. Raised in a moderately assimilated middle class suburban family, it was not until my early thirties that I realized the deep connection I had to my Jewishness. This realization stemmed from seeing the latent anti-Semitism of some of my political comrades—who embraced the cause of every oppressed group but to whom anti-Semitism remained invisible; from getting to know my wife and her parents, who were survivors of the Holocaust; and as a person seeking spiritual development who came to see much of value in Jewish tradition. My studies of the Holocaust connected that event—as warning and lesson—to my understanding of the environmental crisis.[9]

Finally, there is disability. As the parent of a daughter with multiple handicaps, I know that my situation—and hers—cannot be understood without joining both political and spiritual perspectives. The first is needed to comprehend issues of justice and inclusion, and to envision a social order which welcomes rather than shuns difference and vulnerability; the latter to reveal the possibilities of love in the midst of suffering and loss.

Despite their different areas of focus these essays all reflect my attempt at a unified understanding of the human condition. As in the title of this book, I believe that we are all "Political and Spiritual": power and justice, love and compassion, hopes for a better world and a more contented life run through our conscious lives and haunt our dreams. I have sought to use philosophy to make sense of those hopes—for myself, for other theorists, and for those who rather than writing philosophical essays raise food, build bridges, teach children, or heal the sick.

✿ ✿ ✿

In the first two essays of Part I, mysticism and spirituality, often thought to offer ways to escape the burdens and limits of society and history, are shown to be a part of them. In turn, deep ecology is explored as a spiritual connection to nature that enables us to transcend the social ego; but also a perspective in need of correctives from critical social theory to avoid escapist or oppressive stances. I argue that the resources of liberating social movements such as socialism and feminism can serve as antidotes to the limits of mysticism in general and spiritual deep ecology in particular; but that in turn purely political movements too willingly accept the conventional social ego, lack practices of self-transformation, and too often repeat oppressive features of the social forms they seek to overthrow. Mysticism, spirituality, and an ego transcending connection to nature can help overcome these deficiencies.

The third essay roots the socially oriented ethical theories of Levinas, feminism, and deep ecology in the traumas of the Holocaust, male domination, and the environmental crisis. The essay on animal rights emerged from my growing concern with our collective inability to listen to people who have different beliefs. It suggests ways in which spiritually oriented virtues of empathy and self-understanding might help opposing sides in animal rights debates come to improved mutual engagement.[10]

Part II examines the remarkable fusion of politics and religion in religious environmentalism. The theological, institutional, and political greening of religion is one of the crucial—and hopeful—cultural changes of the last thirty years.[11] This remarkable development is a practical confirmation of my argument that politics and spirituality (broadly construed to include certain forms of post-Enlightenment religion) can support each other's shared critique of the injustice and irrationality that characterize so much of modern society. As a motivating discourse for a large percentage of human beings, religion offers a key resource for environmental activism.

After an overview, separate essays explore religious environmentalism's connection to questions of religious diversity, and what the concept of sustainability can mean in a religious context. The final essay describes my attempt to blend the theoretical and practical, verbal and experiential, political and spiritual, personal and objective in teaching a university course on the environmental crisis. The fusion of dimensions typically alienated from each other is, I believe, demanded by the combined immediacy and universality of the crisis.

Parts III and IV focus on the particularities of Jewish identity and on disability. In Part III, the Holocaust—so compelling a challenge to human culture in its own right—offers lessons for our collective response to ecological problems. "Justice in a Time of Madness" and "What Difference Does It Make That We're Jewish?" examine how a Jewish cultural identity shaped by historical experience and philosophical/theological viewpoints may lead Jews to face the environmental crisis in a distinctly Jewish as well as a commonly human way; and may confer on Jews both specific insights and tasks. The concluding essay cautions against dangerously simplistic and overly certain perspectives on the Israeli-Palestinian conflict.

In Part IV we see how the realities of disability and caretaking for the disabled challenge political or spiritual perspectives which ignore these realities. Yet even as they are changed by it, our political and spiritual traditions help us understand disability as a concept, a social identity, and a form of intensely personal experience. "Disability and the Tasks of Social Justice" was written to briefly describe some essential concepts for coming to grips with the subject and to suggest ways of teaching it. "One True Faith" focuses on the religious commonality I share with American Baptist scholar and teacher Bill J. Leonard, who also parents a daughter with disabilities.

Part V examines two questions that challenge the book's overriding framework. First, are the human problems progressive politics and spirituality seek to resolve solvable by technological advances? Second, how can the equanimity offered by a spiritual perspective survive the realization of both personal and mass (environmental) death? My responses are necessarily tentative explorations of questions that we will turn to again and again. If they help the reader think a little more deeply about the first and feel a little comforted about the second, they will have served their purpose.

As dark as our times, as tempting as despair may be, we are still here—still blessed with the miraculous gift of life. In all my writing I have tried to use my philosophical intelligence in the service of that miracle—to face the truth of the world's pain and find in the human passions for justice and spiritual wisdom ways to alleviate our collective suffering. Earth *is* the right place for love. May we find ways to do it better.

NOTES

1. "A Marxian Concept of Ideology," *Philosophical Forum*, Vol. VI, No. 4, Summer, 1975; "Kierkegaard's Ethical Individualism," *Monist*, July 1979, Vol. 62, No. 3; "The Dialectics of National Identity," *Socialist Review*, No. 47,

September–October 1979; "The Concept of Resistance: Jewish Resistance During the Holocaust," *Social Theory and Practice*, Vol. 9, No. 1, April 1983.

2. *History and Subjectivity: The Transformation of Marxist Theory* (Philadelphia: Temple University Press, 1987).

3. Andre Gorz, "Socialism and Revolution." in Roger S. Gottlieb, ed., *An Anthology of Western Marxism: From Lukacs and Gramsci to Socialist-Feminism* (New York: Oxford University Press, 1990), p. 218.

4. I describe their role in some detail in *History and Subjectivity* and the Introduction to *An Anthology of Western Marxism*.

5. My first survey of these ideas can be found in *A New Creation: America's Contemporary Spiritual Voices* (New York: Crossroad, 1990). The book includes my essay "A Dialogue between a Political Radical and a Spiritual Seeker."

6. This perspective is fully elaborated in *Spirituality: What It Is and Why It Matters* (New York: Oxford University Press, 2013).

7. I investigate these questions in more detail in the Introduction to Roger S. Gottlieb, ed., *The Ecological Community* (New York: Routledge, 1996).

8. My first major effort here was *This Sacred Earth: Religion, Nature, Environment* (New York: Routledge, 1995).

9. I explored this connection in several places, including chapters 3 and 5 of *A Spirituality of Resistance: Finding a Peaceful Heart and Protecting the Earth* (Lanham, MD: Rowman & Littlefield, 2003).

10. This theme of listening to the other is a central sub-text of my environmental short story collection: *Engaging Voices: Tales of Morality and Meaning in an Age of Global Warming* (Waco, TX: Baylor University Press, 2012).

11. My comprehensive analysis is in *A Greener Faith: Religious Environmentalism and Our Planet's Future* (New York: Oxford University Press, 2006).

I

Spirit, Justice, Nature

I

THE TRANSCENDENCE OF JUSTICE AND THE JUSTICE OF TRANSCENDENCE

Mysticism, Deep Ecology, and Political Life

Humanity's responses to the perils and pains of existence give rise to many attempts to see the sources of our suffering, to escape or transcend our limits, and to form or recognize communities of solidarity—both with other people and with beings who are not people. The cry of the heart has gone out to gods and goddesses; to totem animals and sacred mountains; and to those with whom we would join on the barricades. In the desperate time of the present, as cynics celebrate the end of alternatives to global capitalism, global industrialism, and global technoaddiction, those of us who are not entranced by the prospect of a fully administered society search for something else. Sensing the bleak and poisonous prospects around us, we shrink from pollution that is physical, psychic, and moral. Surely, we believe (as people have always believed) that there is some other choice we can make. Surely we can find some wisdom with which to confront the soulless intelligence of modernity and the amoral cyberchic of postmodernity. Surely we can touch with our living hearts the Heart of the World, and listen to the secret revelations of its unending beat. Surely, at least as individuals, we do not have to be bound by the endless commodification of the living world. Surely, if we cannot defeat or change, then we can *transcend* that which surrounds us.

One name for that transcendence is mysticism. It has for thousands of years signified the attempt to move beyond the confines of society and history; to break the bounds of normal human interaction, normal consciousness, and normal physical reality. It has been, or has been claimed to be, the foundation for a wisdom beyond—or hidden beneath—"this world." Yet, as we shall see in relation to the present, the world has a way of persisting in the face of the most transcendent of wisdoms. It is the struggle between transcendence and the social world, and the dangers which attend each, that are the subjects of this essay.

MYSTICISM

This term is used to describe a variety of at times overwhelming, often life-defining, experiences, experiences which give rise to fundamental shifts in how we sense the nature of both the universe and our own personal identity. For many those experiences are the heart of the world's religions. Beyond details of dogma, institutional organization, or even ethical teachings, the direct encounter with the divine seems to make possible a temporary release from the boundaries of the social ego and the socially constructed understanding of the body. It is this encounter which promises an alternate possibility to constricted forms of self-definition, and offers an answer to merely local claims about who we are, what we owe each other, and what we can be. The truths contained in mystical experiences seem to dwarf parochial understandings. People see them as "perennial" (as in "the perennial wisdom"), to be hidden from people not mature enough to grapple with the insights that mystical experience can confer, and even containing a hint of danger if misunderstood or misappropriated (as in the Yogic warnings about the perils of developing psychic powers without the appropriate ethical development).

Mystical experiences are celebrated in every religious tradition. Consider, for example, the "Arhat," the type of the Sage in the original form of Buddhism which has come to be known as "Therevada." In his religious practices the Arhat seeks an end to the psychic confinement caused by mistaken identification with a self bound to desires and attachments. Intellectually, the Arhat has come to believe that this identification is the source of great pain (as the Buddha taught in the first of the Four Noble Truths). Yet intellectual acceptance of the first Noble Truth does not necessarily produce a sense of self (or "non-self") which is actually free of attachment. The question arises: is it in fact possible to be alive as a human being and *not* identify with a conventionally understood self, a collection of desires, aversions, etc.? This question is answered—and what we might call mystical wisdom arises—when the student directly experiences a state of mind in which identification with self dissipates. As one early practitioner is reputed to have said, when questioned by a fellow seeker: "During my meditation I reached a point where I had no thought that 'I am this; this is mine; this is my self.'"[1]

Or consider the prophet Elijah. Fleeing for his life from Jezebel's wrath after he put to death the prophets of Baal, he encounters God not in a mighty wind, an earthquake, or a fire, but in a "still, small voice." (I Kings 19:11-12). The voice is "inside him." It is a source of ultimate knowledge; or, in the case of what is typically stressed in Jewish scriptures, of ultimate moral responsibly—a responsibility which takes precedence over all merely social, merely conventional, customs or forms of authority. The experience of God's voice provides an ultimate ethical arbiter which releases us from any conflicting obligations to social powers.

Consider how the poet William Blake saw Christ suspended in air, dancing outside his window. Or the states of ecstatic no-self produced by Sufi dancing or tribal chanting; or the transformations of consciousness which come on a Native American Vision Quest, prepared for by days of fasting and isolation. Or consider the feminist image of a divine interconnection and sharing and mingling of mind, emotion, and body; an interconnection in which God does not speak from the Heavens or even within our hearts, but emerges in the sacred spaces which both separate and connect us.[2]

In all these (and the legion more which could be discussed) we find the wisdom of mysticism. This wisdom provides an end, or at least a temporary alternative to, the ego's twisted identification with a psychic condition of permanent dissatisfaction, insecurity, and violence. From attachment to a particular social role, we move to an identification with a cosmic harmony for which possessions, status, or social group become merely relative, merely historical, essentially contingent. From attachment to our particular, personal, self-owned pains and pleasures, we move to a celebration of the infinite fields of energy which move through us. As in the case of Elijah, we develop a deeply altered and often highly critical sense of the meaning and validity of social life: of its teaching about what is important, of its norms of human interaction, of its models of success or adequacy.

Perhaps most important: while the intensity of the experience fades, and may be hard even to remember at times (it is said that Pascal, having had an experience of God, sewed an image of the sun or a phrase beginning "fire, fire" into his clothes to remind himself), the wisdom of mysticism opens the receiver up to a clarity of understanding about what is of lasting importance in the realms of everyday, non-transcendent life. Variously known as love, grace, peace, or care, the wisdom of mysticism releases us from the bondage to patterns of emotion which ultimately serve neither ourselves nor others. The demands that we earn a lot of money, that we be beautiful, that we make war on our "enemies," that we believe the government, that we manage to be successful at being "men" or "women"—these snarling dogs of desire ("fires" the Buddha called them) become the tame lap-cats of tamed desire. We escape—initially only for a moment but then for much longer if we are able to maintain the power of the memory of that moment—the demands, evaluations, and definitions of our social existence. Maintaining this memory requires stern but rewarding discipline, described in detail in the mystical traditions. If we follow these paths of prayer, meditation, fasting, study, retreat, knowledge, and/or service, the traditions promise, we will be ever more released from the bondage of false attachments.

And it is in just this promise that the danger lies: the place where mysticism can betray itself and deteriorate into self-deception, folly, and escapism. For mysticism can be and has been used simply to evade that which is frightening, confusing, or difficult *in* the social realm. In such cases it is motivated by an inability to face what is threatening in the world-as-it-is, and what the mystic really seeks is escape. In such cases the mystic claims to have experienced—and at times to offer to others—the Truth of the Whole; but he is really simply avoiding what is distasteful.

For instance, we become entranced by, even addicted to, the *experience* of the mystical state. It is so lofty, so sweet, such a relief from how awful we feel most of the time. And when we are under it or in it or up to it, we do not have to take seriously our suffering, anyone else's suffering, or the ways in which it is not only what Buddhists would call the folly of individual attachment, but also social evil which causes that suffering.

This danger of mysticism is that it becomes in Kierkegaard's sense merely "aesthetic": merely a series of experiences which do not contribute to the formation of an ethical and spiritual character. Merely something which, in the end, is another titillation, another object of desire, another way to pacify a self that has not been transformed, but merely thrilled or sedated.

Put another way, the danger of mysticism is that it can become an escape from concerns about other people. Entranced by the cosmic oneness of it all, we end up forgetting or ignoring the other people in the room, on our block, or on our globe. Feeling cared for by an infinite source of love, we forget (inadvertently? to some extent intentionally?) that it is up to us to manifest as well as receive that love. And that if we do not, our own access to the source will become more and more strained, desperate, and attenuated.

[Many years ago a teacher of yoga and meditation instructed me: "Do not be distracted by sounds in your practice, but use them. For instance, if you are meditating and you hear a loud siren outside your window, instead of feeling interrupted you can simply take in that energy, move it up your spine to your crown chakra and use it to further your practice."

A useful tip I thought a first. But then I thought further, and asked him: "Sir, this sounds a fine idea if, for instance, the siren is simply from an ambulance on its way to a nearby hospital. But what if it is the siren of the police vans which, in Amsterdam, took Jews to be transported to the death camps? When is the sound a source of energy to be incorporated into the meditation? and when is it an indication that we need to end the meditation, look outside ourselves, and act in resistance to help innocent people who are being murdered? And what is the source of an ability to discern between the two?"]

What I am saying here is not meant to discredit mysticism. While there are elements which resemble Marx's or Nietzsche's critiques of religion, I do not accept their fundamental antagonism to spiritual life. Unlike them, I believe that mystical experience contains the possibility of Great Truth. *And* I am suggesting that it also contains the chance of Real Error. In fact, it is just because mystical experience contains the

Powers of Truth—relief from suffering, transcendence of social limitations, insights into Connectedness, Grace, Gaia, or God—that we can
use those experiences as distractions, pain-killers, or excuses to Look
the Other Way.

The danger that mysticism may become (merely) aesthetic or serve
as a spiritual by-pass of the moral and the political are not unknown in
religious culture. In traditional Judaism, a person does not approach the
mysticism of the Kabbalah until he is established in family and community relationships. Typically, not until the age of forty. The entire history
of Buddhism is marked by a split over precisely the nature of mystical
enlightenment and the role of the enlightened person in the community. While Theravada Buddhism saw the Sage as ultimately no more
than a person who provides an example to others that Enlightenment is
possible, Mahayana Buddhism arose partly out of the critique of what it
took to be the selfish and ultimately self-defeating character of that
ideal. In its place, the Mahayana offered the image of the Bodhisattva,
who refuses ultimate Enlightenment in order to help all other sentient
beings to achieve it. Such a person is like a strong young man who,
when his household is lost in a dangerous forest, stays with the group to
help them all to safety rather than making his own way home.

Yet the awareness of these traditions is itself suspect in part because
of the duality of all mystical encounters: at once a communion with
energies which transcend society *and also* experiences processed,
understood, and described in words by socially situated human beings.
The pervasive sexism of even the most mystically founded traditions
should remind us that while God or goddess may touch us directly, our
response to that touch will necessarily bear some imprint of our contingent selves. For example, it was not in fact a "person" who, when suit-
ably mature, was allowed by the Rabbis to study the Kabbalah. It was
always and only men. The claim that we speak with truth about, as
opposed to simply that we have experienced, a Truth Beyond Question
has too often been a strategy for Power Over the Uninitiated.

In our time the dangers of mysticism are especially real, because
much of mysticism in the advanced industrial societies is disconnected
from tradition, community, and personal responsibility. It was, after all,
in great measure the widespread use of psychedelic drugs which
brought an interest in ecstatic states back into a society defined by
professionalism, technology, and television. The power of these drugs—

for many people an instant revelation—was precisely their impotence. Since nothing had prepared us for what they offered—and we had not seriously prepared ourselves—the next day's psychic life was often no more holy than the day before. At best, the drug experience was a signal that there was more to life than was dreamed of at Harvard Business School or the National Science Foundation. At best, it served only as a beginning to a long and difficult search.

Further, since the cavalier cultural raids on ancient and tribal traditions of the 1980s, one can learn the secrets of a South American Shaman for the cost of a weekend's time and a few hundred dollars. (This will be a wonderful experience. And next month we can learn witchcraft. Or perhaps the mysteries of the Druids.) The consequence is that far from becoming an alternative to the limitations of social life, mystical experience becomes one more commodity—with no more ultimate spiritual meaning than anything else that can be bought or sold.

In short, while the actual Truths disclosed by mystical experience may in fact be just those truths all of us need to know, our access to them has always been (and perhaps, given the depth and extent of the presence of society, are now even more so) conditioned by the social setting in which they unfold.

And in fact, it is precisely that social setting which has led to a return—on something approaching a mass scale—of a mysticism which takes the earth and all its life as an ultimate truth.

DEEP ECOLOGY

The crucial fact of our time is that we may be destroying the very life support systems which make human life possible. With less uncertainty we can say that we have *already* extinguished countless species, poured millions of tons of toxic wastes into the air, earth, and water, and altered the earth's atmosphere and climate.

A variety of environmental movements and philosophies have arisen in response to this crisis. From the heart of the spiritual impulse and the memories of countless generations in which forest and grassland, bird and wolf and salmon were our home and family and intimate enemy, comes Deep Ecology.

The Deep Ecology of which I speak here is not the version presented in the technical language of philosophical ethics, where debates
about varieties of intrinsic as opposed to instrumental value take place.
Rather, I speak of a passionate, spiritually oriented, mystical communion with the earth and its many beings; a recognition of kinship with
those beings which no more requires philosophical justification than
does the connection we feel with our parents, our pets, or our lovers. As
such Deep Ecology is a spiritual philosophy; and the deepest experiences which animate its adherents are profoundly mystical.[3] What is
"deep" about this perspective is the experience—and the conviction—
that our surroundings are essential to what we are. And this not just
because they are useful, but because we are indeed tied to them by
invisible threads of longing, teaching, learning, connection, struggle for
existence, and memory. Sky and earth, bird and fish, each leaf on each
tree—all these mirror who and what we are; indeed, without them, we
could not be ourselves.

This Deep Ecology is not, nor could it possibly be, a recent creation.
As humans have evolved physically, cognitively, culturally, and spiritually in a setting bounded by beings who are not people, so a recognition
of our delight in them and affinity with them has been present throughout all human cultures.

There is a Midrash (a Jewish spiritual story which aims to enlighten
rather than legislate) which speaks of trees: "When a tree that bears
fruit is cut down, its moan goes round the world. Yet no sound is
heard." Or even more poignantly, in the words of the eighteenth century Hasidic Rebbe Nachman: "If a person kills a tree before its time, it is
like having murdered a soul." The Medieval Catholic Hildegaard of
Bingen saw God in the physical world: "I, the fiery life of divine essence, am aflame beyond the beauty of the meadows, I gleam in the
waters, and I burn in the sun, moon, and stars. . . . I awaken everything
to life." The *Koran* was confident that "the creation of the heavens and
the Earth is greater than the creation of humankind; Yet most people
understand not." And the World Council of Indigenous Peoples stated
in 1977 that in their past "The earth was our nurturing mother, the
night sky formed our common roof, the Sun and the Moon were our
parents. . . ."[4]

This recognition is also found in non-denominational, often explicitly
non-religious, nature writing which celebrates a luminous moment of

seeing in which the natural world speaks to us. In her celebrated essay "Living Like Weasels" Annie Dillard describes a moment when, face-to-face with a weasel: "our eyes locked, and someone threw away the key. Our look was as if two lovers, or deadly enemies, met unexpectedly on an overgrown path when each had been thinking of something else" (Dillard 1982, 14).

Similarly, Aldo Leopold, one of the inspirations of the deep ecological turn in contemporary environmental ethics, speaks of seeing a "fierce green fire" in the eyes of a dying wolf he had himself shot, and of never again thinking of wolves, or mountains, or wilderness in the same way (Leopold 1949).

Considered as a form of spirituality—as a way of moving beyond the conventional social understanding of the self or of the social construction of the body—Deep Ecology articulates a powerful and pervasive sensibility. It unifies and expands our childhood love for an animal, the times as adolescents when only the woods or fields seem to understand us, the moments of grace we feel watching a sunrise, or light glinting over ice-covered branches, or hearing birds sing on a surprisingly warm day in March. Knitting together these moments, a deep ecological perspective simply says: "You are more than your profession and race and religion and even gender. In your cells and sinews and even your atoms there is a tie to all this which surrounds you. Open yourself up to this source of grace and peace and love. More important, open yourself up to the love you feel for it."

Deep Ecology also, as Joanna Macy (1994) observes, signals something of our capacity to love and the reality of our connections to other beings across space and time. Our sadness for the burning rainforests and casually eliminated species is a sign that despite everything we can still love—and mourn. As Deep Ecology sings of the joy we feel in our delight of nature, so it must also have us join in the requiem for what we have ourselves helped to kill. Our pain is not simply that things will be inconvenienced: that recreation will be interfered with because the forest has been clear-cut; that a potential cancer cure has been lost as the rainforest burns; that 40 thousand people in Newfoundland's fishing communities have lost their jobs because mechanized trawlers strip mined the cod fishery. The earth is not just being polluted, deep ecology suggests, it is being *desecrated*. Something more than useful, more than physically pleasing, something *holy* is being torn to bits for what are typically the most trivial, thoughtless, or downright cruel of reasons. Thus Deep Ecology highlights the limitations of a purely instrumental attitude towards nature, an attitude which reduces non-human nature to quantities of stuff to be measured, mastered, and commodified. As a philosophy based in powerful emotional experiences, Deep Ecology expresses simply and directly what many people feel: a love and concern for the natural world. As more familiar mystical experiences might alter our attitudes towards death, our fear of the unknown, or our petty insecurities, realization of our kinship with the earth confirms the need to question any unquestioned trashing of our dear relations. Its insights can teach us to see the familiar in a new way; challenging our taken-for-granted beliefs, practices, and institutions.

Deep Ecology, like all forms of mysticism, comprises knowledge as well as emotionally meaningful experiences. It reminds us of truths which industrial civilization and many forms of patriarchy have obscured; for example, that we are physical beings, made of the same stuff as earth and stream and air; or that we need wilderness because, as Edward Abbey (1977) observed, we ourselves are wild animals. As Paul Shepard argued (1982), we develop a good deal of our language, our sense of ourselves, our understanding of morality, and our very sensory apparatus from direct or symbolic lessons from the natural world. As David Abram (1996) suggests, the boundaries between the human and the more-than-human are the sources of knowledge about balance and integrity for the human community; and for time out of mind wisdom was sought beyond those boundaries, and seen as vested in the shamans, priestesses, and prophets who journeyed there.

Finally, an identification with nature can be the source of deep pleasure and deeper calm. Just as people who hear the voice of God may feel a little differently about a flat tire or being passed over for a promotion, so a felt connection with a tree or a bird can soothe the anxieties and relieve the sense of overwhelming pressure to achieve or possess in the social realm. Such a connection might even, if we let it, help us learn not to be quite so (desperately, compulsively) busy. Experiencing ourselves as natural as well as social, part of a cosmos as well as a community, we can find a remedy for the kinds of neurosis that typically are not part of the lives of ants, birches, or elks.

Even my anxiety over the fate of the environment can be soothed by the experience of connection with it. I can, for instance, see the rainforest not only as an object I am trying to save, but, in John Seed's words: "See myself as *part* of the rainforest trying to save itself" (Seed, Macy, Fleming 1991, 8). And I can then realize that even desperation to save nature need have no place in my life. As the leaves on the trees that I love, I can only do my bit and then drift gently down to the forest floor and make way for more life.

And, once again, here is where the dangers arise. For Deep Ecology (just as other forms of mysticism) can slide too easily into the attempt to escape society, or to bring into the social realm one of the more pernicious forms of religious ideology and practice. There are, in fact, at least four central dangers which face Deep Ecology in this regard.

First, there is the problem that mystical experience can give rise to fundamentalism. Given the long history—and the present resurgence—of religiously motivated violence and narrow-mindedness, this is a bleak prospect indeed. While Deep Ecology is a powerful critic of modernist scientific and economic reductionism, it is, as Michael Zimmerman (1995) has argued, always quite difficult to transcend the limitations of the Enlightenment while simultaneously keeping its accomplishments. We see the consequences of the rejection of those accomplishments in religious totalitarianism of all stripes. Political notions of individual rights and a spiritual understanding that mystical knowledge is essentially metaphorical are both foreign to any form of fundamentalism. The Mullahs of whatever faith are sure they know what God wants; and they have the whips and chains to put that knowledge into practice.

Of course, Deep Ecology remains too institutionally marginal for it to face an exactly comparable danger. However, its form of fundamentalism, I believe, would take the shape of attempting to escape society; to see "nature" as a realm in which people are absent and in the celebration of which people can be ignored. Yet if it is truly nature we love, we must not forget people, for they too are born of the earth.[5] If we would commune with plants, we must not (as Aldo Leopold himself suggested) forget the weeds in a city vacant lot. And we must also show some concern for those kids playing in the city lot—at risk from broken glass and drug dealers and lacking for the most part physical or cultural access to the wilderness we seek to preserve.

In another area, we can recognize that the special virtue of non-fundamentalist contemporary spirituality is its ability to synthesize spiritual insights across traditions. Buddhists talk to Jews, Christians study

Yoga, and everybody wants to know a little bit about Shamanism. The wonderful opportunities of this openness are obvious; but the danger is that certain principles will be lost. While every tradition can be clearly seen for its virtues and powers, spiritual deep ecologists will lose their thread if they let certain clarities be obscured: the equality of men and women, a recognition of the past and present effects of racial domination, the need to frame spiritual truths in the context of a worldwide economy and culture—if these are neglected, the integrity of deep ecology will diminish and it may devolve into a sect of spiritually, and thus socially, irrelevant bird watchers.

Third: All attachment to truth provides the opportunity to hate error. There is thus the possibility—which at times has been realized in practice—of deep ecologists erecting a sharp divide between them and other kinds of environmentalism. Surely there are grounds for alliance between those who (merely) think of the world as deserving of care because it is God's creation, and not in itself sacred. Surely the deep ecologists have enough in common with the stewards of nature to make common cause with them against the pure despoilers. On a practical level, only a mass movement can motivate the government to constrain global capital, and demand international, national, and local programs to recover what we've lost and clean up the mess we've made. Such a movement will require environmentalists of all stripes, and participation will necessitate a long view in which tactical compromise with less radical elements will be necessary to secure the basis of an ongoing collective, and effective, movement. As they relate to others in the struggle to protect nature, spiritual deep ecologists should remember that in our own time we encounter the wilderness with the very accomplishments of our society riding on our back. As E. O. Wilson (1983) observed: no matter how much the naturalist loves the jungle, he had better be very well equipped or before long a host of jungle dwellers will break him down into his constituent amino acids. Every deep ecologist goes to the wilds with his vibram boots on his feet, his nylon back pack, and his Swiss army knife. With all that stuff along, there is little room for arrogance.

What all this adds up to is that just as we experience the mystical touch of God as socially situated existing individuals, so we come to "nature" through social life. We bring our historically defined expectations and needs. We have a concept of nature (as benign or threatening, comfortable or forbidding, infinitely powerful or dangerously at risk) which is very much the product of our own society's level of technological development. Especially in our own time we only *go* to the wilds with the very particular accomplishments of our society riding on our back.

Thus there is, fourth, also the problem that at times the bland images of nature which emerge from Deep Ecology distort what "nature" really is like. For example, our mystically based love of life will not extend to the AIDS virus; and our wariness at tampering with the sacred character of nature may well be suspended when it comes to using genetic engineering to cure cystic fibrosis. Ghetto rats will probably escape the purview which holds all of life as sacred, as might the black flies which cause widespread blindness in Africa. Adopting a deep ecological perspective will not eliminate the hard choices we face—choices about how much to take for ourselves and how much to leave for others; how much to exercise the control we increase day by day, and how much to surrender. And it will not turn the real world into a PBS special on butterflies or dolphins. The love we feel for the more-than-human is not a love that can erase the realities of struggle and conquest—of nature as one long and frequently quite painful food chain.

(There in an old Buddhist tale about two monks who stand on top of a mountain, surveying all of nature. "How horrible!" says one, with tears in his eyes, "they are all eating each other." "Don't be so upset," the other comforts him, "really, they are feeding each other." The point, of course, is that both are correct.)

SOCIAL TRANSFORMATION

In human history, the long counterpoint to ecstasy which takes us out of our social setting is the longing for justice within it. Morality and transcendence are the twin axes along which authentic personal and communal existence develop; and our success at both are the criteria for measuring the adequacy of a humane form of life. This longing for a more just social order can be found in the cautionary words of prophets, social reformers, and revolutionaries. In contrast to the claims of mysticism, the pursuit of justice is very much an awareness of just how socially situated we are; and how our concerns with making things better center on the alteration and improvement of this situation which defines us, grounds us, and sets our tasks.

This pursuit of justice exists, among other things, as a needed corrective to the ahistorical pretensions of mystical traditions—their claims to provide doctrines which originate outside of the social order. From a viewpoint that originated in politics, rather than spirituality, we are able, for instance, to critique the sexist teachings of early Buddhism. For all its self-understanding as a source of truth beyond the ego, it maintained the idea of women's social and spiritual inferiority. While the Buddha may have seen his way clear of the imposed caste system and the empty formalities of ritual sacrifices, he could not escape his own attachment to patriarchy. What source could there be for even recognizing this failing except a socially based political critique? Such a source only rarely emerges from transcendent visions but rather typically stems from the cries of the oppressed themselves. Ultimately, as I mentioned above, the danger here is that mystical *experience* is used as a support for *social authority*. It is then that, inevitably, veracity must be claimed not only for the experience, but for one particular discursive and institutional expression of it. And this expression will *always* give rise to structures of power and privilege—which will be defended with all the typical violence and deceit that hierarchies of power always employ.

In our own time, Deep Ecology in particular and the conservation movement in general have by this time been the subject of extensive critiques: for ignoring the social basis of their own perspectives; for emphasis on wilderness and forgetting of toxic waste dumps; for love of trees and lack of concern for children. These criticisms have helped move deep ecologists towards an understanding that environmentalism needs to embrace the concern of environmental justice: an awareness of and resistance to the unfair distribution of responsibility for and suffering from humanity's attacks on the environment. The radioactive dumps on native lands, the toxic wastes flowing into the poor neighborhoods, the outlawed chemicals exported to the Third world—can we really love nature if these things escape our vision?[6]

Finally, it must be stressed that for many the struggle for justice is *itself* a form of connection which can break the bonds of the ego. While social movements too often have devolved into the brutal tyrannies of a Stalin or the crass appeal to group hatred of a Farrakan, at their best they provide experiences where political solidarity blossoms into a kind of selfless love. At times people struggling for justice are freed from the usual petty isolations, jealousies, and fears. In the very struggle they find the joy of service and the spiritual clarity which comes from knowing the ultimate rightness of what they are doing.

AND YET . . .

Too often confidence in one's ultimate rightness has led political movements into dogmatic violence. The history of too many revolutions is the history of the replacement of one autocracy by another. The history of too many left groups reveals sectarianism, verbal violence, and exclusion of others who deserve solidarity. We have seen the fundamental wisdom of the struggle for justice be obscured by rage, pompous posturing, or simple careerism.[7]

And thus as the political perspective is necessary for both a grounding and a critique of mysticism and Deep Ecology, so their spiritual insights and resources can be a corrective to the excesses of politics.

Mysticism in general can offer relief from identification with theories, rigidly held "positions," and the pursuit of institutional power. An emphasis on compassion, on empathy even for the guilty, on service rather than on the acquisition of personal status within the "movement"—these are values which can be forthcoming from a direct experience of the holy. For from that experience, once again, we may learn that the ego-bound concerns which motivate us towards arrogance and violence, even in the service of justice, are not the only reality. To make the point we need only compare Lenin's practice of threatening to expel any party leader who disagreed with him, to Gandhi's insistence that comrades vote against him if that was what their own inner wisdom dictated. Coercion is clearly a product of any kind of fundamentalism, whether of a religious or a secular kind. Control or cooperation, manipulation or trust, the Grand Inquisitor and Lenin, or Gandhi and Aung San Suu Kyi Sang—these choices face any collection of human beings, any institutional structure, any attempt to bring truth into the world.

From Deep Ecology in particular, the world of conventional human-oriented politics also has much to learn. For one thing, Deep Ecology's emphasis on the value of the non-human offers a measure and a limit of what we are seeking when we pursue an improved "standard of living." The notion of a "sustainable" form of life begins to condition what we are after, becoming an essential defining element along with "justice" and "freedom." And (as difficult as it is to find the right way of putting this), we have before us the prospect that the true subjects of political life are not just people, but people, animals, plants, ecosystems, and perhaps the biosphere itself. Thus for social activities of all kinds new questions arise. What is the ultimate worth of this construction project, these jobs, this or that commodity? Whose needs or wants deserve to be satisfied? And which should be altered?

In the same vein, a mystical identification—or deep relationship—with the natural world allows us to orient political struggle away from entitlement and rage; and in a direction not tied (or at least less tied) by a psychic addiction to the very social system which destroys us. As Marcuse (1967) observed, by rooting personal identity in the ownership of things, the consumer society binds its subjects to the principles of ever increasing production and consumption. The recognition of spiritual values in general and the value(s) of nature in particular gives us a way out of the ecocidal cul-de-sac of the endless mall. We develop, in short, an alternative sense of self. This alternative allows the possibility of a withdrawal of psychic energy from a cultural and economic system which threatens all those subject to it.

In more strategic political terms, concern for nature is a value which can provide the basis for a new kind of solidarity. We might remember that whatever else divides us as human beings, we all need to breathe. And virtually all of our hearts rejoice to the sounds of Spring. These commonalties may save us when the divisions of race, class, gender, ethnicity, or sexuality leave us deeply suspicious of each other.

While those getting very rich off of pollution are not likely to be convinced, as are many of those whose most immediate livelihood depends on exploitation of their surroundings, we have already seen cross class, cross race, and cross nationality coalitions doing serious political work. An enormous dam project slated for India—supported by the World Bank and liable to destroy the habitat of endangered species and indigenous people alike—was stopped by a transcontinental alliance of local people, environmental activists, lawyers, and concerned citizens from India, Switzerland, and the U.S. (Rich 1994, 44-7). In Wisconsin white activists have helped Native Peoples fend off multinational mining interests (Gedicks 1992). These are but a few examples of arenas of cooperation based in the joint concern for the human and the non-human world.

It may actually be that care for the environment will continue and flourish as one of the main motivating forces of politics in the 21st century. The abatement signaled in the U.S. by the Republican victories of the mid-1990s is, I believe, a temporary development. In any event, the "working class," as Andre Gorz (1990, 218) observed many years ago, is not likely to mount a serious challenge to the established social order to get a 10% increase in pay. Concern for the environment—a concern motivated both by "self-interest" and as interest for nature that we love and long for—*could* be a significant element in a major social transformation. If people can truly see what is at stake, they may yet rise to the challenge. And the spiritual understanding of this concern has been and will continue to be an essential element in the process. We have seen it already in the spiritual motivation of the radical ecology group Earth First!, in the convention challenging claims of the new, earth-oriented ecotheology coming out of mainstream religions, and in the politicized versions of spiritual ecofeminism.

Finally, and perhaps most surprisingly, there is in a general "deep ecological" orientation a cognitive corrective to the distortions of centralized, reductionist, commodified knowledge and social practice. In agriculture, for instance, the belief that modernized science and technology can replace the fertility of the earth or the expertise of local groups has led to a series of disasters. As Vandana Shiva (1993) has described it, the imposition of "advanced," commodity-oriented monocultures has erased a wide variety of crops, seeds, productive uses (for food, fodder, herbs, local consumption etc. as well as sale), and ultimately peoples. The result has been polluted soils, drastically increased water consumption, less productive land use, and violent social dislocation. In this approach there is respect neither for the earth nor for the people who have sustainably managed their fields and forests for centuries. A perspective which sees communion with nature as having spiritual as well as instrumental value might look very carefully at any attempt to supplant either natural processes or long-established local forms of culture and practice. Thus as a spiritual view of the ultimate value of persons can provide an orientation for social life (though clearly not a simple way to resolve its conflicts and contradictions), so a spiritual view of nature can offer at least the beginning of an orientation towards production, consumption, and development.

And so, paradoxically, the wisdom of a mystical Deep Ecology can augment the powers and promises of the secular drive for just social transformation. Their mutual support is necessary, I suspect, if the environmental crisis is not to erode the conditions for human life on earth, and simultaneously erode our very confidence in our right to exist on it. If we are to be truly touched by the Holy Spirit, our own spirit of holiness must reach out to the enormous family of life which surrounds us, shapes us, and gives us our own particular place in the vastness of time and space.

CONCLUSION

The vision of mysticism offered here will not satisfy everyone. It is a particularly non-metaphysical view, in which ultimate reality is pretty much exhausted by "ordinary" reality. Of course, when illuminated by the sparks of mystical experience, "ordinary" reality can shine pretty brightly (as in the old Zen story, which identifies true enlightenment with simply seeing "a mountain as a mountain and a river as a river"). But what is absent here is any confidence that the pains of injustice and loss will be compensated for by any Grand Plan, Protecting All-Powerful Source, or Cosmic Pattern of Growth and Development. Speaking quite personally, I never could feel any of those; I believe we just have what we have. Mysticism, on my view, does not mean transcendence, but (again) illumination: not to believe in Something Else, but to See More Clearly (and more brightly) What We Have—and Who We Are. In the end, the work of mysticism is to join us to what we have: in delight, in grief, in life and death. Sometimes that joining will have the force and pleasure of a sexual climax, sometimes the utter peace of spring flower or the caress of a child's hand. Sometimes it will be the knowledge that the only way we can join with what is—is by resisting it; and that "acceptance" must mean, in our struggle for justice, that we fight back. At such times we fully realize our desire to transcend the falseness of our social world not by finding some other realm, but, through acts of solidarity and resistance, by transforming its emotional, moral, and—therefore—spiritual meaning.[8]

NOTES

1. For these and other accounts of Buddhism in this paper see, for example, Conze 1951 and Stryk 1969.

2. For a feminist account, see Heyward 1992.

3. There are many sources here; e.g., Macy 1994, Devall and Sessions 1985.

4. For these quotations, as well as many sources on contemporary and traditional writings on religion and nature, see Gottlieb 1996.

5. This critique is developed more extensively in Gottlieb 1995.

6. Two accounts of these matters are in Gedicks 1993 and Bullard 1994.

7. For an extensive critique of these defects in the history of European and U.S. left movements, see Gottlieb 1987 and 1992.

8. See the account in my forthcoming *A Spirituality of Resistance: Finding Peaceful Heart and Protecting the Earth* (New York: Crossroads, 1999).

REFERENCES

Abbey, Edward. *The Journey Home*. NY: Penguin, 1977.

Abram, David. 1996. *The Spell of the Sensuous*. NY: Pantheon.

Bullard, Robert D., ed. 1994. *Unequal Protection: Environmental Justice and Communities of Color*. San Francisco: Sierra Club Books.

Conze, Edward. 1951. *Buddhism: Its Essence and Development*. NY: Harper.

Devall, Bill and Sessions, George. 1985. *Deep Ecology: Living as if Nature Mattered*. Salt Lake City,UT: Peregrine Smith Books.

Dillard, Annie. 1982. *Teaching a Stone to Talk*. NY: HarperCollins.

Gedicks, Al. 1993. *The New Resource Wars: Native and Environmental Struggles Against Multinational Corporations*. Boston: South End Press.

Gorz, Andre. 1990. "Socialism and Revolution." in Roger S. Gottlieb, ed., *An Anthology of Western Marxism: From Lukacs and Gramsci to Socialist-Feminism*. NY: Oxford University Press.

Gottlieb, Roger S. ed., 1996. *This Sacred Earth: Religion, Nature, Environment*. NY: Routledge.

Gottlieb, Roger S., 1995. "Spiritual Deep Ecology and the Left," *Capitalism, Nature, Socialism: A Journal of Socialist Ecology*, Vol. 6, #4, Fall. Reprinted in Gottlieb 1996.

Gottlieb, Roger S. 1992. *Marxism 1844-1990: Origins, Betrayal, Rebirth*. NY: Routledge.

Gottlieb, Roger S. 1987. *History and Subjectivity: The Transformation of Marxist Theory*. Philadelphia: Temple University Press.

Heyward, Carter. 1992. *Touching Our Strength*. San Francisco: Harper.

Leopold, Aldo. 1949. *A Sand County Almanac*. NY: Oxford University Press.

Macy, Joanna. 1994. *World as Lover, World as Self*. San Francisco: Parallax.

Marcuse, Herbert. 1967. *One-Dimensional Man*. Boston: Beacon Press.

Rich, Bruce. 1994. *Mortgaging the Earth: The World Bank, Environmental Impoverishment and the Crisis of Development*. Boston: Beacon Press.

Seed, John, Macy, Joanna, and Fleming, Pat. 1991. *Thinking Like a Mountain: Towards a Council of All Beings*. Philadelphia: New Society Publishers. 1991.

Shepard, Paul. 1983. *Nature and Madness*. San Francisco: Sierra Club Books.

Shiva, Vandana. 1993. *The Violence of the Green Revolution*. London: Zed Press.

Stryk, Lucien, ed. 1969. *World of the Buddha*. NY: Anchor.
Wilson, E. O. 1983. *Biophilia*. Cambridge: Harvard University Press.
Zimmerman, Michael. 1995. *Contesting Earth's Future: Radical Ecology and Postmodernity*. Berkeley: University of California Press.

2

SPIRITUAL DEEP ECOLOGY
AND THE LEFT

An Effort at Reconciliation

I can see the bright green strip of grass beneath the wall, and the clear blue sky above the wall, and sunlight everywhere. Life is beautiful. Let the future generations cleanse it of all evil, oppression, and violence, and enjoy it to the full.
Leon Trotsky[1]

Often developed in isolation from and frequently opposed to each other, I believe that the more spiritual forms of deep ecology and the left political tradition need each other's insights and sensitivities. They are mutually necessary to help us learn how to respect human and nonhuman nature alike. Uniting their contributions could help mobilize a political response to the poisoning of our environment and root that response in an encompassing spiritual framework that would alter the fundamental ways in which we think about politics, our own identity, and nature.[2]

A fruitful exchange between deep ecology and the left, however, requires that adherents of both perspectives and beliefs suspend certain entrenched prejudices. Leftists need to open themselves to the possibility that a spiritually oriented perspective might actually have something to teach about the ultimate sources of value in our lives, and about limitations in our conventional sense of self. Deep ecologists would do well to suspend their ahistorical arrogance about their own wisdom, their pretensions to being above or beyond political struggles, and their too facile dismissal of left movements as unremitting agents of the exploitation of nature.

IDENTITY

Deep ecology, as I shall describe it here, is not solely about the environment, about protecting the rainforest, or about saving spotted owls. Paradoxically, what may be most important about deep ecology is not just what it says about non-human nature, but what it says about people. For deep ecologists, human identity—who we really are—is not constituted solely by psychological and physical individuality or collective social experience. Rather, deep ecology asserts the direct and ultimate importance of humanity's connection to, and identification with, other forms of life and being. In preserving, respecting, and even loving nature, we are not deferring to an Other, but overcoming a kind of alienation from essential aspects of our own selves. This is a potentially revolutionary claim, because both common sense and philosophical theory have for centuries concentrated on the isolated individual or the social group (or both) as the centers of our personal, social, and political selfhood.

By contrast to deep ecology, liberalism, socialism, feminism, and other social and political movements have focused on resistance to tyranny, exploitation, and injustice, putting individual freedom and/or group interests at the heart of their sense of what is human.

To understand how these two views need each other, and how both are essential elements of our political response to ecocide, we need first to reflect on our understanding of human identity.

WHO ARE WE?

We come to answer this question not (or not *just*) by thinking about ourselves, but by learning particular ways of talking and concrete social practices. From infancy to adulthood, the manner in which human beings are taught to speak of themselves and to act in the world cultivates very specific forms of self-understanding.

In the "modern" age of the last three centuries or so, forms of discourse and social practices have evolved to teach us to think and act as individuals: to live as if the central truth about ourselves is that we are isolated, and that connections with others *follow from* rather than constitute who we are. Political philosophy and psychotherapy, educational autonomy, and the nuclear family all cultivate self-interested independence. In different social settings, we learn to evaluate beliefs and morality with independence of mind, to take personal responsibility for our own moral failings, and to see the possibility of autonomous and creative insights in art, science, or technological development.

Existing in uneasy symbiosis (and at times conflicting) with both the positive and pernicious aspects of individualism are varieties of group identity based on characteristics such as economic class, nation, race, ethnic history, religion, and gender. As members of groups we know ourselves through particular historical "fates": Jews who have faced the Holocaust or blacks with a legacy of slavery. And we know ourselves by the songs, stories, prayers, and food that have shaped *our* communities and which are strange or unknown to others. [3]

Taken together, modern society's individualism and the continuing identification with socially differentiated groups have sharply demarcated human beings from the rest of the natural world. As *individuals* we seem to stand out, and to be separable from, the biological context that makes our lives possible. We can know something, try to control it, approve of it, or resist it. Similarly, as members of racial/ethnic/religious *groups,* our identity is constituted by cultural traditions, beliefs expressed in language, and our own special histories. Social groups define themselves, commemorate their history, and compare and distinguish themselves from others. Such processes are found only among humans. [4]

THE VALUE(S) OF DEEP ECOLOGY

The above practices and discourses teach us, then, that we are individuals and members of groups—and that we are little else.

Deep ecologists challenge these notions of human identity, seeking to add to them by enlarging our sense of our own self-hood. Denying that our essential identity includes only our individuality and our membership in social groups, deep ecologists reject many of the ethical, religious, or "scientific" distinctions between humanity and non-human nature. This rejection is the hallmark of deep ecology. It is sometimes called biocentrism or ecocentrism.

A deep ecological perspective begins by claiming that non-human nature is not here solely for the use of humanity. Individual animals and plants, as well as entire ecosystems of wetland, tundra, or mountain range, have their own integrity, meaning, and importance. Yet deep ecologists do not aim to oppose the value of non-human nature to that of people. Rather, they root the *value* of both in a fundamental sense of the *identity* of both. Water and air, earth and humans, are and can be experienced as strands of an infinite web of life and being where no part has inherent priority over the rest—just because there is no clear way to demarcate one part from another.

This view has been expressed by many people in various forms.[5] My focus here is on those versions that stress a revised view of human identity rather than emphasize nature's "rights" or our "obligations" to preserve it. These deep ecologists recognize, experience, and honor our natural surroundings *as essential to who we are.* Care for nature is not a matter of deferring to the rights of strangers, but of loving a dimension of oneself.

> Ecological thinking requires a kind of vision across boundaries. The epidermis of the skin is ecologically like a pond surface or a forest soil, not a shell so much as a *delicate interpenetration.* It reveals the self ennobled and extended rather than threatened as part of the landscape and ecosystem because the beauty and complexity of nature *are continuous with ourselves.*[6]

To a confirmed anthropocentric—one who feels that human groups stand isolated from nature as the center of historical or cosmic importance—these claims about our connection to nature may seem either false or trivial. While we need air like furry animals, they might say, that does not make either air or kittens *part of ourselves.*

Perhaps the closest thing to an "argument" that deep ecologists might offer the anthropocentric is to point to the many situations in which individuals feel, beyond doubt, a direct and absolutely essential connection *to other people.* Mothers and infants, comrades in wartime, and companions in political, spiritual, intellectual, or artistic journeys may well experience one another with a kind of intimate solidarity, based in care, love, and empathy. In such contexts, our regard for fellow humans is not based on their "rights," but on our bonds with them as companions on this earth, whose lives and well-being are intimately tied to our own. Similar feelings, deep ecologists claim, are both possible and appropriate when we care for the air that we breathe, the water that we drink, or the other species with whom we share this planet. Our regard for non-human nature can spring from an awareness of it as our companion, fellow-traveler, and friend; or, more profoundly, as the matrix which in fundamental ways enables our lives to be what they are. We "identify" with nature when we realize it is what makes our lives possible, and therefore no longer conceive of our "selves" as bounded by our skin.[7]

It is obvious that humans *depend* on non-human nature; the most anthropocentric of thinkers will readily allow that poisoned earth and water are "bad" for people. Agreement on this point, however, does not logically compel any emotional and ethical openness to the environment.

Yet we *can* describe the social practices and historical developments that have given rise to anthropocentrism or biocentrism—just as we can with the beliefs and practices that gave rise to individualism and group identification. We can know and understand the fundamental shifts in social practices and human experience that have created human-centered or deep ecological visions.

We may suppose that their interdependence with the non-human natural world was evident to the hunter-gatherers of the Paleolithic (40,000-15,000 B.C.E.) and early agricultural settlements of the Neolithic (12,000-5,000 B.C.E.). The living earth provided food to gather or hunt, herbs for medicine, and revealed cycles of birth, maturation, and decay. Much of life was spent under open sky and the elements. Viewing their artistic/religious artifacts, we can suppose they felt a strong sense of continuity and community with animals and plants; and that they were in awe of the powers of birth and death. This identification can be traced in the rich and varied symbolism of the mother goddess, which continued in cultural rituals and beliefs well after these societies were supplanted by others.[8]

In short, the daily experience of humans in these settings *itself* gives rise to a particular attitude towards nature.

Yet along with connection to, and reverence for, nature, there doubtless existed a certain degree of dread and fear, stimulated by the lack of predictability of nature's ways, a desire for "easier" ways of meeting human biological needs, and expanding populations. These feelings and conditions motivated new attitudes towards our natural surroundings; especially, they gave rise to the view of non-human nature as alien or separate and also to the desire to *control* nature.

Whatever the initial causes, history from c.3000 B.C.E to the present witnessed the development of more advanced agriculture, increasingly complex social divisions of labor and relations of exploitation, and the continual creation of tools, techniques, and social organization, to delve and shape the earth and its products. Part of this development involved the devaluation of nature, the creation of exclusively masculine symbols for divinity, the subjugation of women by patriarchal control over their reproductive and sexual status, and the evolution of economic and social classes.

The continuous growth of technological and social power, and the attendant religious and political ideologies that supported them, promoted the illusion of our fundamental difference from nature, and gave rise to the desire for *control* in and of itself, as a good thing. This desire played an essential role in evolving, interlocked systems of military, religious, economic, and ideological domination.[9]

Like all deeply embedded illusions, this one was based in a certain truth: humanity did, in certain short-run ways, dramatically increase its capacity to dominate non-human nature. Mass agriculture produced mass surpluses, supporting cultural elites and a complex division of labor. Control of fire, and of water, steam, electricity, and even atomic power perpetuated the image that Nature had become our dominion. With the rise of modern science, mastery has seemed to be virtually limitless. Daily life in the industrialized world now depends on hyper-technological substitutions for and controls over previously natural processes: the ways in which we travel, dress, eat, communicate over distance, labor, and amuse ourselves require an intricate technological system that seems to rely only on human knowledge and organization. Nature, it seems, obeys our will.

At the same time, our powers over nature have always been embedded in gender and class dominated societies in which hard labor, power, status, and wealth are unequally and unjustly distributed, and in which "man-made" poverty and exploitation supplant droughts or floods as the greatest threats to material well-being. While some speak of "man controlling nature," this control is ultimately vested in ruling elites.

And now the dreadful consequences of our presumption of separation from, and superiority over, non-human nature have become clear. Human "control" has evolved into a series of feedback loops in which the controller is himself controlled.[10] The Green Revolution in agriculture depletes the soil, pollutes water tables, and leaves cancer-causing pesticide residues. The convenience of modern refrigeration threatens the ozone layer. The EPA recently declared that ninety-nine major U.S. metropolitan areas have unhealthy air. Wilderness and species vanish. Many who experience these losses no longer trust still newer technological fixes. They want to turn away from the forms of individualism and group identity that fund the juggernaut of technological destruction, and turn toward a sense of community with the non-human world.[11]

Along with our emerging sense of what we have done to the non-human world, and how those actions are affecting us, there are other sources of deep ecological thinking. Our societies seem increasingly inhumane; violence haunts streets, offices, and homes, and is echoed horribly in both popular culture and the military-industrial complex. Against such "man-made" threats, non-human nature may feel much more like "home" than the built environments we in fact live in. The heroes of modern rationality—the scientist, the professional, the expert—do not seem to have produced either reasonable societies or models of personal wisdom. The "scientific" culture which was to have remade the world in the human image now gives us less and less comfort. Consequently, many people have turned to other metaphors and narratives on which to construct ideals of how to live and whom to respect. Instead of the democratic republic of the welfare state, many turn to the biotic community as more attractive and more ultimately plausible. Instead of the scientific "expert" or the detached professional, more people look to the "wisdom of nature," or the ecological traditions of indigenous peoples.

DEEP ECOLOGY AND SPIRITUALITY

Because of the way it expands our sense of what people are, deep ecology can be considered a *spiritual* perspective.

While this term may be alienating to some, I wish to stress that it need not refer either to conventional organized religion or to faith in a vengeful Divine Father. Rather, the sense of spirituality I intend here begins with the belief that it is a grave error to understand ourselves solely in terms of our social roles, possessions, personal successes and failures, individual achievements, or purely social group identities. There are sources of contentment and inspiration which are more lasting, powerful, and benign than anything that can be purchased, measured, evaluated, or socially calculated; in short, anything which can be possessed or accomplished by a purely social being. A spiritual perspective suggests that only with this discovery of a sense of selfhood beyond the ego can we become released from the ego's compulsions and inevitable disappointments. Our social identity itself is not to be eliminated, but rather integrated into a more comprehensive selfhood. We are not to quit our jobs or surrender our zip codes, blending into some faceless, personality-less tapioca pudding of bliss. Our sense of personal identity continues. The difference is that now we have another perspective on the conventional social ego and its foibles.

This sense of spirituality does not require a conventional (Western) religious attachment to a personal God. Nor does it require, as, unfortunately, many have supposed, a spiritual denial of the manifest horrors of human experience from concentration camps to violence against women. Traditional religion and pop spirituality frequently ignore social injustice, and radicals have rightly rejected their politically conservative and sexist tendencies. [12]

But we can no more fully comprehend spirituality if we focus on its lowest manifestations than we can fully understand Marxism if we only look at Stalinism. The model of spirituality I am developing must be understood as distinct from dogmatic religious attachments to particular rituals, creeds, or organizations. From this perspective, the concrete form of spiritual practice or belief is a means to self-transformation, not a way of deciding whom to hate. Further, an authentic spirituality does not ignore social suffering. The more powerful, enduring, and credible spiritual messages counsel openness to the truth: not the rosy security of a blissful avoidance, but a committed involvement with others.[13]

For instance, when we take action on behalf of threatened nature, we may see ourselves not simply as individuals defending the rainforest, but, in John Seed's words, as *"part of the rainforest defending itself."* Such a view may well expand our selfhood beyond the conventionalities of status, money, power, possessions, physical beauty, and purely human narrower forms of self or group interest. It can also help shape political action that transcends the simple pursuit of increased entitlements for particular social groups. In this vein, we see that a spiritual deep ecology can help counter consumer society's addictive preoccupation with individual consumption and ownership and provide an alternative, non-commodity centered framework of "self-realization." All it asks is that we give up the illusion that we are *only* our social selves.[14]

As we sense our continuity with leaf, stream, and butterfly, we manifest a global or ecological consciousness far from the domineering and consumptive obsessions of modernity. Accumulation of real money or the symbolic capital of status, endless self-evaluation or crippling high anxiety, paralyzing despair, or entrenched loneliness—all are soothed by the reassuring sense of our participation in the web of life.

As promising as such personal changes might be, there is also the profound effect that a spiritual deep ecology could have on some of the basic ways in which we think about politics. It can help overcome the limitations of progressive or radical political organizations whose aims seem to be stuck in attempting to satisfy the conventional ego of individuals or collectivities.

Although committed to overturning unjust systems and ending oppression, leftist or progressive political movements have often reproduced, rather than opposed, the conventional ego. Classical liberalism emphasized personal rights, enshrined individual economic activity at the heart of its system, and believed that the central purpose of society was to protect and further ownership and consumption. Surely this view will not help us face the environmental crisis.

Sadly, more "radical" political movements of the West—despite their emphasis on community, class, or racial experience, and their attempt to generate an ethic of collective solidarity and struggle—have *also* often presupposed an individualistic, consumerist ego. The practical politics of the left have frequently aimed to provide more things, money, and prestige. They have too often represented the interest of one segment of the oppressed while claiming to represent all. And they have repeatedly failed to challenge the individualist premise that a higher standard of living will make for greater happiness. It has been a rare progressive party that called for less, not more, consumption—at least until the Green Parties of Europe came into being; and there has been little assertion that human fulfillment may be directly opposed to high consumption life-styles.

Moreover, concern for nature as a dimension of being in its own right has been absent in most progressive politics. The left has usually opposed consumerism for reasons of "pollution and conservation." The individual rights of the Lockean agrarian capitalist are in this sense pretty much the same as the overthrow of alienation sought by the Marxian communist. One grows crops for cash, and the other seeks fulfillment in an egalitarian and rationally ordered society. Both seek justice; yet both have little or no sense that there also may be norms for which the fulfillment of human beings is not the sole goal.

The exceptions to these trends—from Michael Lerner's "politics of meaning" to the hippies "turn on, tune in, drop out," from certain elements of early Socialist-Zionism to radical elements of spiritual feminism—have been minority currents.

For the radical tradition—even at its best, when it sees the integral connections between humans and their environment—nonhuman nature has value or integrity only by reference to its relation to human beings. We should use it for our own good; if we pollute it we will suffer; and our access to scientific knowledge gives us the right of mastery. Ultimately, however, our destruction of it carries meaning just insofar as it affects us.[15] The problematic consequences of such views are revealed not only with every breath we take, but also in our inability to feel at home in our own world. Our dominion over the earth and its creatures leaves a bitter taste.

I do not mean to invalidate the enormous courage and self-sacrifice expended in trying to bring either the working class or oppressed minorities into a reasonable standard of living, protect their political and social rights, or give them a "place" in capitalist society. Nor do I wish to ignore the way ecological issues center at least as much on structures of production—over which the mass of the population have virtually no control—as on consumerist personal orientations. I am suggesting, however, that a politics which identifies human good purely or mainly with the acquisition of things or the achieving of social status of whatever kind is no longer adequate. The economism which has always pacified mass left movements—from the craft workers in the early decades of this century to the industrial unions of the 1930s to the inner-city insurgency of the 1960s—not only spells the inevitable continuity of ecocide but is self-defeating for the movements themselves.[16]

Thus when progressive political movements take the conventional social ego for granted and seek to fulfill it, they are typically unable to counter our society's suicidal preoccupation with success, consumption, and spectacle. Without an attempt to construct a sense of identity along more spiritual lines—as something not reducible to the ego of social consumption, social status, or active control—the left may have little to offer individuals or groups whose main preoccupation is greater wealth and power. Such "progressive" groups are unable to progress beyond the unending use of—and so alienation from—nature. There is no consistent alternative vision of a form of life which is either ecologically sustainable (or even sane) and personally fulfilling. We see examples of the left's failure here in the way the political uproar of the 1960s too often devolved simply into demands for more transfer payments. Comparably, the vibrant movements for democracy and human rights which toppled the tyrannies of communism are now tripping over each other in their haste to effect a capitalist restructuring. Hopefully, the emerging ecologically-oriented left will continue to develop sensitivities in all these areas. Strands of the left that have stressed the material and spiritual costs of consumerism already will surely be strengthened and broadened by an infusion of deep ecological thinking.

With the acceptance of an essentially human-centered model of identity, rights, and fulfillment, the traditional left has also accepted models of interpersonal relations based on self-righteousness and rage. There has been little critical distance from the driving emotional force of entitlement: to justice, goods, or power. Within progressive organizations, these failings have too frequently given rise to relational styles that make interpersonal cooperation and organizational coalitions impossible. While a spiritual view stresses compassion and the transcendence of desire, the endless emphasis on personal and group entitlement, flavored with generous helpings of self-righteousness and pretentiousness, fracture every attempt to hold together an elusive "rainbow" of oppressed social groups. Competition over who is most oppressed, masculine leaders who pump up their own egos and position at the expense of the group, endless controversy and conflict leading to endless splits—all these riddle the history of progressive organizations. [17]

Spiritual deep ecology can help us begin to understand ourselves as natural, rather than purely psychic, social, and symbolic beings. We not only come to value non-human nature, we also come to think of *ourselves* in radically different ways. In doing so, we may realize that we live not just socially but also in an ecologically bound biotic community. The particular needs and interests defined by our place in social life may no longer exhaust our vision of what we want or deserve.

Spiritually, this means that basic values such as a birth and death (rather than murder or destructive consumption or commodification), identifying with other life forms, a sense of connection to, and participation in, one's place, may begin to inform not just spiritual reflection and mystical experience, but our prophetic political demands. We can enter into political life with a greater compassion for both comrade and opponent. We can see the goal not as endlessly raising consumption, but as re-orienting the distribution of wealth and the process of production and consumption so that future generations of plants, animals, and people can live simply and in harmony. We can begin to be self-critical about ourselves, our particular ethnic, religious, or economic group— for we find our identity is not totally rooted in any human location or connection. We are part of nature, of tree and sky, as much as we are our bank account or racial history. Surely this realization will help free us emotionally from some of our compulsions to dominate other people or the earth, to be forever and in every instance "right," "in control ," in "power." Surely this will help us learn to live with others—and with our own fears and greeds—and a much more sustainable, and even loving, way. [18]

THE RETURN OF THE SOCIAL

Yet thinking of nature alone will not do. We are creatures of history and society as well as of earth and air. We hunger for justice as we hunger for food and water. And without a compelling memory of class, gender, racial, and national forms of oppression, spirituality in general and deep ecology in particular will be blind to complex and painful issues of social injustice and political reorganization. [19]

To begin, one must observe that just as it is morally significant that species are made extinct or habitats poisoned, so it is critical to remember that humans are *also* sickened by environmental degradation, and that the contamination disproportionately affects the poor, people of color, and the "Third World." There is surely a terrible "human" folly in using carcinogenic pesticides in agriculture. But while ultimately that folly affects us all, in the short run the toxins surround the migrant farm workers in the fields, and their sale makes money for owners of the chemical companies who produce them, owners who work and live far from the contaminated substances they create.

The difference between the farm worker and the chemical company industrialist, between the World Bank executive who supports a destructive "development" loan for a massive dam and the indigenous tribes whose villages are destroyed by it, between the timber companies eager to clearcut and the native peoples whose lives and culture depend on the forest—these differences must be kept in mind when we speak of what "humanity" has done to the earth. [20] Clearly the responsibility for the domination of nature does not lie equally on all humans—any more than racism, sexism, or colonialism are equally the work of all whites, men, or Europeans.

Of course, the complexities of coercion and cooptation may make it difficult to decipher how responsibility is distributed. When peasants deforest a hillside because they have no other source of firewood, are they no different from clear-cutting timber companies? When a housewife flushes a toxic cleaner down the sink, how is she like—and unlike—an oil company negligent in a major oil spill? How do the greenhouse gases released by our daily commute—including my own—compare to DuPont's continued production of ozone-destroying CFCs a full decade after their effects were known?

These questions are not easy to answer. Yet in a world of ruling elites and ideological mystification, in which some genders and races are identified with nature while others are considered nature's masters, it is necessary to approach ecological devastation with an understanding of the distribution of social power that makes a small number of people initiate and—to an extreme degree—profit from it; and of the social constraints that lead the mass of people to accept it.

Another problem arises when deep ecologists suggest that because humans are a *part* of the natural world we can therefore discover how we ought to live by observing how non-human nature operates. It is suggested, sometimes directly, sometimes indirectly, that were we simply to live "naturally" we should thereby end the environmental crisis. The wisdom of nature would guide us, replacing the follies of a purely human view.

This approach faces several difficulties. First, it should be recognized that "nature," for all its seeming self-sufficiency and objectivity, is *also* a social category. Our very sense of what is "nature" rather than human, "natural" rather than artificial, is partly a product of social factors. The particular conceptual system out of which any sense of "nature" emerges will reflect, as do all such systems, a particular distribution of power and a pattern of social experience. Perhaps the most obvious historical example of such a mistake occurred when "Social Darwinists" applied the notion of the "survival of the fittest" to social life and thus identified the existing social elite with the genetically most successful animal species. Comparable errors arise when our supposedly immutable biological nature is used to justify some form of social domination; e.g., militarist aggression or patriarchy. In all these cases, the meaning given to "nature" is pretty clearly a product of social interests.

A deep ecologist who uses a politically unanalyzed sense of "nature," may well make similar errors. A lack of attention to class privilege may be a reason why some deep ecologists put so much stress on the existence and experience of wilderness—a locale and an encounter of limited cultural and economic accessibility—as the hallmark of a deep ecological sensibility. An authentic, as opposed to a self-indulgent, deep ecology will find "nature" in city pigeons or slum children playing in a vacant lot as well as in an old-growth forest. Equally important, the ultimate fate of the wilderness depends at least as much on relations among human beings as it does on our attitudes towards non-human nature itself.

Another fallacy of an uncritical reliance on the idea of "nature" is revealed if we ask why non-human nature cannot itself follow *our* rules, live as we do, since after all it is "connected" or a part of us as surely as we are a part of it. Why cannot we ask predators to consider the justice of their kill, or bacteria to think twice before they invade someone's throat? Why can't sharks and smaller fish, robins and worms, spiders and flies, make peace with each other?

These questions reveal that different things may be "part" of each other and still have their own distinct principles of organization, structural necessities, and proper states of being. Non-human nature and humans are, for all their connections and similarities, in some ways fundamentally different. (So are stars and beetles.) What humans have, and what non-human nature does not, is the capacity to interrogate both self and other, to raise questions of moral or cognitive validity, to examine purposes, to organize and *re*-organize the way we interact with nature. People do not live solely by instinct or need, but by rules, norms, values. We seek to understand and evaluate our lives, and to alter them in accord with changes in our understanding and judgment.

Thus human self-realization is (alas?) more complex, dangerous, and troubling than that of animals, plants, or rivers. Unlike other life forms, we can ask for justice, for compassion, for decency—and respond with rage or grief when they are absent. Thus the "proper" state of being of humanity is not simply to act "naturally" in an ecosystem, but also to manifest *justice* among humans. [21]

Justice *is* our proper condition, the fitting form our nature should take. [22] Paradoxically, it is a nature we often fail to achieve. This ability to fail shows that our nature is "ours" in a very different way than the "nature" of a rosebush or a wolf is theirs. Roses and wolves *live* their nature. From those lives we can determine what their natures are. Humans, by contrast, strive to fulfill their nature; that is, to organize a social form which meets the implicit demands of our unique—and historically evolving—capacities and drives.

We are beings who need others and can also question the rightness of the way our needs are met. Because we have the gift for complex language use, we can make claims to power and property—and also challenge those claims. We manifest complex emotional states that emerge—as the fulfillment of love and trust or as violations which give rise to hatred and anger—out of our natural social bonds. In these ways the anticipation of a just society is built into our basic physical, emotional, and cognitive need for others and our basic capacity to speak, surely the elements of our existence that make us distinctly "human." [23]

The longing to realize our nature can be found in our dreams and prayers, our critical reflections on society, and our dissident movements. From the prophets of the *Old Testament* to the Bodhisattva ideal of Mahayana Buddhism, from Plato's ethics to Marx's critique of capitalism, in countless well-known and anonymous rebellions, uprisings, and acts of resistance, we have sought love and justice. It is this importunate longing—and our sadness for our failures—which nonhuman nature cannot have, and therefore which no amount of deep ecological reflection can ever fully assuage.

Thus our membership in cities, tribes, communities, nations, races, genders—and not merely our "natural" identity—is critical in our response to the environmental crisis. And if that crisis represents a profound failure of all basic social and cultural systems, then a tremendous amount of temporary pain must follow any attempt to set things right.

Who will bear the brunt of the pain? Who will initiate it? Who will resist? Who should be forced to pay the greatest price?

When we demand that logging be curtailed to save a rainforest, concern for the unemployed loggers must accompany our passion for owls and trees. Only if the costs of the transition to ecological sustainability and respect for nature are truly *socialized,* can such issues not take their present form of desperate, win-lose battles. Without a radical democratic political system and a rational economy, efforts to create a sustainable society will place vastly unequal burdens on the socially powerless. If technology is not shaped by the needs of the human and the ecosystem community as a whole, ruling elites will continue to combine the domination of nature with the domination of human beings. The choice between loggers and owls is like some of the bogus choices forced by affirmative action programs in which working class whites and minorities are pitted against each other. When conflicts are posed in these ways, deep ecologists will always lose, because they will always be a tiny minority.

To further complicate matters, consider Bill McKibben's claim that our present alteration of the global climate gives all life on this planet a human imprint. [24] As we change the world's temperature, we change the growth conditions of every living thing. Further, man-made pollutants are found in the depth of the oceans and on top of the tallest mountains, in the most isolated deserts and glaciers. All areas designated as "wild" now exist as such only on the sufferance of some nation or community. Forests and species and ecosystems must have our blessing to live, otherwise they will go the way of the buffalo, the vast Redwood forests of 19th century California, or the long lost wild lands of Western Europe.

In this most practical of ways, then, humanity and nature have truly become one. With the poisoning of the environment, plagues such as cancer, immune-system disorders, and hunger take ever great tolls on humanity. With the use of the environment as an infinite source of expanding economic accumulation, and a source of commodities designed to compensate otherwise empty lives, non-human nature will be continually and increasingly degraded. Unjust power, private wealth without social responsibility, rulers who sustain themselves by military terror or the promise of more "things" to a demoralized population—none of these can do anything but continue to destroy the earth. Ecocide is their stock in trade.

Because of the necessary interdependence of all that lives, there are fundamental connections between respect for ecosystems and respect for people. As stated by the loose coalition of popular environmental and social justice groups in the Philippines, ultimately "The environmental movement is a struggle for equity in the control and management of natural resources." Such equity means that economic development must be fully participatory. Therefore, to work for "environmentally sustainable development requires working for human rights."[25] Similar conclusions are reached in a detailed study of efforts to save African wildlife. The two most successful conservation programs in Africa

> are two of the least expensive. What makes them successful is that they are premised on the needs of people. All we have to do to preserve Africa's wildlife heritage is care about the people as much as we care about the wildlife.[26]

As Ramachandra Guha puts it, the grass-roots Indian environmental movements focus not on "environmental protection" in itself, but on who should use and who should benefit from the environment.

> If colonial and capitalist expansion has both accentuated social inequalities and signaled a precipitous fall in ecological wisdom, an alternate ecology must rest on an alternate society and polity as well.[27]

These quotations derive from movements of people who are far more immediately connected to non-human nature than those thinkers of the industrialized world who created deep ecology. In fact, however, every person must exchange with non-human nature every moment of his or her lifetime. Even the most devout deep ecologist must relate to nature by some degree of consumption and displacement—or else die of starvation and exposure. We can choose to make that exchange one of rapacious folly or respectful community, but we cannot exempt nature from its effects. We cannot, in Edward Abbey's desperate cry about Yosemite, "Keep it like it was."[28]

Conversely, however, deep ecology's struggles to preserve at least some of the pristine, pre-human wild should not be dismissed as the self-indulgence of the privileged. The wilderness has its own integrity and purpose, and the world would be a poorer place for us all if that were lost. A balance *can* be struck between *preserving* the wild and *reorganizing* our transactions in cities, suburbs, and countryside. Properly grounded in the social world as well as the wilderness, our reverence for non-human nature can be lavished on the birch tree next to my house in Boston as well as on the ones in the White Mountain National forest, the vegetables I ate for dinner as much as the wildflowers of the rainforest.

PROSPECTS

The reconciliation of deep ecology and radical politics, then, must not stress non-human nature *at the expense* of human beings. This would simply continue the painful history of divisiveness of left movements, in which suffering groups are pitted against each other in self-destructive competition over needs, degrees of self-righteousness, and entitlement. The goal, rather, is to widen our sense of community, including but going beyond our current human limits of race, class, gender, or nationality.

There remain, of course, daunting social sources of experience which impede the rise of a deep ecological consciousness—just as there are comparable experiences obstructing the development of socialist/progressive group consciousness. In the case of ecological awareness, at least two barriers are crucially difficult to overcome, which I can mention here only in passing.

First, there is in the industrialized world the addictive quality of our relation to consumption. The idea of a form of life in which consumption plays an increasingly diminished part seems to threaten our very selfhood. Our anthropocentric economy offers so much to so many—and tantalizes the rest with the possibility that they too might one day enter the golden land of consumerist bliss—that the inevitably more austere prospect of a sustainable, ecologically respectful society is deeply troubling. It is difficult to imagine the success and power of a political party calling for less jobs, production, energy use, and consumption being successful; or that Americans or Europeans or Japanese would willingly part with air conditioners, cars, nuclear power, or the freedom to shop till you drop.

Second, our economies are so tied to an endlessly exploitative relation to non-human nature that altering them involves a confrontation with our ultimate economic—and hence social and political—powers. Any brief glimpse of what deep ecological society might look like is immediately clouded by the dark shadows of the powers that depend on the exploitation of both people and nature. These powers include not only the capitalist state and the corporations, but also entrenched authorities in science, technology, and culture.

As difficult as these obstructions are, they at least reveal once again the commonality of interest between deep ecology and the left, for surely these two barriers to deep ecology also deflect attempts to imagine or put into existence a democratic, socialist-feminist society.

NOTES

1. Leon Trotsky, shortly before his assassination. Quoted in Isaac Deutscher, *The Prophet Outcast: Trotsky: 1929–1940* (New York: Vintage, 1963), p. 479.

2. This article benefited greatly from suggestions by Bettina Bergo, Miriam Greenspan, and the Boston area *CNS* editorial group. Daniel Faber and John Wooding were kind enough to respond to two different drafts.

3. I have discussed social differentiation in *History and Subjectivity: The Transformation of Marxist Theory* (Atlantic Highlands, NJ: Humanities Press, 1993), Chapters 12–14.

4. Even gender, which appears to some to be given by nature, varies so much over history and culture that it is clearly in many ways a social product itself.

5. Sources here include Joanna Macy, Warwick Fox, Theodor Roszak, Starhawk, Aldo Leopold, Dave Foreman, Gary Snyder, and Riane Eisler. Despite my support of deep ecology, I reject the way some of its voices have placed undue primacy on wilderness preservation, promoted an apolitical understanding of population issues, and been blind to political and social inequalities.

6. Paul Shepard, "Ecology and Man—a Viewpoint," in *The Subversive Science,* edited by Paul Shepard and Daniel McKinley (Boston: Houghton Mifflin, 1969), p. 2, emphasis mine.

7. Even such a bounded self involves non-human nature, for our health requires the presence of billions of microbes that function *within* our bodies.

8. See Riane Eisler, *The Chalice and the Blade* (New York: Harper and Row, 1987); and Marija Gimbutas, *The Goddesses and Gods of Old Europe* (Berkeley: University of California Press, 1982).

9. For sources describing the simultaneous emergence of patriarchy, class society, and dominating attitudes towards nature see Gerda Lerner, *The Creation of Patriarchy* (New York: Oxford, 1986); Marilyn French, *Beyond Power* (New York: Ballantine, 1985); Robert Pogue Harrison, *Forests: The Shadow of Civilization* (Chicago: University of Chicago Press, 1992) pp. 13–60; and Michael Mann, *The Sources of Social Power: Volume I* (New York: Cambridge University Press, 1987), pp. 34–129.

10. Andrew McLaughlin, "Marxism and the Mastery of Nature: An Ecological Critique," in Roger S. Gottlieb, ed., *Radical Philosophy: Tradition, Counter-Tradition, Politics* (Philadelphia: Temple University Press, 1993).

11. Theorists describing new forms of social organization—including bioregionalism, organic farming, ecological educational practices, tax codes restricting pollution, etc.— are thus depicting social practices which can further a deep ecological perspective.

12. Too many spiritual traditions also enshrine hierarchy and power within their own organizations.

13. For a fuller account of spirituality, see my Introduction to Roger S. Gottlieb, ed., *A New Creation: America's Contemporary Spiritual Voices* (N.Y.: Crossroad, 1990); and *Marxism 1844–1990: Origins, Betrayal, Rebirth* (N.Y.: Routledge, 1992), pp. 197–220.

14. Adopting a deep ecological view will not solve particular conflicts of interests between humanity and nature; it will not tell us which houses or dams or diet are necessarily justified. But in this way it is no different from either

liberalism or socialism, neither of which can exclude painful conflicts among legitimate interests.

15. Marx, Engels, and Marxism's views on nature are more complex and controversial than I can do justice to here. Clearly, the major strength of the Marxist tradition's account of environmental issues lies in its analysis of the causes of ecological devastation. As for Marx's own attitudes to nature: even a defender of his ecological wisdom such as Howard Parsons notes that "Marx . . . shared the faith of a spectacularly successful nineteenth-century capitalism in material and technological progress" and "called for a *social mastery of nature* for the sake of *man.*" In Parsons, ed., *Marx and Engels on Ecology* (Greenwood, CT: Greenwood Press, 1977), p. 69. Much more negative critics, such as Stanley Aronowitz, Murray Bookchin, and Isaac Balbus, consider Marx to be a full-fledged representative of the worst excesses of Western Philosophy's and modernity's attempt to endlessly dominate and exploit nature. See, e.g., Isaac Balbus, *Marxism and Domination* (Princeton: Princeton University Press, 1983).

16. This position is developed at some length in my treatment of the Communist Party and the CIO in *History and Subjectivity,* op. cit.

17. I have discussed these problems at length in both *History and Subjectivity* and *Marxism 1844–1990,* op. cit.

18. A deep ecological sensibility thus corresponds to forms of interaction stressed by feminism.

19. I have explored relations between spiritual and political viewpoints in "Heaven on Earth: A Dialogue between a Political Radical and a Spiritual Seeker," in *A New Creation* , op. cit.

20. As others have observed: cf., Murray Bookchin, *Remaking Society: Pathways to a Green Future* (Boston: South End Press, 1990); Tim Luke, "The Dreams of Deep Ecology," *Telos* 76 (1988); Ariel Salleh, "The Ecofeminism/ Deep Ecology Debate: A Reply to Patriarchal Reason," *Environmental Ethics* , Vol. 14, Fall 1992.

21. Sadly, these two conditions do not entail each other. We have seen cultures that practice a high degree of ecological sustainability—and even reverence for non-human nature—and are also quite patriarchal.

22. "Justice" here includes both institutional norms and face-to-face interpersonal relations, and is founded both in abstract principles and the cultivation of the capacity for care.

23. 1 am drawing here on both the communicative ethics perspective of Jürgen Habermas and the stress on emotional interdependency and care developed by feminist ethicists and psychologists such as Carol Gilligan, Jean Baker Miller, and Nel Noddings.

24. Bill McKibben, *The End of Nature* (New York: Anchor, 1989).

25. Robin Broad, *Plundering Paradise: The Struggle for the Environment in the Philippines* (Berkeley: University of California Press, 1993), pp. 137–39.

26. Raymond Bonner, *At the Hands of Man: Peril and Hope for Africa's Wildlife* (New York: Knopf, 1993), p. 286.

27. Ramachandra Guha, "Radical American Environmentalism and Wilderness Preservation: A Third World Critique," in Lori Gruen and Dale Jamieson, eds., *Reflecting on Nature: Readings in Environmental Philosophy* (N.Y.: Oxford University Press, 1994), p. 249.

28. Edward Abbey, *The Long Journey Home: Some Words in Defense of the American West* (New York: Penguin, 1991), p. 145.

3

ETHICS AND TRAUMA

Levinas, Feminism, and Deep Ecology

How do the sorrows and terrors of personhood, rather than the demands of impersonal reason, shape our ideas of morality? What dark mysteries of history are ethics designed—consciously or unconsciously—to solve?[1]

I hope to shed some light on these questions by juxtaposing three broadly construed ethical perspectives: Emmanuel Levinas's attempt to surmount the rationalist and ontological biases of Western philosophical ethics; the cultural feminist revaluation of ethical theory in light of women's culturally shaped personality structure and socially allotted tasks; and deep ecology's emerging holistic and spiritual orientation toward moral value and human identity. Though I will focus a good deal of critical attention on Levinas, and less on cultural feminism[2] and deep ecology, I believe all three frameworks have something important to tell us. The pressingly important feature they share is a common motivation of *trauma;* i.e., a sense that life is threatened by times of terror and helplessness in which conventional restraints, resources, and forms of understanding are inadequate.[3] I believe that ethical frameworks open to tasks set by the distinctive experiences of our century must comprehend the traumas of mass industrialized genocide, ecocide, and collective personal violence toward women and minorities. Ethics not aimed at somehow "solving"—or permitting us to live with—these dark mysteries are simply not relevant to our horror, our pain, or our scant hope.

LEVINAS: ETHICS OF IRREDUCIBLE CONCERN

Levinas seeks to overcome the fundamental rationalist, egocentric presuppositions of Western philosophical ethics. His project centers on a basic assertion about human relationships, which can be summarized thus: Other philosophies of human existence have tended to describe our ethical obligations as consequences of historically, conceptually, or developmentally prior structures of social life, rational thought, or experience. These philosophies generate the need for ethics out of the contradictions of a life without ethics (as in contract theory or, to some extent, Hegel); or out of the dialectical development of self-consciousness; or out of ontological assumptions about the nature of humanity, nature, reason, or God. Traditionally, in short, ethics is secondary to knowledge of "things" (with that term construed as broadly as possible), including knowledge of or concerns about oneself.

It is this sense of knowledge of things that Levinas tries to capture under various rubrics—most importantly, in his two major philosophical works, as "totality," "essence," and "being." (Levinas believes that the attempt to generate ethics out of self-knowledge or interest is simply a form of war.) For him, knowledge is necessarily aimed at or inevitably leads to objectification, alienation, and domination. Therefore knowledge cannot be the basis of ethical life—that is, of a kind of transcending concern for other people, a concern untouched by our own needs, desires, or attempts to control. As Hume could not get an "ought" from an "is," Levinas finds an unbridgeable gap between knowledge and ethics. If we begin with knowledge—in the guise of science or philosophy, technique or ontology, rational reflection or psychoanalysis—we will never respect the other person as irreducibly other. Knowledge is something acquired, dispensed, and instrumentally used by us. Consequently, knowledge of others necessarily reduces the other to something we possess, something we have acquired, and something—ultimately—we will use.[4] If the foundation of our relation to others is knowledge, the other will be reduced to the same. Otherness will not be allowed to coexist with the agent of sameness.

What Levinas poses as an alternative is the irreducibility or underivability of our concern for the other. This concern does not stem from an empirically or conceptually based sense of the "facts" or the ultimate ontological structures of the universe. It does not come from an expansion of self-interest through identification with the other, either practically (as in contract theory from Locke to Rawls) or transcendentally (as in Kant). Nor does it come from the discovery of common interests in the realm of historical struggle (as in Marxism, feminism, or antiracist movements). Levinas leaves little doubt that the terrain of history, in the sense of political conflict, is too implicated in the wars of self-interest to be a site for ethics.

Like a negative theologian, Levinas is most effective in characterizing what the grounds of our concern for the other are *not*. They are neither a consequence of our knowledge of things (totality) or of the ultimately knowable character of things themselves (essence); nor are they how the things appear to us or exist in their truth (being). Working through, behind, and beyond essence and totality, being and knowledge, and leaving a subtle trace of itself in our capacity to speak with care, the call of the other simply breaks through and across the barriers of science and philosophy and the greedy attempt to satisfy my desires by "knowing" about the world and others.

We do witness the other in the face-to-face relation. The naked vulnerability of the other person, the sense that this person speaks *to us* (whatever is actually *said*), the imperative to leave this person alive and not to murder constitute for Levinas the basis of an ethics outside the limitations of totalizing thought. The face of the other is not an empirical face, reducible to generalizations provided by sociology or psychology. Rather, our sense of the other's vulnerability and need, together with the other's call to justice—neither of which is reducible to any particular empirical, historically defined situation—represents the "trace" of the infinite. The infinite can only be a trace, irreducible to the empirical person in front of me, because, as Robert Bernasconi observes, Levinas is urging us to remember our experience not (as in Heidegger) of "being" but of "the good beyond being," which he also calls "metaphysical exteriority," "transcendence," and "infinity." The good surpasses "being," "objectifying thought," "objective experience," "totality," and history.[5]

This primordial experience constitutes our capacity to function as human beings: "the face of the other is the primordial signification, from which all other signs take their meaning; the perception of the other is the true one, from which all other bodily perception ultimately derives."[6]

Responding to the other's call leaves us infinitely concerned with the other, with the way our very existence on earth takes up her space, with our unlimited responsibility which constitutes or makes possible—rather than follows from—ego-bound interests, communication, or subjective freedom. Only by responding can we give up our attitude of domination; but knowledge of the world always involves a comportment of domination, and Levinas therefore rejects the aggressive imperial gaze of detached reason which has been the hallmark of Western thought from Parmenides to positivism.[7]

Thus, if we are to have ethics at all, it must be, in Levinas's phrase, our "first philosophy." The capacity to speak and to know, to haggle over questions of truth and evidence are *signified by* rather than *signify* this ultimate responsibility for that which cannot be knowingly reduced to myself: the other for whom I must act and be concerned; the other in answering whose call I receive the distinctive imprint of my humanity.

The basis of ethics is thus the sheer fact of "otherness"—that which somehow penetrates my psychic and ethical space from outside.

> The freedom of another could never begin in my freedom, that is, abide in the same present, be contemporary, be representable to me. *The responsibility for the other can not have begun in my commitment, in my decision.* The unlimited responsibility in which I find myself comes from the hither side of my freedom, from a "prior to every memory."
>
> The knot tied in subjectivity, which when subjectivity becomes a consciousness of being is still attested to in questioning, signifies an allegiance of the same to the other, *imposed before any exhibition of the other, preliminary to all consciousness*—or a being affected by the other whom I do not know and who could not justify himself with any identity, who as other will not identify himself with anything.[8]

What motivates Levinas's philosophy? What do we receive and what do we escape from, if in fact my obligation to the other, especially to those most in need, does not follow from who I am or who they are, but precedes those contingent identities? What trauma has led Levinas to this conclusion?

FEMINISM

We will approach this last question indirectly, beginning by noting that there are many problems posed by Levinas's categorical assertions of human responsibility without knowledge, emotional connection, or self-interest. Why, for instance, *must* all knowledge be objectifying, tied to domination and the eradication of difference? Why does Levinas feel compelled to accept the instrumental view of knowledge and leave our ethical connections to a realm beyond essence and outside of knowledge?

What would he make, for instance, of Habermas's attempt to situate forms of knowledge in relation to distinguishable human interests in the control of nature, communicating with others, and social emancipation? Of these three, certainly the first and possibly the second—but not, it would seem, the third—serve the tasks of domination or control. For Habermas the very idea of a free consensus presupposes a kind of knowledge that enables us to distinguish between exploitative and non-exploitative human relations, between domination and justice. That such knowledge takes a different form in natural science is not surprising, because it is motivated by a different—but equally inescapable—human project. Nevertheless, unless we remain under the sway of positivism, we can see that it *remains a form of knowledge.* That is, it is part of a context of discourse and practice in which concepts such as truth, correctness, evidence, argument, reality, and illusion have a place.

Similarly, there is the Western Marxist concept of *praxis,* in which self-knowledge, knowledge of the world, and emancipating political action reinforce each other. In Lukacs, for example, the proletariat's knowledge about its own social status as a commodity helps undermine that status, enabling it to make the transition to different beliefs about and practices in society.[9] This process of achieving self-knowledge about one's social position and then being motivated by that knowledge to change one's position has been relevant in many social contexts, most notably in the political movements of women and of ethnic/racial minorities. The feminist process of consciousness-raising, for example, involves women's transcending their objectification by patriarchy in the process of coming to see that objectification. A kind of knowledge of the self—that the pain one thought was personal, for instance, stems rather from one's social/political condition—makes it possible to initiate relationships and practices which will change the self.

From a rather different source, we might ask Levinas why self-interest cannot lead, by a Kierkegaardian existential dialectic, toward the choice of ethical life, principles, and commitments to the good. Kierkegaard's subject begins in the aesthetic realm (self-interested, without principles, totally egotistical); however, boredom, repetition, and a sense of personal emptiness inevitably lead the aesthetic subject to confront the possibility of ethical life. The outcome of this confrontation is not guaranteed; for Kierkegaard personal choice is always a necessary ingredient of significant personal change. But the self has undergone a kind of premoral education, has acquired a kind of knowledge— of what the inevitable consequences and limitations of a purely selfish life will be. This knowledge does not reduce the other to the same, but allows us to recognize our obligations to principles which involve commitments to care for and respect the other.[10]

Of all such questions about Levinas, I have been most struck by his obliviousness to the feminist counterview that his radical disjuncture of self and other simply consummates a culturally male perspective on human relationships. The idea that our ethical connection to others is possible because the other to whom I am "ethical hostage" leaves a "trace" in the objective realm is at odds with what a host of cultural feminist writers have, in a variety of ways, described. This feminist view is not monolithic (all the more reason Levinas and his commentators should have seen it); its range can be roughly summarized, however.[11]

The culturally male ego is predominantly formed through a process of separation, toward an ideal of autonomy, and results in a bounded, competitive, and dominating self. By contrast, the female ego is shaped through affiliation, toward an ideal of "self-in-relation," and results in an empathic, nurturing, and connected self. Women's selfhood stems from women's role as primary caretakers of infants and their responsibility for emotionality and nurturing in adult relationships. Consigned by patriarchy to the "labor of relatedness," to the production of sexuality, emotional intimacy, and affection, women approach the moral realm from a radically different sense of themselves and others than men. Partly as a consequence of their distinctive ego structures, men and women reason differently about moral problems: men favor abstract principles of justice, while women think in terms of concrete relatedness, and reason via empathy rather than abstraction. Feminist ethicists have developed the concept of an ethics of care, of "maternal thinking," to refer to moral perspectives based in a sense of emotional kinship between self and other, as distinguished from those stemming from abstract principles, self—as opposed to other—interest, or Levinas's own infinite obligation across an irreducible gap.

Cultural feminists have further argued that, because social domination and hierarchy express highly individuated and competitive egos, political injustice and economic exploitation are male forms of relationships. These evils cannot be overcome by the application of abstract principles of liberal democratic-rights theory, or by Marxist-oriented strategies of class struggle, since both these perspectives reproduce the individualism, abstraction, and aggression endemic to the male styles embedded in the evils themselves. Neither, clearly, are they addressed by Levinas's view that we must serve an Other who is categorically so separate. Rather, a social order based in the cooperative, nurturing, noncompetitive style of female identity might overcome the antagonisms and oppressions of male-dominated society. The "feminine virtues" of relationality, empathy, and cooperation could make possible a social order which escapes the domination, exploitation, and violence endemic to both capitalist and bureaucratic state societies. It is further suggested that the image of rigid ego boundaries between people is largely the product of a masculine prejudice inflicted on psychological theory. Certainly women, and no doubt men as well, develop not as self and other but as "selves-in-relation"—so that even theoretically we must speak of persons in the contexts of their relations, unknowable outside those relations. [12]

It is not hard to see that feminism presents a vision of ethical life rooted in a recognition of the fundamental trauma of male domination. The insights of cultural feminism are products of and reflections on the exploitation and devaluation of women. An ethic of care, compassion, and emotional inter-identification is not simply a conceptual alternative to one based on (supposedly) disinterested reason or metaphysical foundations. Rather, this ethic is a desperate cry *for* the recognition of women; and *against* a masculine world which wields impersonal categories in one hand while it ravages women with the other. Feminist ethics celebrates what masculinity has consigned to women and (therefore) devalued. It posits as a strength what men have tried to kill in themselves while they exploit it in women: a sense of emotional connectedness. Feminist ethics is thus a post-traumatic ethics, an imperative exclamation against the hypocrisy and violence of masculinity. If you do not see *who* you are, and you do not learn to understand your own emotions and your emotional relations to others, this ethic warns a patriarchal culture, you will continue to violate women and the men you dominate as well.

In other words, Levinas is lost in a world in which we know the other and answer the other only through this imponderable call to a responsibility divorced from every other facet of my being—*just because he accepts the basic premises of masculine theoretical culture.* On these premises human identities are formed in rigid isolation and opposition to one another; and bridging the gap between self and other always requires some extended process of reflection, self-development, or transformation. In this culture we start as isolated owner/producers (Locke) or isolated minds (Descartes) or aesthetic enjoyers of amoral experience (Kierkegaard) or isolated ego-id-superego complexes whose struggle for mastery and sex can lead, at best, to the autonomous ego of bourgeois adult masculinity (Freud). In patriarchal thought we never start in connection to others. We are not seen as beginning, as we in fact do, as babies at our mother's breast, after having come out of her body. Or if the beginning is there, that image of connection is not carried into the heart of the theoretical representation of adult ethical life. Men have tried to obliterate the memory of their own relation to their mothers. [13]

Ironically, Levinas does have a sense of our beginning with our mothers, but in his view precisely that beginning needs to be overcome if we are to achieve the full ethical identity of someone answering the "call" of the other. Like other patriarchal writers, Levinas sees motherhood as an embracing warmth of care, that which makes a house a home. But the relationship of mothering, just as the figures of mothers themselves, is conceived of as separate from the world of men, of maturity, of the ethical. Women do not provoke our utter responsibility, they do not call for justice or demand honesty; they provide relief. [14]

Further, Levinas makes it clear over and over again that the ethical relation is with a being who is in some sense "foreign" to us. I may owe care to my neighbor, but that neighbor is (strangely) unknown. In discussing a passage of the *Talmud* he states:

> Nothing is more foreign to me than the other; nothing is more inti-
> mate to me than myself. Israel would teach that the greatest intimacy
> of me to myself consists in being at every moment responsible for the
> others, the hostage of others. *I can be responsible for that which I
> did not do and take upon myself a distress which is not mine.* [15]

Between real mothers and children, however, the other's "distress" belongs to the self just because the fluid boundaries between them, as
well as the emotionally based knowledge each has of the other, make
the rigid distinction between self and other much more problematic
than it is in patriarchal thought. [16]

Unfortunately, Levinas's image of the face-to-face relation, a relation meant to overcome the egotism and totalizing reason of traditional
Western philosophy, is ultimately a relation with a being whom we do
not really know. For him, personal identity can be either wrapped in an
inescapable egotism *or* exist in thrall to a superior moral force which
derives from the vulnerability and neediness of the other. Since knowledge is always domination, we cannot "know" that other; rather, his
appearance is what makes knowledge, communication, and, ultimately,
my identity possible.

That the Other is placed higher than I would be a pure simple error
if the welcome I make him consisted in "perceiving" a nature. Sociology, psychology, physiology are thus deaf to exteriority. Man as Other
comes to us from the outside, a separated—or holy—face. His exteriority, that is, his appeal to me, is his truth. In the face to face the self has
neither the privileged position of the subject nor the position of the
thing defined by its place in the system; it is apology, discourse *pro
domo*, but discourse of justification before the other. [17]

Levinas's self—cruelly abandoned in a world of objectifying knowledge and self-interested war—answers the trace of the Divine in the
other's face, and sees the obligation to answer—to put the self in the
other's place and seek the other's good. The basis of this movement, for
Levinas, cannot be the kind of inter-identification described as the basic feminine ego structure by cultural feminism. The use of emotion—
as empathy, compassion, or intuition of the other—reeks to Levinas of
simply another form of egoism. In his view, empathy begins with the
self. Further, the self on an emotional—i.e., for him, empirical and
social—level cannot help but be self-centered. Therefore, the move of
empathy must be a move out of the self-centered self, a move which,

for Levinas, is impossible. We do not respond to the other because of who we are; rather, we are possible as truly human beings only because we first heed the other. Because I respond, I am able to speak, to reason, and to know. The call of the other unifies a self out of the chaos of self-interested action, action which itself reflects varying emotional conditions and desires.

> There is an anarchy essential to multiplicity [of selves]. In the absence of a plane common to the totality . . . one will never know which will, in the free play of the wills, pulls the strings of the game; one will not know who is playing with whom. But a principle breaks through all this trembling and vertigo when the face presents itself, and *demands justice.* [18]

In a theoretical world of purely masculine possibilities, Levinas's solution may be the best alternative possible. But would the whole edifice come crashing down if he realized that it is possible to see human identity as based in a relation to the other *from the start?* that the other is not a trace, not an uninteriorizable "outside," not something which can only get flattened into sameness if it is brought "in," but rather that the other has been known, connected to, and made part of ourselves from the beginning? if he could have conceived of a self so implicated in the other that the Face we see is in some sense our own, because the boundaries of self and other—far from being obliterated by a reductionist or instrumental knowledge—are fluidly constructed by the reality of a shared relationship in which both find their selves?

Even when Levinas seems to be hinting that we have some kind of direct relation with others, that relation seems to me abstract, constructed, distant, formal; in a word, metaphysical rather than emotional or psychological. We may, as he insists in the crucial chapter in *Otherwise Than Being,* necessarily "substitute" ourselves for the other, in fact, for the whole world. But in that substitution there is no real connection to the other, just (once again) that limitless responsibility for the whole universe of suffering and vulnerable others. "Responsibility for my neighbor dates from before my freedom in an immemorial past, an unrepresentable past that was never present and is more ancient than consciousness of . . ." [19]

Just because our responsibility is so absolute—preexisting to everything in our personal life or social world—it never seems to shine with any direct connection to another real human being with whom I, as (in Kierkegaard's words) an actually existing human being, am in an actually existing relationship.

But what is then left for us to relate to? or with? For Levinas the empirical self is always so implicated in struggles for domination that he must appeal to some "other" realm of identity: a primordial, hypothetical, speculative, and ultimately metaphysical notion of a self formed in response to the other's call. Such a self has no basis on which to mobilize a response. In this reliance on a self out of time, mind, and body, Levinas simply repeats the culturally masculine rejection of the particularities of identity. From a feminist viewpoint, such a rejection accumulates authority for the speaker at the expense of the reality of the situation, which is that we can never reach beyond our actual position to a viewpoint which is other than that of an embodied, concretely located person.[20] The greatest fear of masculine thought is that the speaker is simply a single person, bereft of sources of authority such as Objective Reason, Human Nature, or, in the case of Levinas, a "time-out-of-mind" phenomenological essence of selfhood found in response to a reified other.

What is missing from Levinas, then, is a kind of conceptual humility, a humility found not just in the rejection of dominating reason but in the recognition that we are situated, partial, finite, empirical. Further, from the feminist standpoint, our empirical identity is implicated in the other in the very psychological foundation of its being.

HOLOCAUST

It might seem, then, that Levinas's work simply lacks a feminist viewpoint. And while this is true, the matter as a whole is not that simple. Like the best of the feminist writers, Levinas is not simply a theorist, but a person responding to the traumas of our time. His ethic is at once an intellectual edifice *and* an extended prayer. He can—does he realize this?—prove nothing. He can only beg that it be so. And this returns us to the question of motivation. Why does he so want us to feel—or if not to feel, to have it true about ourselves—that beyond knowledge and history, we are ethical hostages for the other whom we do not know?

The answer, I believe, is the trauma of the Holocaust.

In Levinas's world, the destruction of the Jewish people is the basic fact: more basic than theory, more basic than self-interest, more basic than the conventional forms of ego development or psychic, emotional, familial, or even communal inter-identification.

Ethically, what were the Jews of Europe during the Holocaust but the irreducibly other? What were the Jews but the other with whom the gentile world could so little to identify, share so few interests, know so little about? The Fascist world did not know the Jews, or did not know them as Jews, but only as the enemy, as vermin, traitors, insects, germs. The only "knowledge" which was possible was the knowledge of genocide, to reduce the other to the same . . . by murder.

Even more particularly: why does Levinas violate the conventions of symmetry that are virtually ubiquitous in philosophical ethics—i.e., why does he insist that our obligation to the other is in some sense greater than the other's obligation to us? Consider, quite simply, what it meant in Nazi-dominated Europe to side with the Jews. To shelter or protect—to stand against the regime of evil—meant, with few exceptions, torture and death, possibly for one's family, friends, and village, as well as for oneself. To be responsible, as many were, was to reach out to those who could not reach back to you.

In such a world one might well pray with Levinas that we feel a kinship, a bond, to the other we do not know. Or that we feel an infinite obligation of care, holding us hostage before any choice on our part, to that other of whom we know nothing. We are bound solely to the fact of otherness.

For Levinas, only this prayer will do; only this prayer really speaks to that terrible loneliness of the Jew who is not known by the gentile world, or known only in a way that sets in motion the technology of the death camps. Levinas is not just arguing for a new philosophical system; he is praying or dreaming or simply hoping against hope that what he says might be true: that out of the sheer fact of otherness, there is hope of ethical life. Nothing else, as he has seen, can protect the "widow, the stranger, the orphan"—the Jew. In a different setting, yet another group will be the otherness that is grist for the mill of power and murder.

In another of his talmudic readings, this one centered on the question of what Judaism has to give to the world, Levinas suggests that:

morality belongs in us and not in institutions which are not always able to protect it. It demands that human honor know how to exist without a flag. The Jew is perhaps the one who—*because of the inhuman history he has undergone*—understands the suprahuman demand of morality, the necessity of finding within oneself the source of one's moral certainties."[21]

Even more telling, when he points out the way in which the face is beyond any sign or representation, he describes it as "a trace of itself, given over to my responsibility, but to which I am wanting and faulty. It is as though I were responsible for his mortality and guilty for surviving."[22] Here we see Levinas not only as prophet of the murdered people, but as guilty survivor who feels his own survival as a burden.

In a world in which no one seems responsible for me, my choice is simple: I can either reciprocate their immorality or create a moral framework in which concern for the other is built into every basic framework of human life as its metaphysical precondition. If I cannot find such a framework in history, in self-awareness, in knowledge of self or other, it had better be there in a way so basic that it is inescapable. Without it, the result will be . . . the history of the Jews as well as the countless other murders which history has provided. (As Elie Wiesel has remarked: "Has mankind learned the lessons of Auschwitz? No. For details, consult your daily newspaper."[23]) In short, because Levinas finds himself in a world of cultural masculinity—of violence and domination toward the other, of the use of instrumental knowledge to reduce the other to the same—he *must* create a vision of moral responsibility across an unbridgeable gap. Because he is stuck not simply in the theory of cultural masculinity but in its reality, he is compelled to theorize an unrationalizable moral connection based simply in the fact of otherness. In a culturally masculine world every other is, *a priori,* a kind of enemy. Having seen how such a world operates, Levinas is praying that the opposite might somehow come to be—that is, against all appearances to the contrary, the other, far from being the object of hostility, is the unknown and infinitely deserving subject of our ethical devotion.

This world of the Holocaust pervades the nightmares not just of the Jews, but of anyone not stuck in denial. After Stalinism, Cambodia, the economically induced mass starvations in Africa, Latin America's bloody civil struggles, and too many more tragedies than can be mentioned, mass industrialized murder cannot be dismissed as an aberration of the 1940s; it is the defining characteristic of the twentieth century. The enormous power of Levinas's thought, its attraction despite his hopelessly dense language, resides in the fact that it speaks to this condition, offering a prayer of hope during a century of death camps. That prayer does not describe what we know or could ever know. From the standpoint of the best in cultural masculinity, it describes what we must be if we are to survive. Reaching out beyond the self-imposed isolation and loneliness of the masculine ego, of a patriarchal society which relegates empathy and emotional inter-identification to a devalued female caste, Levinas's philosophy seeks a source of ethical life in what must be a metaphysical mystery to the lost self of male culture: the voice, the face, the very presence, of the other.

ECOCIDE

Is there then no way out? Are Levinas's failings simply those of patriarchy? Is his reaction to the Holocaust all that we can expect in a traumatized world? Likewise, is the feminist critique hopeless in the face of historical reality? Is it perhaps not Levinas who is the dreamer but the feminist? After all, in a world made by men empathy, connection, and inter-identification have little chance or place. Does feminism's answer to male domination remain within the privatized and domesticated realm of the family or the intimate relationship, at least until patriarchy is ended? Is the feminist response to the trauma of male violence necessarily marginalized until social institutions come to reflect the logic of feminine personality styles and forms of relationship? Is the feminist dream of an ethical cosmos of care and compassion as alien to the real world of exploited wives and sexually abused children as Levinas's dream of infinite obligation is to the real world of the Holocaust? Are both these frameworks, different as they are, trapped by history, leaving us no way out? Are they simply lanterns waving dimly in a shrouded night of endless trauma?

Perhaps.

But perhaps not. Perhaps there is in progress another, even more encompassing Death Event, which can be the historical condition for an ethic of compassion and care.

I speak of the specter of ecocide, the continuing destruction of species and ecosystems, and the growing threat to the basic conditions essential to human life. What kind of ethic is adequate to this brutally new and potentially most unforgiving of crises? How can we respond to *this* trauma with an ethic which demands a response, and does not remain marginalized?

Here I will at least begin in agreement with Levinas. As he rejects an ethics proceeding on the basis of self-interest, so I believe the anthropocentric perspectives of conservation or liberal environmentalism cannot take us far enough. Our relations with nonhuman nature are poisoned and not just because we have set up feedback loops that already lead to mass starvations, skyrocketing environmental disease rates, and devastation of natural resources.

The problem with ecocide is not just that it hurts human beings. Our uncaring violence also violates the very ground of our being, our natural body, our home. Such violence is done not simply to the other—as if the rainforest, the river, the atmosphere, the species made extinct are totally different from ourselves. Rather, we have crucified ourselves-in-relation-to-the-other, fracturing a mode of being in which self and other can no more be conceived as fully in isolation from each other than can a mother and a nursing child.

We are that child, and nonhuman nature is that mother. If this image seems too maudlin, let us remember that *other* lactating women can feed an infant, but we have only one earth mother.

What moral stance will be shaped by our personal sense that we are poisoning ourselves, our environment, and so many kindred spirits of the air, water, and forests?

To begin, we may see this tragic situation as setting the limits to Levinas's perspective. The other which is nonhuman nature is not simply known by a "trace," nor is it something of which all knowledge is necessarily instrumental. This other is inside us as well as outside us. We prove it with every breath we take, every bit of food we eat, every glass of water we drink. We do not have to find shadowy traces on or in the faces of trees or lakes, topsoil or air: we are made from them.

Levinas denies this sense of connection with nature. Our "natural" side represents for him a threat of simple consumption or use of the other, a spontaneous response which must be obliterated by the power of ethics in general (and, for him in particular, Jewish religious law).[24] A "natural" response lacks discipline; without the capacity to heed the call of the other, unable to sublate the self's egoism. Worship of nature would ultimately result in an "everything-is-permitted" mentality, a close relative of Nazism itself. For Levinas, to think of people as "natural" beings is to assimilate them to a totality, a category or species which makes no room for the kind of individuality required by ethics.[25] He refers to the "elemental" or the "there is" as unmanaged, unaltered, "natural" conditions or forces that are essentially alien to the categories and conditions of moral life.[26]

One can only lament that Levinas has read nature—as to some extent (despite his intentions) he has read selfhood—through the lens of masculine culture. It is precisely our sense of belonging to nature as system, as interaction, as interdependence, which can provide the basis for an ethics appropriate to the trauma of ecocide. As cultural feminism sought to expand our sense of personal identity to a sense of inter-identification with the human other, so this ecological ethics would expand our personal and species sense of identity into an inter-identification with the natural world.

Such a realization can lead us to an ethics appropriate to our time, a dimension of which has come to be known as "deep ecology."[27] For this ethics, we do not begin from the uniqueness of our human selfhood, existing against a taken-for-granted background of earth and sky. Nor is our body somehow irrelevant to ethical relations, with knowledge of it reduced always to tactics of domination. Our knowledge does not assimilate the other to the same, but reveals and furthers the continuing dance of interdependence. And our ethical motivation is neither rationalist system nor individualistic self-interest, but a sense of connection to all of life.

> The deep ecology sense of self-realization goes beyond the modern Western sense of "self" as an isolated ego striving for hedonistic gratification. . . . Self, in this sense, is experienced as integrated with the whole of nature.[28]

> Having gained distance and sophistication of perception [from the development of science and political freedoms] we can turn and recognize who we have been all along . . . we are our world knowing itself. We can relinquish our separateness. We can come home

again—and participate in our world in a richer, more responsible and poignantly beautiful way.[29]

Ecological ways of knowing nature are necessarily participatory. [This] knowledge is ecological and plural, reflecting both the diversity of natural ecosystems and the diversity in cultures that nature-based living gives rise to.

The recovery of the feminine principle is based on inclusiveness. It is a recovery in nature, woman and man of creative forms of being and perceiving. In nature it implies seeing nature as a live organism. In woman it implies seeing women as productive and active. Finally, in men the recovery of the feminine principle implies a relocation of action and activity to create life-enhancing, not life-reducing and life-threatening societies.[30]

In this context, the knowing ego is not set against a world it seeks to control, but one of which it is a part. To continue the feminist perspective, the mother knows or seeks to know the child's needs. Does it make sense to think of her answering the call of the child in abstraction from such knowledge? Is such knowledge necessarily domination? Or is it essential to a project of care, respect and love, precisely because the knower has an intimate, emotional connection with the known?[31] Our ecological vision locates us in such close relation with our natural home that knowledge of it is knowledge of ourselves. And this is not, contrary to Levinas's fear, reducing the other to the same, but a celebration of a larger, more inclusive, and still complex and articulated self.[32] The noble and terrible burden of Levinas's individuated responsibility for sheer existence gives way to a different dream, a different prayer:

Being rock, being gas, being mist, being Mind,
Being the mesons traveling among the galaxies with the speed of light,
You have come here, my beloved one. . . .
You have manifested yourself as trees, as grass, as butterflies, as single-celled beings, and as chrysanthemums;
but the eyes with which *you looked at me this morning tell me you have never died.*[33]

In this prayer, we are, quite simply, all in it together. And, although this new ecological Holocaust—this creation of planet Auschwitz—is under way, it is not yet final. We have time to step back from the brink, to repair our world. But only if we see that world not as an other across an irreducible gap of loneliness and unchosen obligation, but as a part of ourselves as we are part of it, to be redeemed not out of duty, but out of love; neither for ourselves nor for the other, but for us all.

AND YET . . .

That last sentence would make an elegant finale to this essay. Unfortunately, our trauma is so great, and exists on so many levels, that no such simplicity is possible. The movement from Levinas through feminism to deep ecology is not a dialectic of success. Rather, each moment must be preserved, at least until the traumas which gave rise to them have been forgotten—or we have created a world in which their recurrence is impossible. Thus it would be fitting for someone to point out that I have taken for granted that nature—as a totality structured by principles of interaction—is nurturing and benign. Yet nature—whether as the drama of an earthquake or the quiet tragedy of crib death—can be as brutal as any hired killer. How are we to structure an "ethic of nature" in the face of such brutality, unless we ignore the pain nature causes and think only of blue skies and daffodils?

The answer is that brutality exists only from the standpoint of the isolated ego. It is true that nature cares nothing for individuals; yet nature as a totality provides the inspiration for deep ecology. In that inspiration, we must look not at how this or that person, animal, or plant has fared. We must look at the whole and pronounce it fitting or horrific or indifferent: the brutalities of nature are inevitable consequences of cycles of birth and death, renewal and destruction. Unlike the nightmare genocides or everyday viciousness of human cruelty, they are essential to a totality of life which we judge proper, beautiful, and ultimately moral. In that totality each process has a productive role: when one animal eats another, one animal feeds another. The "injustice" of defective life is simply part of the price of living in an imperfect world. An appreciation of these principles of life is possible, however, only if we give up the standpoint of the isolated, self-interested ego. To practice deep ecology is to practice the art of such vision. Without it, the ecological revelation makes no sense.

But such revelation cannot replace Levinas's concerns: care for the human neighbor is a call still to be heard in the councils of deep ecology. However much we identify with the earth and nature, the effects of ecocide are not felt equally by all. The poisons disproportionately affect the poor, people of color, and the Third World. Without a commitment to social equality, efforts to create a sustainable society will place vastly unequal burdens on the socially powerless. Deep ecologists must beware of identifying with all of life while ignoring the compelling differences that are structured by social relations and theorized by conventional anthropocentric perspectives. The widening circle of ethical concern must not skip over human beings, but move through them. We are responsible, as Levinas tells us, "for all who are not Hitler."[34]

Yet it is our final continuing trauma that the demarcation of this responsibility is terribly, at times tragically, unclear.[35] What is to be our ethical stance in a world which may contain yet another—and another—Hitler? Knowing that the Holocaust is not a grotesque fantasy but an established fact, and that the world repeats this fact and threatens more, how are we to know where the boundaries of ethical responsibility—of a Levinasian, feminist, or deep ecology sort—lie? When is my enemy a neighbor for whom I am responsible? and when is he a Nazi, savagely and madly bent on my death? When are people to be offered empathy, compassion, and compromise? and when have they so violated the bounds of humanity that they—as in those who threatened nuclear war for thirty years or who continue to produce ozone-destroying CFCs—are no longer my neighbor, or someone with whom I can identify, or anything but a rabid cancer on the body of the ecosystem?

The ethical perspectives examined here leave off where these questions begin. The loneliness, terror, and hope we feel in responding to them marks us all as human beings trying to live ethically in an age of trauma.

NOTES

1. The author acknowledges helpful comments from Richard A. Cohen and Mario Moussa.

2. For a critical discussion of cultural feminism see my "Broken Relations: Some Barriers to the Triumph of Feminine Virtue," in Roger S. Gottlieb, ed.,

Radical Philosophy: Tradition, Counter-Tradition, Politics (Philadelphia: Temple University Press, 1993).

3. For a clinical and social account of trauma, see Judith Herman, *Trauma and Recovery* (New York: HarperCollins, 1993).

4. Levinas is relatively untouched by environmentalist critiques of instrumental knowledge applied to nature. He rejects the Heideggerean concern with Being, except insofar as our concern with that abstraction signals our own moral dimension. Concerning Levinas and animals see John Llewelyn, "Am I Obsessed by Bobby? (Humanism of the Other Animal)" in Robert Bernasconi and Simon Critchley, eds., *Re-Reading Levinas* (Bloomington: Indiana University Press, 1989).

5. "Levinas and Derrida," in Richard A. Cohen, ed., *Face-to-Face with Levinas* (Albany: State University of New York Press, 1986), 185.

6. Robert Gibbs, *Correlations in Rosenzweig and Levinas* (Princeton: Princeton University Press, 1992), 186.

7. The phrase and the point come from Susan A. Handelman's insightful *Fragments of Redemption: Jewish Thought and Literary Theory in Benjamin, Scholem, and Levinas* (Bloomington, Ind.: Indiana University Press, 1991), 211.

8. *Otherwise Than Being or Beyond Essence* (Boston: Kluwer Academic Publishers, 1974), 10, 25, my emphasis in both quotes.

9. Georg Lukacs, *History and Class Consciousness* (Cambridge, Mass.: M.I.T. Press, 1971).

10. Søren Kierkegaard, *Either/Or*, 2 vols. (Princeton: Princeton University Press, 1964).

11. The proliferation of feminist viewpoints makes it hard to speak of any "general" feminist position. My focus is on the trend often called "cultural" feminism.

12. Some central texts on the relation between female psychology, women's social role and feminist ethics and social theory are Jean Baker Miller, *Toward a New Psychology of Women* (Boston: Beacon, 1976); Miriam Greenspan, *A New Approach to Women and Therapy* (New York: McGraw-Hill, 1983); Nancy Chodorow, *The Reproduction of Mothering: Psychoanalysis and the Sociology of Gender* (Berkeley: University of California Press, 1978); Carol Gilligan, *In a Different Voice* (Cambridge: Harvard University Press, 1983); Susan Griffin, *Women and Nature: The Roaring Inside Her* (New York: Harper & Row, 1979); Carolyn Merchant, *The Death of Nature* (New York: Harper & Row, 1980); Eva Feder Kittay and Diana T. Meyers, eds., *Women and Moral Theory* (Totowa, N.J.: Rowman and Littlefield, 1987); B. Andelson, C. Gudorf, and M. Pellauer eds., *Women's Consciousness, Women's Conscience* (New York: Harp-

er & Row, 1987); Nancy Hartsock, *Money Sex and Power: Toward a Feminist Historical Materialism* (Boston: Northeastern University Press, 1983).

13. This last phrase comes from Miriam Greenspan.

14. The sexism of Levinas's early and middle work is somewhat muted by his use of mothering as a model of supportive relationship in *Otherwise Than Being*. However, his awareness of feminist issues remains minimal at best

15. *Nine Talmudic Readings* (Bloomington, Ind.: Indiana University Press, 1990), 85.

16. Space precludes a discussion of Levinas's concept of fecundity. In brief, that account, while tremendously interesting on its own terms, replicates many of the problems of the material discussed here.

17. *Totality and Infinity* (Pittsburgh: Duquesne University Press, 1969) 291, 293.

18. *Totality and Infinity*, 294, my emphasis.

19. "Ethics as First Philosophy," in Sean Hand, ed., *The Levinas Reader* (London: Blackwell, 1989), 84.

20. I have made a similar critique of various Marxists in *History and Subjectivity: The Transformation of Marxist Theory* (Philadelphia: Temple University Press, 1987).

21. *Nine Talmudic Readings*, 81–82, my emphasis.

22. *Otherwise Than Being*, 91. See also Handelman's *Fragments*, 212–14, 270, 276.

23. I cannot recall the precise location of this statement

24. See *Nine Talmudic Readings*, 83.

25. *Totality and Infinity*, 120–21.

26. See *Totality and Infinity*, 130–34; and "There Is: Existence without Existents," in *The Levinas Reader*.

27. The literature is very large here. For a beginning on eco-feminism, see: Irene Diamond and Gloria Orenstein, eds., *Reweaving the World: The Emergence of Ecofeminism* (San Francisco: Sierra Club Books, 1990). For deep ecology, see Christopher Manes, *Green Rage: Radical Environmentalism and the Unmaking of Civilization* (Boston: Little, Brown) 1990, as well as the works by Vandana Shiva and Joanna Macy referred to in later footnotes.

28. Bill Devall and George Sessions, "The Development of Natural Resources and the Integrity of Nature," *Environmental Ethics* 6 (Winter 1984): 302–3.

29. Joanna Macy, *World as Lover, World as Self* (Berkeley: Parallax Press, 1991), 14.

30. Vandana Shiva, *Staying Alive: Women, Ecology and Development* (London: Zed Books: 1989), 41, 53.

31. See Sara Ruddick, *Maternal Thinking* (Boston: Beacon Press, 1989).

32. See the account of the "loving eye" as opposed to the "arrogant eye" in Marilyn Frye's *The Politics of Reality* (Freedom, Calif.: Crossing Press, 1983), 75–76.

33. "The Old Mendicant," by Thich Nhat Hanh, quoted in Joanna Macy, *World as Lover, World as Self*, 14.

34. *Nine Talmudic Readings*, 87.

35. I develop this point in my Introduction to Roger S. Gottlieb, ed., *Thinking the Unthinkable: Meanings of the Holocaust* (Mahwah, N.J.: Paulist Press, 1990).

4

CAN WE TALK (ABOUT ANIMAL RIGHTS)?

Animals suffer for lots of reasons: they freeze to death in bad winters, get torn to shreds by predators, and grow old and starve because they can no longer hunt. If you put enough sad music on the screen as we witness such moments, doubtless many an eye will fill with tears. But such tears are easily remedied by a moment's reflection on the endless and necessary cycles of life and death.

But there are other forms of suffering that do not go down so easy. The sea birds covered in oil, the fox caught in a fur hunter's trap gnawing off its leg, the long, long lines of cows waiting to be bludgeoned and then to have their throats slit, the millions of mice to be used for God knows what, including the ones who have been scientifically, genetically *engineered* to get cancer ("onco-mice," they are called). Not to mention whole species, thousands of them, dying off because humans have taken or contaminated their habitat, or brought in exotic species against which they have not evolved defenses, or just eaten too many.

What happens when we look at their pain? Quite often, not a whole lot, because most of us do not bother to look. Or, if we do, what we see is an abstraction: x million killed in experiments, x thousands of species lost. What if we do look, carefully, slowly, willing to accept whatever feelings arise, at—say—polar bears forced to cannibalize each other because global warming has melted so much ice they can no longer hunt. Look at them—magnificent creatures clad in thick white fur, superbly adapted to the frigid ice and snow, at home even in the sea. They are mothers that protect their young, playful cubs and powerful hunters of seals. They are dying, not from old age or from a struggle with predators or competition in the herd, but because we are killing them. Through global warming. Reckless sport hunting. Human-made toxins that build up in their flesh.

The point is that it is not just the suffering of the individual polar bears that gets to us, or even the potential loss of this majestic species. It is *how hard it is to look at ourselves.* To save the polar bear, and the big cats, and the cows on the assembly line, how much would *we* have to change? How much of our economy, our culture, our family life? How many laws would we have to pass? How many Thanksgiving get-togethers would feel (and taste) different? Would we have to give up our dream of endless economic expansion in order to leave some room for other species? Would we have to convince all those folks who believe that charbroiled steak equals a good time that tofu is just as good? Would we have to say that the whole human enterprise of the last ten thousand years—seeking more and more power, wealth, control, technical expertise, and possessions—should be (deeply, seriously, essentially) restrained?

Between the intensity of the pain we feel, the guilt over our own complicity, and the seeming impossibility of what *all* of us would have to do to transform, we are left in a difficult and contorted moral position. Guilt for ourselves and rage against "the others" who "just don't get it." The need to do something to "make it all stop" and the certain realization that we can't. A life which seems hard enough already, but to which those "animal rights types" want to add *more* concerns, problems, things to feel upset about.

There is no way out of this conflict and confusion. That is, no way that will lead to a simple fix of the problems, or a universally accepted way for people on different sides to come together and create a calm, reasoned, agreeable moral conversation. The truth is that we have extraordinarily powerful feelings on this subject, and these gut responses can translate into very strong moral intuitions. These opposing intuitions can be summarized this way:

> *Animal Rights Activist Intuitions.* Animals suffer, just like us. They love their mates and their children, they romp in the grass and tussle with each other. They delight in soaring across a dawn sky, running through the forest, chewing their cud. And despite the occasional time when they hurt people, they are pretty much defenseless

against us. And think of how much suffering we cause them: in labs, in farms, at the meatpackers. If you really, really look at them, listen to their screams, take in their wounds, how can you continue to do this to them?

People First Intuitions. People are more important than animals. They just are. And, besides, life is hard enough already—if I want a steak or fried chicken, I'll just have one. They taste good. And the idea that some rat or pigeon has rights is just, well, ridiculous. People need food. Science needs lab animals. People all over the world are starving and sick, and you want me to worry about a cow or a mouse? Get real. If you want to go gaga over your labradoodle, that's fine. But leave the rest of us alone. Most people, most of the time, are going to use animals for whatever they want. It'll never change.

Things might ease off a bit if we could all just "agree to disagree." Why can't each of us get along with people who have different opinions about eating meat, using animals in experiments, or the amount of space a veal calf should have in his cage before he's slaughtered? Yet, this will not work, because whether or not a particular "difference" is allowable is part of the problem itself. As individuals, as a society, we have to draw lines: between differences that are a matter of taste (like a really bad wardrobe) and differences that will put you in jail (like abusing your kids). Although the option of tolerance for differences is surely a *possible* option, animal rights and animal care just might *not* be a toleration kind of issue.

At the same time, even if we think our views are so morally right that people on the other side are not just different, but wrong—and *so* wrong that what they do should be illegal and considered an ethical outrage—whichever side *we* are on, there still are an awful lot of people on the *other* side.[1] If we are going to get along with each other morally—thinking of those on the other side as moral agents who deserve respect for their choices just as we do—at the very least we had better try to understand each other. What's more, such understanding might lead us to a bit of common ground.

When views have a long-standing, broad acceptance—as human superiority, eating meat, and the scientific exploitation of animals do—we have to take them seriously on their own terms. Similarly, when so many people are moral vegetarians, or oppose using animals in science, it will not work to write them off as overly sentimental hippies. If either side is dismissed at the beginning, attempts to communicate with—or even to comprehend—these different people will be doomed from the outset. And where would that leave us? A truly moral conversation—in which we open ourselves to what the other person is saying and find as much truth in it as possible—seems to be called for.

Let's first acknowledge that we relate to animals in so many different ways. Consider: we use animals for food, for work, for scientific experiments. There are pets and wild animals and zoo animals. Animals are prey for hunters, sacrifices for some religions, and companions to the blind. How are we to make sense of all these different contexts? I will not offer a simple, universal rule.[2] However, we can compare two very different contexts and see how the differences affect our responses.

Here is the first scenario: When you order a delicious veal parmesan at a fancy Italian restaurant, you are consuming the flesh of a living being who was confined in a cage so small that it could barely move, always in the dark so that its flesh would be pale, without any company (which it needs, being a social animal), and, to preserve the delicacy of its taste, was never fed the solid food it requires.

Clearly, there are all sorts of *cultural* reasons to keep eating that veal parmesan. It has been a delicacy for a very long time. It tastes great. People earn a living raising, cooking, and serving it. Yet, if you lean in the animal rights direction, as I do, it might seem pretty easy to dismiss all such defenses of veal by pointing out that slavery was culturally supported and that people made money off of the Holocaust. But the vast majority of people simply do not equate cages for veal calves with concentration camps, so while comparing the treatment of animals to the horrors humans have inflicted on each other might be morally valid, it may not seem so to many of the people you need to convince.

But, it *is* very hard to defend the way veal calves are raised without saying flat out that the pain of animals is morally meaningless. This position is a kind of orthodox anthropocentrism: people are the center of all things and the beings on the periphery do not count for very much. Interestingly, though, even people who believe this sort of thing typically do not believe it *completely*; and it is that lack of completeness which leaves an opening for the other side. For example: a good number of the veal parmesan eaters (or servers) doubtless have their own special, favorite pets that they would not dream of treating the way veal calves are treated: animals whose welfare, happiness, and pleasure count for something. The fundamental inconsistency here creates a deep logical hole that is very hard to climb out of.

So when we look at veal—and, indeed, at meat eating generally— what we have is a deeply entrenched social practice that is, when examined, pretty much without any moral justification. What can the veal eater say in response? Not much, which is why his or her response is generally laughter, contempt, ignoring the truth, not looking at films of factory farms and slaughterhouses, saying "that's just the way we do things around here," and repeating "it tastes good," as if that were sufficient *reason* to keep eating it. One usually gets a lot of attitude, but very little argument. If the cheerful meat eater does not want to engage seriously with an animal rights advocate's claims, what are we to do?

Well, we can start by recognizing that the moral failure of modern meat eating is not the end of the story. There are *many* things we do that do not add up morally. I certainly have my own ethical weaknesses. Indeed, every animal rights activist lives in a way that harms animals. Such activists drive their cars and plug into the power grid, thus contributing to the global warming that is eradicating countless species. Even their fully vegan diet involves large-scale agriculture that displaces animals. And when their children are sick, they do not reject "out of principle" medicines that have been developed through testing on animals.

One of the things that distinguishes ethics in an age of global warming is that, short of dropping out completely, we cannot help but be part of the problem. Certainly we will be less of a part if we stop eating animal products and refuse to buy consumer products tested on animals. But so long as we are functioning members of this society, we will be in this bind.

And the sad truth is that a lot of people who cherish animals deeply can at the same time be pretty uncaring about other people and other important, moral concerns. They might think of and speak to animal-eating humans with hatred and verbal violence. They might take refuge in a comforting sense of superiority, endlessly taking the moral inventory of everyone else's failings while never seriously examining their own.

This line of thought does not eradicate the tensions between the "two sides." It does, however, enable the morally critical animal rights activist to approach his or her adversary with a less arrogant and more modest posture.[3] We might also be able to see that a partial improvement is better than no improvement at all. In some countries, there has been agreement on legal restrictions on how you can raise veal, and in other matters relating to animals as well. If these new laws are not enough for the moral vegetarian, I completely understand. But moral life is often, perhaps typically, not a case of "enough." It usually is, at best, a case of getting a "little bit better."

Now let's consider a second scenario: Your child has been born with cystic fibrosis (CF), a generally fatal genetic condition in which a missing enzyme leads to lung and digestive problems. While CF used to spell a quite early death for everyone afflicted, recent research has now enabled many to live into their thirties and forties.

If it is your child, doomed to a life of frequent lung infections, rounds of seemingly endless coughing, near constant chest physical therapy to clear the distinctly thick and immovable CF mucous, do you care how many lab animals have to die to find a cure, or even just a treatment that will enable your child to have a somewhat longer, somewhat more tolerable life? In forty years, the median survival age for CF has gone from ten to thirty-seven. *That's* what you're counting, not the number of mice that were used to develop treatments, and potentially a cure, for your child.

If meat eating, in particular veal, is an immoral self-indulgence, the use of animals for research to cure deadly diseases is something else. Here we have what at least looks like a clear choice: allow a child to suffer and die young, or do what needs to be done for the human at the expense of animals. If you are that parent—or the child himself—do you think you will put much stock in accounts of animal suffering?

Of course, the animal rights defender can simply say that there is no reason to prefer the human to the animal, or to raise questions of degree and scope.[4] Further, and more powerfully, it can be argued that using animals for research costs money, that money for health care is limited, and that there are a lot of other things that we can do with that money that are good for people's health and do *not* involve animal cruelty. We can clean up the environment so fewer people get cancer from pollution; we can teach people to have better health habits so lifestyle diseases diminish; we can encourage people not to eat animal foods, since they are a big contributor to ill health. These measures will not hurt animals at all; in fact, they will help both animals *and* people, a win-win solution.

Yet even the best environmental regimes and an entire population doing yoga, meditating, and eating nothing but salads, brown rice, and lentil stew will not end genetic health problems like CF. We will still have the desperate parent and the sick child, the people with a terrible illness and the animals whose lives we will want to sacrifice to find better treatments.

Perhaps, once again, the only approach with a reasonable chance of success is to try to make things a little better. First, stop all the stupid, wasteful, even insane animal experiments: the ones that drip cosmetics into rabbits' eyes until they go blind; or that smash monkey's heads into walls to see if having heads smashed into a wall will injure the brain; or that test how long it takes to make animals crazy by randomly subjecting them to electrical shocks.

As for the cystic fibrosis experiments? Well, perhaps we could agree to talk about them later. There is a lot that can be done to limit or eliminate animal experiments *before* we get around to stopping the research aimed at curing lethal illnesses.

In a moral life we are often faced with difficult choices. Sometimes these are really false choices, and we should make sure we know who or what has said "Choose between A and B." Maybe there is an option C that would work out for us all—like the holistic and preventative health measures described above. Still, at times, and sadly, there are instances when there is no way out of painful alternatives. We will have pain in this life, and so will everyone else, and no amount of moral goodness will ever take that away. Just as the "I can do anything to animals I want" types might have pets they cherish, animal rights supporters still privilege their own children, or other people, over animals. That is one reason this issue of animal experiments is both very difficult and a place where agreement across real differences might be reached.

The practical truth of any moral claim—animal rights, women's rights, gay marriage, what we owe to people starving far away—is only as powerful as the level of moral development of the people we are talking to. No matter how right a moral claim is, if humanity is not ready to take in its truth, it will have no social consequence. It may be that according full respect for animals is just something that is not psychologically, and hence morally, possible now.[5] Every minute of every day our civilization may indeed be committing monstrous crimes, and perhaps the anguished, "extremist" cries of animal rights activists are just what we need to wake us up. However, I suspect that in this case, whatever changes we make will necessarily be gradual, based more on quiet understanding and slow, moderate improvements than on wholesale moral condemnations.

Probably some animal rights activists, and perhaps even the animals themselves, would think this is a cowardly cop-out in the face of mass slaughter. But we should remember that the long struggle for women's social and legal equality is far from over; and that while the slaves were freed in 1865, more than a century later African Americans were still fighting for even basic civil rights. With all important change that has taken place, it is hard to know how much was accomplished through anger, verbal violence, and coercive laws, and how much by the slow, patient work of moral conversation—by doing our best to understand "the other" despite bitter disagreement. Perhaps reflecting on this history will help us to be a little more satisfied with limited gains that make life a little better, rather than clinging with rage and bitterness to an impossible ideal. Like it or not, big changes are slow.

In the meantime, those of us who pay attention can at least acknowledge how upset this makes us. We can commiserate with other people's moral limits, knowing we have plenty ourselves. We can ask ourselves what the difference is between the golden retriever who sleeps on our bed at night and the bacon we eat for breakfast. And if we are really willing to feel the full range and intensity of our emotions about our animal cousins, to take in their pain and our responsibility for it, and to have compassion for them and for our fellow humans at the same time, who knows what might result? Not enough, to be sure. But surely enough to make a difference.

NOTES

1. Though the animal rights position might still represent a small minority, the vast majority has been wrong about issues in the past that were at first opposed by only tiny minorities. Moreover, the animal rights position is making something of an inroad in social life. Vegetarians are a steadily growing number, there are more limits on animal labs than there used to be, and we have—however inconsistently applied—an Endangered Species Act, which says that

normal property rights can be suspended if activity on privately owned land threatens to erase a species. And there are more examples.

2. Any such rule would be so abstract that we would not really know what it meant until I described how it operated in each context.

3. Comfort for both sides can be found in an unexpected source: the vegetarian perspective of Rabbi Abraham Isaac Kook (d. 1935), the chief rabbi of pre-state Israel. Though Kook functioned in a community in which meat eating was the accepted rule, he argued for future vegetarianism from the perspective of biblical history. He never issued an absolute rule, but he pointed out that there are many biblical rules restricting what and how we eat; thus, the way we eat is a matter in which God's commands operate. Thus, humans are in a very long process of moral development, which starts with some restrictions on what we can do to animals, but will end up in an ideal of respect and care, including a refusal to use animals for food.

4. Questions such as: How many animals would you sacrifice for a cure? A million? A hundred million? A hundred billion? And for what disease? For one, like CF, which afflicts some 300,000 in the United States? For one that afflicts 300? Or 3? Is there no limit at all?

5. I liken it to calling for women's equality in the seventeenth century (as a very few did) or to demanding the end of slavery in 1820.

II

The Promises of Religious Environmentalism

5

RELIGIOUS ENVIRONMENTALISM

What It Is, Where It's Heading, and Why We Should Be Going in the Same Direction

My topic is the important and unprecedented phenomenon of religious environmentalism.[1] In its most compressed form my message is simple: religious environmentalism is good for environmentalism, good for religion, and good for earth community. I'll also hazard a few thoughts on the role scholars can play in this movement. [2]

I

To begin, religious environmentalism offers the broader, secular environmental community a language in which to express the depth of our relationship to the rest of the natural world and the gravity of the disastrous policies and misguided values which have led to damage already done. When we read, for instance, that the placental blood of newborns contains 287 toxic chemicals, it will not do simply to say that this is unhealthy, inconvenient, or a damn shame.[3] The magnitude of the violation of what should be a human being's safest place calls forth a more powerful, more visceral, response. We want, I believe, to make it clear that this kind of desecration is absolutely intolerable. In this context most people would find even a language of rights inadequate to the severity of the problem, and one of "consumer preferences" patently absurd. And thus we might turn to Bartholomew, head of the Eastern Orthodox Church, who stated flatly that "To pollute the environment is a sin."

Of course the language of sin—and related concepts like reverence, holiness, or the sacred—may be alienating to many: especially since such language seems to come so easily from the mouths of religious conservatives eager to cast the first stone. Yet when used with a self-reflective humility which includes the person speaking, it invokes a kind of moral seriousness that seems particularly appropriate to poisoning children before they are born. And it is a typical feature of religious environmentalists that along with vigorous criticism of current environmental practices, goes an honest admission of their own failings. They make it clear that they are not talking about simple mistakes, inconveniences easily rectified, or strategic errors; that we are confronting a profound and wide-ranging failure of virtually every aspect of modern society; and that a problem this deep and systemic necessarily involves some complicity on the part of virtually all of us. The sin is collective, and the need for repentance is as well. Whether or not one makes sense of these terms religiously or not, they communicate what we feel as well as, or perhaps better than, any other language. In terms of religion itself, Protestant theologian James Nash has pointed out that "Ongoing repentance is warranted. . . . For most theologians . . . the theological focus has been on sin and salvation, the fall and redemption, the divine-human relationship *over against* the biophysical worlds as a whole. The focus has been overwhelmingly on human history to the neglect of natural history. . . . "[4] Or as Christian Creation theologian Matthew Fox bluntly argued: "The anthropocentrism of ecclesial titles like 'People of God' is appalling. . . . What about the four-legged people? The cloud people? The tree people? The winged and finned people? Are they not also integral to the love of the Creator?"[5] For western society as a whole, we might note how Thomas Berry—a leading figure among the new ecotheologians—summarized the western attitude towards nature in one word: autism.[6] He elaborates: "After dealing with suicide, homicide, and genocide, our Western Christian moral code collapses completely: it cannot deal with biocide. . . . Nor have church authorities made any sustained protest against the violence being done to the planet."[7]

Further, religious environmentalists can draw on traditional religious culture for value-oriented resources that are positive as well as
critical. When secular environmentalists rail at out-of-control consumerism, consumerism that is doubtless an essential element of our collective inability to live more sustainably, they often come off sounding
like shrill spoilsports. Religious people, however, can appeal to the simple (and comparatively non-polluting) joys of religious community as
alternatives—ones which are both more fulfilling and, quite literally,
cannot be bought. In general, I believe, people will not give up pleasures, even self-destructive ones, if they cannot see that a better life will
be possible when they do so. The joys of Sabbath rest, or the comfort of
a congregational community, provide alternatives to the Mall and Ama-
zon.com. Of course one need not be religious to appreciate the nurturing aspects of community and rest. Yet these values are perhaps most
familiar to us as presented by the culture of religion—i.e., by a framework of beliefs and values which, as Bill McKibben puts it, offers something else than accumulation as the highest goal of life.[8]

Finally, at their most moral and socially engaged religious traditions
can offer models of humane and compassionate activist politics that are
particularly appropriate to environmentalism. For environmentalism to
succeed, it must offer a universal vision of community, one which includes all people and all of life, not mere interest group politics applied
to old-growth forests. It therefore needs a sensibility which is, in the
broadest of senses, at least spiritual if not religious. Otherwise environmentalism will remain a minority movement, just one more partial political "party" which has to take its place in the line of claimants somewhere between feminism and welfare rights. This new sensibility must
translate into a distinctive political style—one which is committed to
nonviolence, respect for opponents, principled pursuit of goals, and
rejection of desperation created by despair. Because we cannot effect
the massive changes needed without the active support of vast numbers
of people, we need to appear as both principled and humble, clear
about what is right but not self-righteous. It is no accident that the
political movements led by *religious* figures Gandhi, King, and Ang San
Suu Kyi have been the best at embodying these virtues—marked by
nonviolence, openness to disagreement, and a broadly welcoming sensibility. These qualities emerge directly from these figures' essentially
religious beliefs about what human beings are; and the style of politics

to which they give rise would be beneficial to any progressive movement, and *especially* to environmentalism.[9] Spiritual social activists
have been the most successful at living out this attitude in political
contexts. Of course this is not guarantee that religious political actors
will be any better than anyone else. Indeed in the case of many "fundamentalist" groups we find a good deal of rigidity, inability to tolerate
difference, and tendency towards simple hate.

To those who would say that fundamentalist religions' violent repres-
siveness proves that the *last* thing we need is more religious involvement, I would simply remind them that secular threats to
democracy have been at least as dangerous as religious ones. If we think
of Stalin, the CIA, and the World Bank, we can see that secularism is no
guarantee of political good will. Any unbiased examination of history
shows that the world of religion contains as wide a variety of political
positions—and of basic humanity—as does the world of the secular. We
simply cannot know in advance if a political movement will further
democracy, human rights, good will or simple sanity by knowing whether it is or is not religious. Of course religious groups, just like secular
ones, have tendencies towards self-righteousness, careerist leaders,
male posturing, and irrational claims which ignore evidence to make a
point. But this just means that religious environmentalism is like every
other political movement, since every political movement contains such
tendencies. My argument is not that religious environmentalism is perfect or pure, but that it is important, and that liberating versions of
religion—the ones most religious environmentalists tend to espouse—
provide a basis for overcome these tendencies, a basis often lacking in
secular politics.

II

That religious environmentalism is good for religion, or at least what I
(and many others, I suppose) believe is good for religion, can be shown
by what happens to religions as they become more environmentally
friendly or concerned.

First, as we have already seen, they tend to become more self-aware
of their own limitations. Religious thinkers have spoken frankly about
the failures of their own traditions to see the ecological problems of

modern civilization until they were alerted by scientists and secular environmentalists. Also, taking secular environmentalists and scientists as comrades rather than opponents opens up religion's participation in political life in a fruitful direction. In particular, they have developed openness to sources of knowledge to which they were previously closed. Further, seeing problems with some of their own basic ideas—for example, a rigid separation of body and soul, or of earth and divinity—leads to the recognition that the spiritual traditions of many indigenous peoples contained valuable attitudes and values. Public statements by leaders of the Catholic Church, for example, testify to a new-found respect for earth-honoring traditions of "the natives"—of precisely those groups who had been subject at earlier times, with the Church's frequent blessing, to cultural and physical genocide precisely because they were "primitive pagans."[10]

Similarly, religious environmentalism is almost always ecumenical and/or interfaith. The universality of the crisis, and the sense of a shared fate across communal boundaries, leads to easily formed and sustained alliances between people of many different faiths and of no faith at all. Thus we see both effective interfaith coalitions and remarkable joint projects with leading scientists and powerful secular environmental organizations.[11]

Third, religious environmentalism, just like the secular kind, has learned how to link concern with nature (wilderness, species loss, etc.) with concern for people; i.e., with issues of environmental justice. To do so ecotheologians have had to develop a comprehensive social and ecological vision of the interconnection of all of life. This vision is profoundly new, if for no other reason than that over the past century "nature" has become "environment." There is no part of the earthly web of life that is not affected by human beings; no social relation of oppression that does not have some role in ecological degradation; and no form of ecological degradation the effects of which are not made worse by social inequality. To honor nature we need not only new prayers and rituals, but a radical alteration in our basic social structures. And we cannot heal social injustice without transforming our relations to nature. Therefore a concern with the social order is now essential to religious ethics and false dichotomies between nature and humanity, and between religion and politics, have been swept away.

Finally, this "ecojustice" perspective very often drives religions to a more progressive, leftist, even at times (dare I say it?) anti-capitalist political position. When the head of the World Council of Churches charges world leaders to create a "new economic paradigm"; or the Bishops of Alberta, Canada criticize an "economic model of maximizing profit in an increasingly global market" and the move to "large-scale corporate agriculture" something, we might say, is definitely up.[12] If these kinds of challenges have been seen before, the scope of the environmental crisis and therefore the scope of the religious social critique has not. Even for those religious environmentalists who remain firmly within the ideological orbit of capitalism (most Evangelical environmentalists, for example), a *more* critical attitude emerges. In other cases a serious confrontation with environmental problems leads to a critical stance towards corporate power and the culture of consumerism. In fact, when we compare the statements on economic globalization by the AFL-CIO with that of the World Council of Churches, we might well come to think that not only is Marx turning over in his grave, but that religious environmentalism could be the new socialism. To those who think this might be a reckless overstatement, consider that in 2003, in preparation for a meeting with the World Bank, World Council of Churches general secretary Konrad Raiser questioned "the allegedly irrefutable logic of the prevailing economic paradigm." Simultaneously representatives of 70 member churches signed a document stating that "nothing less than a fundamental shift in political-economic paradigms is necessary."[13]

Of course some would respond that state socialism's typically dismal ecological record means that any move in this direction is bad for religion, and for nature, not good. Religious environmentalists, the argument goes, should embrace the free market, since only the free market allows for the unfettered technological development needed to improve our ecological situation, the political freedom to challenge whatever bad practices exist, and the political space to initiate ecological reforms. My short response to this extremely involved question is that the vast majority of those in the anti-capitalist environmental movement do not wish to replace whatever we call the current system with a one-party communist dictatorship, but with a democratic and sustainable society that is geared to human needs rather than compulsive economic growth. Whatever we call the system under which this change would occur, it is clear that only a dramatic social constraint of global corporate power has a chance of reversing trends of deforestation, global warming, species extinction, or the toxification of water, soil, and air. If this is not "socialism" it is certainly much more like it than the present system. It is western Europe, with far more government involvement in economic life than the U.S., which has the more effective environmental controls. Further, the "freedoms" associated with capitalism have been, at best, selective (consider Chile under Pinochet for example). As well, ecological reforms under capitalism are themselves not necessarily long-lived. As the Bush administration has shown, policies can be reversed and protected spaces opened to development. Finally, in countries not yet modernized only a policy of some kind of collective democratic control of the pace and form of development offers hope that past mistakes will not be repeated indefinitely. Interestingly, when resistance to unfettered economic (mal)development occurs it is often under the leadership, or at least with the support, of the local religious community or of religious beliefs. In Sri Lanka, for example, the anti-globalization group Sarvodaya pursues a kind of mild-mannered Buddhist socialism. In Mongolia the chief of state and various Buddhist groups have tried to make development ecologically sound by invoking Buddhist principles of interdependence and respect for life. [14]

III

Ultimately, religious environmentalism is good for the planet, for the simple reason that religions continue to command the assent, or at least the sympathy, of vast numbers of people. In response to religious calls for sustainable living, people often rise to the challenge in ways they do not when called on by governments or ecologists. Madagascar fishermen stopped the ecologically damaging practice of dynamiting fish only because the local Sheik told them the ecological damage was forbidden by the Qur'an. The Sikh community has committed itself to 300 years of reduced energy use and pollution. The evangelically based "What Would Jesus Drive?" campaign in North America confronted automakers as it caravanned through the south, and ended up at the nation's largest Christian rock festival. [15]

In these cases and countless others religious environmentalism is creating new environmentalists and new environmental initiatives—and offering, in a typically dismal and depressing world, a source of hope. How effective all this effort will ultimately be is still up for grabs. But that is certainly true of any political movement. And it is certainly the case that in hundreds of local environmental struggles religious ideas or local religious figures have had a powerful and beneficial effect.

To take one striking example: the fundamental concept of environmental racism owes much (many would say "most") of its origins to research and public meetings organized by the United Church of Christ: specifically its role in the 1983 Warren County struggle in North Carolina, its sponsorship of the groundbreaking study of environmental racism *Toxic Wastes in the U.S.*, its convening of the Environmental Summit for environmental leaders of color, and its promulgation of the principles of environmental justice created at the Summit.

The integration of the idea of environmental racism into environmentalism has decisively enlarged a conservationist ethic which had focused almost exclusively on the fate of nature and more traditional political agendas that had been limited to people. For secular environmental organizations which place environmental justice alongside nature preservation it means a potentially much larger constituency. Socially marginalized groups of African Americans in East St. Louis, or Latinos in New Mexico, or Native Americans in Wyoming can now feel that environmentalism concerns their lives as well as the lives of pandas and rainforests. In general, recognition of the class and racial nature of the environmental crisis was among the most important steps in helping environmentalism move into the mainstream of political life as a potentially unifying focus of political action, rather than remain the province of comparatively privileged groups.

The emergence of an ecojustice perspective did not stem from world famous theologians or the somewhat impersonal rhetoric of an Earth Day celebration. It came, rather, because of direct connections among people who knew each other and faced environmental threats together. And the church's role in promoting this new perspective depended on its moral rootedness in the everyday lives of communities.

Countless comparable actions, less well known but equally the result of the simple moral ties between local religion and the daily life of community throughout the world, could be added. In India the Sankat

Mochan foundation, led by Hindu Priest and civil engineer Veer Bhadra Mishra, has received international recognition for pioneering work in organizing to restore ecological health to the Ganges River.[16] In Southern Brazil local church activists joined in an anti-dam movement first to help protect peasants' land and later in support of a more inclusive concern with the regions' ecology.[17] As the most important institution of civil society—poised uneasily between the formal structures of government and the private life of families—religion is at times the most powerful resource in any struggle against entrenched injustice.

And indeed several commentators have argued that for environmentalism to succeed it must be rooted in community life, moving beyond centralized organizations, national laws or policies, and single issue campaigns keyed to a particular wilderness area, pollutant, or endangered species. Labeled by some "civic environmentalism," this model relies on informal networks of people concerned with the enduring existence and sustainable development of a particular locale.[18] It involves creative planning for the future as much as stopping some practice that is damaging, and the health of the human community as much as the health of the land. It focuses precisely on what is close at hand, in the hope that this *particular place* can be restored and sustained. Civic environmentalism can be found in a neighborhood coalition in Oakland, locally based conservation in rural Colorado, urban agriculture in Boston's Dudley Square—and in Africa when natives are integrated into ecotourism of national parks instead of being expelled so that the "wilderness" will be purely "natural" (except for the white tourists).[19] Religious environmental activists, connected to their neighbors through myriad congregational activities, church suppers, and midnight masses, are particularly suited to be active participants in civic environmentalism. They have done so throughout the world already.

IV

The task of scholars in this setting, I propose, is to be religious environmentalism's "organic" intellectuals.[20] That is, we should use our particular talents and positions as writers, teachers, and members of universities to analyze, chronicle, advance, publicize, and when necessary criticize this movement and its various manifestations. This is not about dumbing down what we say or becoming hacks for some limited political agenda. It is about having the horizon of our intellectual work be the struggle to respond to the environmental crisis; and if we are scholars of religion, that it be focused on the religious participation in that struggle. It is about having the criterion of what is or is not a significant theoretical problem be set by efforts to heal the world, rather than by disciplinary tradition or academic fads. If we wish to preserve our scholarly objectivity, that is all to the good. But we cannot pretend to detachment, for ultimately who could be detached from the conditions that make his or her life possible? The autism and disassociation which would permit such a posture are part and parcel of the problem itself. We are members of an ecologically murderous civilization which must be replaced by a sustainable one. Only then will babies come into this world with blood as pure as their souls (or, for those who shudder at exhortative religious language—as pure as their blameless individual rights-bearing persons!).

NOTES

1. For an elaboration of the ideas presented here, see my *A Greener Faith: Religious Environmentalism and Our Planet's Future* (New York: Oxford University Press, 2006). For excerpts from a wide range of source material, *This Sacred Earth: Religion, Nature, Environment* Second Edition (New York: Routledge, 2004) and *The Oxford Handbook of Religion and Ecology* (New York: Oxford University Press, 2006).

2. This essay is based on a panel presentation from the first meeting of the International Society for the Study of Religion, Nature and Culture. It benefited from criticism and encouragement from Bron Taylor and anonymous reviewers.

3. See "Body Burden—The Pollution in Newborns," Body Burden Website, http://www.ewg.org/reports/bodyburden2/execsumm.php.

4. James A. Nash, *Loving Nature: Ecological Integrity and Christian Responsibility* (Nashville, TN: Abingdon Press: 1991), p. 72, emphasis added.

5. Matthew Fox, "How the Environment Can Assist Us to Deconstruct and Reconstruct Theology and Religion." Friends of Creation Spirituality website: http://www.matthewfox.org/sys-tmpl/htmlpage5/.

6. Thomas Berry, *Dream of the Earth* (San Francisco: Sierra Club Books, 1988).

7. Berry, *Dream of the Earth*, p. 77.

8. Bill McKibben, "Preface," *Daedelus*, Fall 200, p. i.

9. For an extended version of this argument, see my account of "what politics has to learn from religion" in *Joining Hands: Politics and Religion Together for Social Change* (Cambridge, MA: Westview, 2002).

10. For a document which contains all these elements, see "What Is Happening to Our Beautiful Land?" a statement by the Catholic bishops of the Phillipines. "Tribal people all over the Philippines, who have seen the destruction of their world at close range, have cried out in anguish. Also men and women who attempt to live harmoniously with nature and those who study ecology have tried to alert people to the magnitude of the destruction taking place in our time. The latter are in a good position to tell us what is happening since they study the web of dynamic relationships which support and sustains all life within the earthly household." *"And God Saw That It Was Good": Catholic Theology and the Environment*, ed. Drew Christiansen and Walter Grazer (Washington, D.C.: United States Catholic Conference, 1996), pp. 309-310.

11. As one example, consider the Interfaith Global Climate Change Network, itself a joint project of the Eco-Justice Working Group of the National Council of Churches (NCC), Coalition on the Environment and Jewish Life (COEJL) and the National Religious Partnership for the Environment. Together, NCC and COEJL have organized 18 statewide interfaith climate change campaigns. These groups see themselves squarely in the emerging tradition of religious care for the earth and concern for the connections between humanity and nature. The North Carolina chapter, for example, is a coalition of "various spiritual traditions" committed to "turning human activities in a new direction for the well being of the planet" and for the sacred task of *preserving all eco-systems* that sustain life." The effects of global warming, the coalition warns will "fall disproportionately upon the most vulnerable of the planet's people: the poor, sick, elderly . . . " The thirty-six signers listed on the group's website include Rabbis, Buddhist Priests, Roman Catholic and Episcopal Bishops, and ministers from the Lutheran, Unitarian Universalist, Quaker, Baptist, Methodist, and United Church of Christ denominations. The frequent use of the term "spiritual" in the groups call signals an acceptance of the variety of paths to God; the acknowledgement of the sacredness of the earth announces an end to theological anthropocentrism; naming the special vulnerability of the poor opens the way for an account of irrational and unjust social institutions and for common work with secular liberal to leftist organizations. The challenge to existing political and economic arrangements is direct and serious. See: Web of Creation website: http://www.webofcreation.org/ncc/climate.html.

12. See detailed accounts in *A Greener Faith*, Chapter 4.

13. World Council of Churches Website: http://www2.wcc-coe.org/ pressReleasesen.nsf/09c9d22d54ad7a37c1256d0a004ebd7d/ c0cc4cb160ebf5b6c1256da40051b72f?OpenDocument.

14. See George D. Bond, *Buddhism at Work: Community Development, Social Empowerment, and the Sarvodaya Movement* (Bloomfield, CT: Kumarian Press, 2004); "Prime Minister of Mongolia to be first International President of ARC," Alliance of Religion and Conservation Website: http://www. arcworld.org/news.asp?pageID=6.

15. Information on the Madagascar fishermen and the Sikh community can be found in Martin Palmer, *New Approaches to Religions and the Environment* (Washington, D.C.: The World Bank, 2003). For the WWJD? Campaign, see http://whatwouldjesusdrive.org/.

16. Mishra was identified as one of seven "Heroes of the Planet" by *Time* Magazine for his work in protecting the fresh waterways of the earth. See Sankat Mochan website: http://members.tripod.com/sankatmochan/index.htm.

17. Franklin Rothman and Pamela Oliver, "From Local to Global: the Anti-Dam Movement in Southern Brazil, 1979–1992," in *Globalization and Resistance: Transnational Dimensions of Social Movements*, ed. Jackie Smith and Hank Johnston (Lanham, MD: Rowman and Littlefield, 2002), pp. 119–123.

18. William A. Shutkin, *The Land that Could Be: Environmentalism and Democracy in the Twenty-First Century* (Cambridge, MA: MIT Press, 2000). See also Robert Gottlieb, *Forcing the Spring*; Dewitt John, *Civic Environmentalism: Alternatives to Regulation in States and Communities* (Washington, D.C.: Congressional Quarterly Press, 1994).

19. Raymond Bonner, *At the Hand of Man: Peril and Hope for Africa's Wildlife* (NY: Knopf, 1993).

20. As opposed to traditional intellectuals whose concern derives from the self-enclosed realm of elite cultural life. The distinction was made by the Italian Marxist Antonio Gramsci.

6

YOU GONNA BE HERE LONG?

Religion and Sustainability

The EPA tells us that "common use of the term 'sustainability' began with the 1987 publication of the World Commission on Environment and Development report, *Our Common Future*. Also known as the Brundtland Report, this document defined sustainable development as 'development that meets the needs of the present without compromising the ability of future generations to meet their own needs'" (Environmental Protection Agency, n/d).

"Sustainability" then, expresses a commitment that the future should be like the present, that whatever changes we are making should coexist with an underlying stability. At least in this definition, it presupposes that we can distinguish between needs and other motivators—such as desires, wants, or greed—and that our ecological concerns can or should be captured by a term which suggests constancy rather than change. Let us ask how much sense any of these presuppositions make, as we also ask whether achieving some kind of social and ecological sustainability has anything to do with religion.[1]

I.

Whether or not they use the word, most religions commit themselves to the value of their own sustainability. Whatever their theologies assert about how everything will change when the messiah comes or how individual egos will snuff out like extinguished candles when they achieve Enlightenment, religions create and maintain powerful, well-supported *institutions* so that the faithful of the future will be able to meet their (spiritual!) needs with as much instruction and support as those in the present. Through the church, the sangha, and the Sunday school religious groups establish collective identities over time and try to insure that their traditions will continue indefinitely. The faithful's "needs" to know Ultimate Truth will be met by clergy and educators, to have spiritual fellowship by the physical and social solidity of local houses of worship, to connect their daily lives with God by a repository or prayer and ritual passed down from generation to generations. Sustainability is therefore a religious question at least to the extent that religions are almost always investing in their own futures.

Ecological sustainability is therefore a religious issue first off simply because without it the institutional and doctrinal dimensions of *religious* continuity—i.e., religious sustainability—will become impossible, or at the least much more tenuous than they are at present. This means that if religions do want to persist into the future, it would behoove them to devote some measure of focused attention and concern to the ecological conditions under which they live. (Unless, of course, religious authorities come to think that the secular world can handle this one without their help—but I doubt that even the most devout could muster that much faith.)

To put it another way: "belief" or "faith" may be thought of as a purely mental or a spiritual act. When we think of "believing in God," then, we may typically forget the physical conditions which are required if such a belief is to be even possible.

By contrast, however, "being a believer" most certainly is, under practically any description whatsoever, in the first place a physical act. We have to have brains to have minds, and beliefs—including belief in God or Spiritual Truth—exist only in minds. Explicitly or not, religious institutions have always known and more importantly acted on this knowledge. From a willing embrace of their tax exempt status in the U.S. to the Buddhist monk with his begging bowl, from giving sacrificial leftovers to the high priests of ancient Israel to having a tag sale to raise money to repair the church's aging heating system, religions have "sustained" themselves as physical entities. As familiar as these dimensions of religious sustainability are, the environmental crisis—which is of course the occasion of this discussion—adds something new and particularly challenging.

Religions are familiar with external threats to their own existence, and with people leaving the fold in favor of another religion or a purely secular life (for instance in the case of Jewish assimilation or the fading of Catholicism in Latin America in comparison to evangelical Protestantism). Still, it is hard to think of many instances in which devout members of a faith put their own faith's future in jeopardy.[2] And yet to the extent that devout Christians, committed Muslims, and Orthodox Jews continue to drive their gas guzzlers, pay taxes to militaristic governments, and store their pension funds in oil and chemical companies they are doing just that. If we continue to meet the physical needs of the present generation of people of faith as we have been doing, and to increase consumption at the present rate, future generations of Christians, Jews, Muslims, Hindus, and Buddhists will not. This inability may take a truly cataclysmic form; for example, cascading feedback loops of climate change or genetic engineers who let the wrong genie out of the bottle. Alternatively, ecological degradation and consequent social unrest and deterioration might simply proceed as a long, slow decline, one in which we don't have a dramatic collapse but simply "apocalypse as way of life" (Buell 2003).

Quite simply, then, if sustainability is not a religious issue, then religious people are ignoring how they themselves are destroying the necessary conditions for their own faith to exist in the future. If sustainability *is* a religious issue, however, then religions cannot continue as they have in the past, they cannot "sustain" their own complicity in our civilization's unsustainable form of life. They cannot relegate ecological concern to a secondary status as it is now, but must take it at least as seriously as sexuality, poverty, war and peace, and tithing to the church. Actually, given the severity of the environmental crisis, it may be necessary to take environmental issues *more* seriously than these other issues. As sea levels, cancer rates, and the prices of oil and food rise, religious sustainability demands that a full and direct confrontation with our collective and individual ecological practices take pride of place.

In this confrontation, one in which world religions have been deeply engaged for more than two decades, religious people are faced with more than the crucial question of the physical condition of their own bodies. What is at issue is the effect of human actions on the entire web of life on this planet—including but not limited to other human beings—and how we are to take responsibility for that effect. Sustainability is thus not only a practical question, capable of being reduced to asking whether "the church" can deal with more expensive electric bills and higher cancer rates. It is also a question of *moral* sustainability—as we ask whether this or that faith is morally relevant to the actual conditions of suffering, threat, and collective denial and irresponsibility in which we find ourselves. If religions cannot help illuminate the moral conflicts created by the environmental crisis, of what use are they?

This issue is all the more pressing because unlike many other moral issues in which the "church" is either comparatively blameless and/or powerless, religion's relation to the environmental crisis raises questions of its *own* moral integrity and authenticity. Bishops cannot declare war, rabbis by and large do not take illegal bets, and most Imams have little wealth. By contrast virtually all religious people in developed or developing nations—from the Pope right down the humblest parishioner—are by virtue of their participation in ecologically damaging economies part of the problem.

2.

Even as we energetically pursue sustainability, seeking to insure that future generations will get their needs met as we do now, we might simultaneously be aware that the whole enterprise of sustainability is a losing game. In the very long run the sun will explode and in that explosion destroy the earth—at which point all human accomplishments, beliefs, organizations, and memories will be swept away.

While the sun's future as a nova is pretty remote in time, other concerns—doubts about the stability of the stock market or the continued fertility of the U.S.'s Midwestern breadbasket—loom closer on the horizon. If we step back from the myriad immediate anxieties which arise when we awaken each morning and glance at the newspaper, what hope do we have that sustainability could ever be more than a stopgap measure? Do we really think that humanity, to paraphrase an ironic dialogue from novelist Joseph Heller's (1996) *Catch-22*, will last as long as the frog? There have been frogs on earth for approximately seventy million years. Do we want to stack up our nation states, universities, cultures, languages, and even, yes, our religions against that kind of cosmic time? Whatever technological cleverness we come up with, do we really think it will protect us for as long as its own natural adaptability protected the frog? Certain Native Americans famously asked how their current decisions would affect the "seventh generation" down the line. It certainly would be a vast improvement if the U.N., the Chinese Minister of Economic Development, or General Motors used the same rule to guide their decisions. But let's be clear that "sustainability" makes no sense if we think of 700, or 700 thousand generations to come. We just are not going to be here that long. It is all temporary.

3.

Is nature *itself* "sustainable," even without the presence of ecosystem altering human cultures? Since around ninety percent of species which have existed on earth have gone extinct, most before humans started in on everybody else, the answer would seem to be "not very much." Evolution is, after all, a process of deep change; and long before people arrived on the scene the natural world stopped meeting the "needs" of the dinosaurs, to take just one example. Even the non-living elements of the earth and *its* surroundings are not marked by anything remotely like permanence, but by endless alteration. The placement of the continents, the creation of the atmosphere, the landscape altering paths of rivers and tides and rain—all these suggest a series of changes to planetary settings and therefore to ecosystems and species. To ask of such a system that the future be like the past is to fundamentally misunderstand it.[3]

How are human beings to sustain what nature cannot—does not even desire to sustain? Is sustainability perhaps a distorted term, expressing mostly the human psychic need to control and preserve that which it values, a term unsuited to the essentially dynamic process of evolution and the interaction between the living and the inorganic in ecosystems?

Is the idea of sustainability, despite the good intentions which animate it, an expression of the same old human fear and lack of acceptance of death: of individual death which leads us to imagine a home in heaven for ourselves after earthly life, or of species death which leads us to imagine ourselves especially favored by an infinitely powerful benign force, or of cultural death which leads us to imagine that our nation or religious group or ethnic bonds will last "forever"? All of these will surely not last even a fraction as long as the frog.

4.

On the other hand, as temporary as all this may be due to factors outside of human control, and as shaped by arising and passing away like the rest of nature as we are, we still have to ask how we should live. And how we should live *given* the fact of our impermanence. Consider the frog again. While frogs have been doing pretty well for a very long time, in recent decades they have been doing, to say the least, not so well at all. Throughout many places in the U.S. and the planet as a whole, frogs have been in decline. Consider but one of the hundreds of studies that have documented this troubling trend: in 1996 in the upper Midwest and parts of Canada frogs with severe birth defects were discovered. These included

> frogs with missing legs, extra legs, misshapen legs, paralyzed legs that stuck out from the body at odd places, legs that were webbed together with extra skin, legs that were fused to the body, and legs that split into two half-way down. . . . One one-eyed frog had a second eye growing inside its throat. (Montague 1996)

The causes of these and related problems for frogs stem from what we are doing to their ecosystems: plausible agents include UV-B radiation, chemicals, pollution, pesticides, climate change, and habitat disruption and disappearance.

The question then is not whether we can keep the frog around forever. After all, *nothing* is forever. The question, rather, is whether we want to be the ones who *cause* a continuing worldwide decline in frogs; who place, as it were, the eye in the frog's throat. A world with no, or with dramatically fewer, frogs means, among other things, a world in which insects and other pests dramatically increase, and in which there are many fewer frog predators—including large birds, snakes, hedgehogs, fish, and foxes. A world without, or with dramatical-

ly fewer and fewer types of frogs means the loss of the brilliantly col-
ored tropical "golden frog," now extinct in the wild (Revkin 2008), or
the Ecuadorian tricolor frog whose poison serves as a painkiller many
times more powerful (and with fewer side effects) than morphine (N.Y.
Times 1998). It means the loss of yet another evolutionary miracle of
vibrant and unique potentiality.

If we live unsustainably will future generations fail to have their
"needs" for frogs met? Do we actually "need" frogs? Can we have high
schools, malls, Christmas trees, the Koran, the Red Cross, and
American Idol without them? Probably. Will we starve to death if we
decimate the frog population? I don't know, and I suspect not. So
perhaps we can live "sustainably" without them.

If, that is, you call this "living."

And is it a life *worth* living if we are knowingly (for the news about
frogs has been out for at least a decade) and willfully (because the
means to stop a good deal of what is killing frogs is already available to
us) depriving them of life?

5.

Framed in this way there can once again be no doubt that sustainability
is a religious question, for what if not religion is in the business of
telling us when and why life is or is not worth living? Political democracy, at least on the current narrow view which identifies it with voting,
can only aggregate preferences. Science and technology can only tell us,
in the true fashion of instrumental reason, how to get what we want
already. An economic and social system dominated by global capitalism
will necessarily encourage us to the accumulation of wants felt so intensely that we cannot help but mistake them for needs.

That leaves religion, which has as a central task instructing us in the
value of things.[4] Simply to say that we must live sustainably so that
future generations can meet their needs as we meet ours is, for religion,
only the beginning of a long conversation about learning how to tell the
difference between what we really do need, and what we might think—
mistakenly—that we need. Authentic religious voices have for a very
long time had some critical things to say about the claimed "needs" of
the surrounding culture. On the level of material wealth, or what we

nowadays call "consumption," Isaiah (5:8) railed against those "who add house to house and join field to field till no space is left and you live alone in the land." The Talmud (*Avot:* 4:1) defined wealth as "being satisfied with what one has" and Mohammad claimed that "A man's true wealth is the good he does in the world."

The task of religion, then, is not just to be "sustainable" but to tell us what should be sustained, even to the limited degree to which humans can keep anything alive. When we are told by economists, politicians, civic leaders, and our own addicted consumerist psyches that we "need" growth, it is the function of religion to ask us: "growth *for what*" and "growth *of what*" and more simply "*why*?" If religion in the developed world takes it for granted that we need all that we currently have, if its moral challenge is limited to helping others get to where we are, then it will have committed itself to moral irrelevance. To sustain itself *morally*, then, religions have to contest the widespread expectation that "more" is "better."[5] They have to trust the value of religious virtues and forms of life as sources of true human betterment, and advocate the spiritual value of "less." Unless "need" becomes synonymous with "want," then, we therefore cannot pursue "sustainability" without some comprehensive understanding of what people are and what should be important to them.

And they have to mean it, and show by example that they do. If people of faith are not to be exterminating frogs in exactly the same ways as secularists, atheists, and communists, etc. they must demonstrate by word and action that they have found themselves wanting and are willing to change.

6.

Is a human form of life that causes frogs to be born with eyes growing in their throats a life worth sustaining, even for the next few centuries or so?

Two decades of ecotheology have provided us with a wide range of resources to say that in many respects religion clearly commits itself to a resounding "no." Scripturally based assertions that the earth is a gift from God, that other creatures deserve respect, that a lifestyle centered on accumulation of wealth and transitory pleasures is a profound spiritual mistake—all these serve as negations of our current global environmental regime.[6]

But while I salute the many creative and critical accomplishments of theologians—and even more the environmental activism which has been expressed by religious groups worldwide—is it, I ask myself, enough?

Is there, I wonder, some more profound religious change that is needed: something besides seeing that ecological virtues—like caring for the poor, developing personal humility, or eschewing violence—are essential religious obligations. Can it be that as any serious concept of sustainability needs to take into account the ultimate and final reality of change, so religion has to take into account the transitory quality of its own presence on earth?

We are physical, we are finite, and we will not last forever: not our churches, or our holy books, or our insights, or our visions. *This* thought, which we come to by reflecting on the true nature of sustainability, is perhaps the most demanding one that confronts religion as it faces the environmental crisis. Our *religious* identity, as part of our *human* identity, is no more sustainable than the maple tree, the bald eagle, or the local river ecosystem, or the frog.

Seeing people as subject to the same temporal limitations as the rest of life runs counter to the dominant presuppositions of the world's dominant religions, each of which in their own way proclaims that we are not natural, or not purely natural; and that we at least stand out if we do not stand above. Made in God's image, possessors of a soul, capable of Enlightenment or union with Godhead, we are not like frogs.

And yet looking at our human institutions, the present chaos of our social relationships, the recklessness of our economically oriented actions, can we really suppose—once again in comparison to the frog— that we are (very) long for this world? Such realization does not rule out the eschatological promise of Hinduism or the Abrahamic religions. The messiah may come and lead us to heaven; our unity with Brahman can be complete. And these things may indeed last for an eternity. But our life on earth will not. And therefore neither will our religious institutions, our Holy Books, our cherished traditions, our memories, or the people we know ourselves to be. This sense of our own impermanence can—and should—be incorporated in our sense of earthly religious practice and institutional life.

In answer to the question, "You gonna be here long?" then, the answer is—"For a while, that's all."

And therefore we should ask, not "what can we sustain forever, for every future generation that's coming down the pike" but "given that our time, personally and collectively, is limited, how do we want to live? Even if the frog is going to be extinct sometime no matter what we do, do we want to be the ones that hasten its end?"

7.

Why can't we live forever? Why can't our souls dwell in eternity? Quite simply because that is not who *we* are—at least, not as we actually experience ourselves in our daily lives, our families, our work, our struggles against scarcity and competition with other life forms. *We*, as we actually know ourselves, rejoice in new life and mourn for the dead. We sense the preciousness of our own sentience and, in the face of our approaching dotage, feel most acutely what will be lost as that sentience diminishes. We defend ourselves from assault, nourish our babies, and buy an awful lot of vitamin pills. Outside of the occasional profession of faith in our immortal souls, we talk and act like the very mortal creatures we are. Whatever we may aspire to or hope for, our lives are permeated by realizations of vulnerability and finitude. If there is a part of us which is immortal, it is known only very fleetingly and through a much darkened glass.

Two philosophers make this point clearly. Martha Nussbaum (2006: 132-33) argues against Kant's rigid dualism between reason and nature rather than religious splits between soul or spiritual essence and nature, but her position is perfectly relevant here. She asserts that human dignity or worth "just is the dignity of a certain kind of animal"; much of what we value about ourselves that has worth we share with other animals; morality and rationality are "thoroughly material and animal"; it is a mistake to think of the "core of ourselves as atemporal . . . since the usual human life cycle brings with it period of extreme dependency." Or as David Hume (1779) put it: "All the sentiments of the human mind, gratitude, resentment, love, friendship, approbation, blame, pity, emulation, envy, have a plain reference to the state and situation [i.e., the frailties and limitations] of man."

When knowledge of ourselves as vulnerable and finite coexists with aspirations to immortality and claims that we are essentially "eternal spirits" of some kind," we live in what Hegel (1997) called the "unhappy consciousness": one in which an identification with the infinite is always haunted by a suppressed awareness of the crushing reality of the finite. Our understanding of the inevitable evolutionary finitude of life, and the imperfect and short-lived nature of human institutions (even religious ones), means that such awareness, or at least the truth towards which it gestures, is inescapable. Like everything else, and precisely because it is part of everything else, religions arise, have their day, and then will pass away.

8.

Despite protestations of good intentions by everyone from the Pope to the leaders of the World Council of Churches, from the (Koranically oriented) environmental ministry of Saudi Arabia to the chancellor of the Jewish Theological Seminary (Gottlieb 2006a), I suspect that somewhere we know that what is at stake is a little closer to home than a generalized "human" temporality and limitation. It is not just that humans have been, and will continue to be, imperfect; it is that we *in particular* will be as well—the author and reader of this essay, the priest and the local parish, the rabbi who reads from the Torah on Sabbath morning, the Patriarch of the Orthodox Church who flies around the world on ozone-layer-destroying, fossil-fuel-consuming jets to make his (truly inspiring) environmental pronouncements. We will *not* do everything we should; we will not sustain for as long as we could as much as we could. Along with the destabilizing forces of evolution sustainability is limited because human beings are limited, because our addictive psychology, lust for power, fascination with technology and ease, and plain moral laziness leave us acting, let us say, far below an ideal moral standard.

So the chain of ethical reflection which begins with sustainability brings religion—after serious reexamination—down to earth. It challenges us to end or at least limit our endless pretensions to being moral exemplars, our arrogance about our insights about what God thinks and wants, our repeated demands that other people listen to us. It thrusts center stage the often recommended but rarely practiced virtue of humility. If we cannot teach and practice humility *now*, after all the mistakes we've made and facts we've ignored and in so many ways *continue* to ignore, we never will.

If humility (which given our collective track record is certainly warranted in secular contexts from progressive politics to technological innovation as well) actually arises, a deeply serious alteration in religion's self-understanding will have taken place. For it would mean that religious leaders and theologians, along with their customary assertions about The Nature of it All, will admit to *not* knowing an awful lot: not really understanding, for instance, how their own faiths could have been blind for so long, or what kind of economic changes are necessary, or what the politics, education, or technology of a Brave New Sustainability should look like. A sustainable religion is thus first of all one that admits its sizable limitations, asks a lot of questions and truly wishes to learn. This learning cannot take place purely internally, for religions cannot begin to answer these questions without enlisting the aid of political theory, environmental economics, and the psychology of addiction (for a start). A Catholic bishop cannot understand the forces which motivate the environmental crisis without some understanding of social theory any more than he can build his own computer by reading Matthew. Religious morality, as an autonomous form of normative knowledge, simply ceases to exist.

Even more dangerously, religion has to admit that it has only just begun to take seriously some of the most troubling moral dimensions of the environmental crisis. For example, it still does not know how to treat wealthy parishioners who make money from polluting industries. While a local church or a national religious organization would in all likelihood be loath to have a morally and psychically polluting pornographer as one of its lay leaders, such a stricture has yet to be applied to the equally dangerous practices of physical pollution. That the church endowment may be invested in polluting industries makes the moral question here that much more complicated. It is no wonder that religions haven't figured this one out yet. Indeed, they are still hesitant to be direct about the simple fact of their own moral confusion about it.

9.

When the good times roll for Jews—at a wedding, a bar mitzvah, the beginning of any important holiday—we say the "Shehechiyanu" prayer: "Blessed are you, O Lord our God, master of the universe, for sustaining us, and keeping us alive, and bringing us to this season."[7] The Shehechiyanu prayer expresses the fundamental realization that we do not sustain ourselves and that the simple fact of being alive calls for a celebratory blessing. It is about appreciating how much it took to get us here, admitting that there is no cosmic necessity that we survive as long as we have, acknowledging everything it took to get us here, and savoring the moment.

These sentiments are rooted in both a true understanding of the human condition and a life-affirming commitment to making the most of that condition. If religion is to be sustained for as long as possible, which is a good deal less long than we are used to presupposing, it will help to cultivate these sentiments in some form or another. Without some delight in existence, even an existence tarnished by human aggression and thoughtlessness, human life cannot be sustained in a meaningful way. Without an acknowledgment of all that supports us, we are not likely to care for it. Without a realization of human finitude and contingency, the grace of our moments of celebration dwindles to noticing the passing of time or mere "pleasure." Obligation and guilt and even fear will only take us so far—and in all probability not far enough. To stop poisoning the frogs, or at least poison them less, we also have to enjoy them.

How can we connect religion's moral obligation to understand and challenge the social forces which are causing the environmental crisis with its vocation for spiritual delight in existence? Not easily, to be sure. But there is one link that is clear: the essential religious intuition that moral action is meaningful even if it does not "succeed" in an instrumental or strategic sense. The hour is so late, the forces arrayed against really significant change so great, our own powers so weak and inconstant, that it often seems that the game is already up. It would thus not be surprising nor unwarranted if we turned to helplessness and despair. From the *Talmud* to the *Bhagavad Gita* religions reject this kind of moral depression. Rather, spiritual perspectives assure us that God is always watching, moral life is its own reward, and every spark of kindness matters. Different faiths will tell different stories about *why and how* it matters, but variations in metaphysical mechanics are much less important than the general agreement shared across traditions. And while the general spirit of this point of view is not *necessarily* religious, it is contingently more associated with religious culture than with secular political commitments, which tend to focus on close calculation of results. A religious spirit, in just this sense, can be enormously useful to the wider movement for ecological sanity. That is not necessarily because secularists will come to adopt a religious view on the ultimate powers governing the universe. It is that the faithful who live out their faith with a modicum of joy and delight in simply being alive, even as they immerse themselves in the gritty, boring, or dangerous world of environmental activism, can provide inspiring examples of politically committed compassion to offset the partisan, egotistical belligerence which too often marks political struggles.[8]

10.

Where does this leave us? Doubtless in a state of grave uncertainty. We do not know for how long we will sustain ourselves and the web of life on earth, what actions will succeed in lengthening that time, and if we have the moral and psychological courage to do what needs to be done. And yet . . . is it not the task of religion precisely to give us faith at such a time? Not faith that guarantees a happy outcome, but faith that human beings can carry on when things are at their most bleak and that despite the bleakness it is truly worth carrying on. Abraham striding up the mountain with Isaac, the Apostles not on that glorious Sunday afternoon when Jesus had returned but in the silent hours of Saturday night when He was so far away, the Buddha facing down the weapons of Mara. All these spiritual personalities must be understood, as Kierkegaard (1985) tells us, not during the successful outcomes of their trials but while they dwelled in the oppressive shadows of fear and doubt. If we wait for a sign that the outcome is guaranteed, that the right thing will be done and that we in fact will do it, that the final result will be a nice one, we will have misunderstood the nature of religious life. Such a life is truly about love without any concrete guarantees whatsoever. If we can sustain our love *now*, then whatever our future, we will have made our present something worth living. That worth need not be "forever" to be real.

NOTES

1. I am grateful for helpful comments from Willis Jenkins, Margaret Bullit-Jonas, and an anonymous reviewer.

2. The closest comparison which comes to mind is the religious community's tacit acceptance of the development of nuclear weapons.

3. For a related critique of ecological morality on the basis of what nature is "really" like, see Sideris 2003.

4. Philosophy, free-lance spirituality, forms of social theory, and art also face these tasks. However, my focus here is on religion, which as a social force has an enormously greater impact than any of these others.

5. The phrasing, which he explores in his usual intelligent way, comes from McKibben 2007.

6. For an overview of religious environmentalism as a movement, see Gottlieb 2006a; for a wide-ranging collection on religion and ecology, including ecotheology, see Gottlieb 2006b.

7. This is similar in intent to the traditional Jew's first thing in the morning prayer thanking God for keeping us alive while we slept.

8. See Gottlieb 2002 for an account of what "politics can learn from religion" on this score.

REFERENCES

Buell, Frederic. 2003. *From Apocalypse to Way of Life: Environmental Crisis in the American Century*. New York: Routledge.
Environmental Protection Agency, n/d:http://www.epa.gov/Sustainability/basicinfo.htm#what.
Gottlieb, Roger S. 2006a *A Greener Faith: Religious Environmentalism and Our Planet's Future*. New York: Oxford University Press.
Gottlieb, Roger S. 2006b. *The Oxford Handbook of Religion and Ecology*. New York: Oxford University Press.
Gottlieb, Roger S. 2002. *Joining Hands: Politics and Religion Together for Social Change*. Cambridge, MA: Westview Press.
Hegel, G. W. F. 1979. *Phenomenology of Spirit*. Oxford: Oxford University Press.
Heller, Joseph. 1996. *Catch-22*. New York: Simon and Schuster.
Hume, David. 1779. *Dialogues Concerning Natural Religion*.
Kierkegaard, Søren. 1985. *Fear and Trembling*. New York: Penguin.
McKibben, Bill. 2007. *Deep Economy. The Wealth of Communities and the Durable Future*. New York: Times Books.

Montague, Peter, 1996. "Frogs Give Warning." in *Rachel's Environment & Health Weekly,*
    No. 515. 10 October, 1996, quoting Washington Post, September 30, 1996.
New York Times, 1998. "Poison From Frog Skin Leads to a Painkiller" January 2, 1998.
Nussbaum, Martha. 2006. *Frontiers of Justice: Nationality, Disability, Species Membership.*
    Cambridge, MA: Harvard University Press.
Revkin, Andrew, 2008. *N.Y. Times* March 24, 2008, "Vanishing Frogs, Climate, and the
    Front Page."
Sideris, Lisa, 2002. *Environmental Ethics, Ecological Theology and Natural Selection.* New
    York: Columbia University Press.

7

ALL IN THE SAME BOAT?

Religious Diversity and Religious Environmentalism

Whoever sheds human blood, by a human his own blood is to be shed; because God made human beings in his own image.
Genesis: 9:6

By this everyone will know that you are my disciples, if you love one another .
John 13:35

I vow to achieve Full Enlightenment, for the benefit of all sentient beings.
Bodhisattva Vow, Diamond Sutra

In some perspectives religious diversity is a regrettable problem. According to this view, truth and error are clear-cut categories. Here diversity is to be stamped out, or if that is impossible, to be lamented. Here we can speak of the "one true faith" (1TF), and the need to spread or at least teach this faith to the non-believers. Given the premises of this view, such proselytizing would seem to be completely justified, at least if we take for granted that religion is about something important. If we possess the truth about what God wants, the Afterlife, moral values, and the Meaning of Life, we'd be selfish and derelict if we didn't try to spread it around. Here diversity in religion makes about as much sense as diversity in science. And while there are areas of scientific controversy and countless unsettled questions, we tend to believe that we can identify what we actually do know. We don't usually tolerate diversity over what we take to have been settled.

A rather different view proposes that religious diversity, and the related term "pluralism," are conditions to be acknowledged, accepted, and perhaps even celebrated. And this for two reasons. *First,* a multitude of religious traditions is an ineluctable fact of modern life. In a globalized world, rife with the legacies of imperialism and rising rates of emigration, we simply will have a variety of religions in many of our nations. And even nations that are religiously homogenous will still be forced to deal with people of other faiths in international affairs. If we cannot muster a little acceptance, a little tolerance, for the Other, then our social life and international affairs will be an endless cycle of conflict and bloodshed. If, as some say, diversity is the fact and pluralism is the acceptance and/or celebration of the fact,[1] we have a choice between pluralism and war. Given that we can't wipe the Other out, we'd better learn to get along.

Second, however, is a position that goes one very large step further. Rather than offering mere acceptance, we should value diversity. Learning to happily coexist with other religions actually teaches us something we need to know about religious life. Exactly what that something is will vary but some of the candidates are:

- *Non-coercion* (NC) We will learn that religious faith by its nature must be freely given, and therefore any attempt to force a person to believe something fundamentally mistakes the nature of faith (Locke: 1689).
- *Learning from the Other* (LO) We will see that even if other people's core religious beliefs are different from ours, we can still learn something from them that will help us in *our* spiritual life. In recent years American Christians, for example, have been utilizing Buddhist meditation techniques and Yoga.
- *From Many to One* (FM1) We will shift our understanding of our own faith, realizing that what is essential to it is something that is common to other faiths. Whatever the differences in scripture, God language, or rituals, the core values of love and respect for others unites us. In this sense an appreciation of religious diversity turns, ironically, into the end of diversity. This perspective deval-

ues a faith's traditional metaphysics in favor of its more philosophical ethics, spiritual yearnings, or "life cycle" (birth, death, marriage, etc.) concerns. Or at least it interprets those metaphysics
metaphorically and in motivational terms rather than literally. Exactly what God is, what He or She is called, and what books
appear on the cosmic CV diminish in significance compared to
general imperatives to love one another, lessen our attachment to
desire, develop humility, kindness, and compassion, and nurture
our children.

As a religious liberal of the first order, whose attitude towards faith in
general is tolerant, if not politically and psychologically opportunistic, I
am mainly concerned with how religious environmentalism serves as a
negation of OTF and moves faiths, like it or not, towards LO and FM1.
Precisely because the environmental crisis, if honestly and openly
faced, shows us a degree of commonality perhaps never before faced,
other aspects of what we share become clearer and our differences
diminish.

II. WHAT DOES THE ENVIRONMENTAL CRISIS HAVE TO DO WITH RELIGION?

The environmental crisis negates many central principles of traditional
religion; for the environmental crisis is first of all a crisis of our biological, and thus essentially our *physical* reality. To take but one telling
example: a random study of 12 newborns in 2004 revealed a horrific
average of 197 toxic chemicals in their placental blood. These included
known carcinogens, endocrine disrupters, and neurological threats (Environmental Working Group 2005). As a process which inscribes itself
on the very inside of our bodies as well as on the landscape and other
species, the environmental crisis assaults us at the very lowest common
denominator of our existence—our existence as bodies. But much of
world religion has denied the importance or reality of that dimension of
our existence—at best emphasizing the need to regulate, restrict, and
transcend it.

The environmental crisis undercuts this devaluation and dismissal of
the body. For while religions were teaching that an immortal soul ex-

isted outside the body, or that our bodily impulses had to be controlled by our higher selves, they were simultaneously trying to insure the generational continuity of believers. Such continuity required great attention to sexual reproduction, food supply, buildings in which the bodies of believers could gather, economies to support physical needs, and so forth. Bodies were taken for granted theologically, but given a tremendous amount of attention practically.

The environmental crisis makes this posture if not impossible, at least a good deal harder. For now the future of the earth as a habitable planet for our species is in doubt. This is a global threat which dwarfs any war, famine, flood, or drought of the past.[2] Once we see that there might not be future generations, or that instead of hope we face the prospect of a slow but irrevocable decline in which apocalypse is a "way of life" (Buell 2003), the denigration of the body becomes that much harder to maintain.

To put it another way: *all* our children are being born with toxins in their bloodstreams. In just this fact we now have a common problem with people of all other faiths and non-faiths. The enormous emphasis we placed on differences in beliefs and practices may remain, but alongside it is the new reality that the cancer ward or special needs school of ill, defective children will not be defined by beliefs, but by malformed and damaged physical structures.

It may be argued that this sense of commonality is no different than, say, people of different faiths realizing that they shared a threat of any natural disaster or invading army. I believe first that the very magnitude of the threat means that even if it resembles the past in conceptual structure it has a different impact. As well, there are other issues which make the environmental threat distinct.

For one thing, the environmental crisis is something we are *bringing on ourselves*. The Protestants, Jews, and Catholics of 1940s England might have shared a sense of threat from Hitler's military aggression, but they were not the cause of that aggression. To the extent that ordinary people of faith, as well as the leaders of their religions, support the current environmental regime by their participation and complicity, they share not only a common threat but a common (failure to take) responsibility. As a Jew I am, just like my Catholic and Methodist friends (and as my atheist, secularist ones as well) poisoning my own children. Guilt and shame over our past blindness and present moral laziness give me something in common with people whose theology is alien to me. Like people of wildly different classes, ethnicities, and personal beliefs who meet at a 12-step meeting to confess the many harms they have done as addicts, religious people gathered to focus on environmental issues will spend less time agreeing *or* disagreeing about "religion," and more about admitting and commiserating their own and each other's moral failings.

This is especially significant for people of faith, for yet another thing people of faith have in common historically is precisely the attitudes which attend OTF: that is, the idea that religious people, institutions, texts etc. have a special moral insight, cosmic knowledge, and ethical value. Religions are forever telling everyone else what to think and what to believe. The basis for this presumption, supposedly, is the idea that religious people act more rightly and know more than others. The Bible, the Koran, and the meditation cushion give us special insights before which, in some fashion or other (as a traditional Jewish prayer would have it) "every knee must bend."

The dawning awareness of the environmental crisis undercuts this self-evaluation. What a surprise to find that religions have done no better than anyone else. The world's religious communities were almost without exception supporters of modern industrialization, blind to the effects on humans and other species, and dependent on secular forces for understanding what is going on. It was free-lance spiritual types, some single individuals with religious values rather than recognized theologians or faith leaders, German existential phenomenologists, anti-communist western Marxists, post-beatnik hippy types, and disgruntled social critics who sounded the alarm. If this is no longer the case, if religions are now among world leaders in environmental awareness, that is both a big and a recent change.

Facing the magnitude of this change is extremely important, in part because the most important group of people to whom we endlessly proclaim our wisdom and virtue are our own children. Every religion which instructs its young, which means every religion whatsoever, now faces a situation in which any student at any Sunday School can say, with no small justification, "Who are you to teach me anything? Look what you've done, or allowed to be done, to the earth." If all religions don't acknowledge their past failings, they will, however subliminally, be perceived by many of their own young as hypocrites and moral failures.

The environmental crisis also threatens some of the basic physical practices of religious life. Again, while the more philosophically oriented theology of our traditions tend almost exclusively to privilege the mental or spiritual aspects of religious life—experiences of God, beliefs about God, the mental transformations involved in Enlightenment—the actual practice of religion typically involves a great deal of physicality.[3] What does it mean then, to take communion when the wafer contains pesticide residue, or to sanctify Sabbath wine made with genetically engineered grapes, or to focus one's attention on the breath (as basic Buddhist meditation technique) when the air is so unhealthy that people are cautioned not to go outside and exercise—in a sense, that is, not to breathe?

Thus to the extent that the environmental crisis is a crisis of our past and our future, of our moral status and our ability to instruct our children, of our basic theological self-conception and our essential rituals, the environmental crisis is indeed a crisis for religion as a whole. In that sense it is a crisis that turns religion outside itself to the wider world of politics, economics, and culture. For if religions had a serious part in creating the crisis, they certainly did not do it all by themselves. Therefore if the crisis is to be met religions need to involve themselves in the wider worlds of legal structures, government economic policy, public control of corporations, and cultural meanings. Religions necessarily will see that the point is not just to lament what we've done to the earth (and each other) but to change what we are doing. Whatever their theologies, they now must become agents of political and social change. They are catapulted (if they are not there already) into difficult political strategic questions of how to balance tolerance and principles, reform and revolution, coalition building with different groups and the need to publicly witness the truth regardless of the strategic benefits.

Since this reality implicates all organized world religions they are all, as it were, in the same boat. Their theologies may be no more similar than they were, say, forty years ago, but they won't be thinking about theology quite so much just because they have to think about this other stuff as well.

IV. HOW DO WE KNOW IT'S POSSIBLE? BECAUSE IT IS REAL

Doubtless there are theoretical criticisms that can be made of the above. All these things may be what religions *should* do, but that doesn't mean they will do them. Clearly there are a lot of religious leaders and (often self-appointed) spokespeople who are still spending a great deal of time distinguishing between their (true) faith and everyone else's. OTF may be getting a lot of bad press in some circles, but in others it is alive and well.

However the simplest way to establish that a historical development is possible is to point out that it is actual. Let us, therefore, examine some interesting examples of religious cooperation and spiritual solidarity in response to the environmental crisis, cooperation that unfolds in the face of a still highly diverse religious world. These examples come from the global movement of religious environmentalism, a movement which involves deep theological change, profound institutional commitment, and thousands of examples of real world political action.[4]

In southern Zimbabwe a remarkable coalition of independent African Christian churches and indigenous "spirit" worshiping groups worked in response to a ravaged landscape. Erosion, damaged stream banks, and above all deforestation had left the region's agriculture in a perilous condition. Formed by the initiative of a South African professor of theology who had studied the role of Zimbabwe's churches in the struggle for independence, the organization (ZIRRCON) eventually involved more than 30 paid employees, over a hundred local churches with a million plus members, as well as women's and youth clubs. In less than a decade it planted over eight million trees, altered local attitudes towards political activism and soil control, and provided countless contexts in which otherwise very different groups could interact productively (see Daneel 2005, 2001).[5]

The most instructive fact about ZIRRCON is the theological *distance* between the participants, which was far larger and more serious than among participants in ecumenical efforts among varieties of Christians or even interfaith connections among different kinds of monotheists. In the context or the ecological struggle, profound religious differences were put aside. As the president of the African Association of Earthkeeping Churches, the Bishop Machokoto, put it:

> We must be fully prepared to recognize the authority of our krall-
> heads and chiefs. For if we show contempt for them, where will we
> plant our trees? . . . Let our bishops in their eagerness to fight the
> war of the trees not antagonize the keepers of the land . . . Let us
> fully support our tribal elders in this struggle of afforestation. . . .
> (Daneel 2001: 155)

Given what was accomplished by the disparate elements in ZIRRCON
it is not surprising that for umbrella organizations such as the National
Council of Churches and the World Council of Churches collective
action on behalf of environmental causes has now become commonplace. These actions range over educational and liturgical innovation,
well publicized proclamations concerning important environmental
problems, and local efforts. Since these are the flagship organizations of
world Protestant Christianity, and since many of the coalitions in which
they work involve non-Christians as well, this is no small matter.

While the generally liberal Protestants of the NCC and WCC might
be expected to engage in common environmental action, a more surprising development is the emergence of a profoundly different attitude
towards alien religious traditions by the Catholic Church. In a range of
pronouncements by important Catholic leaders, we have, as it were, the
example of at least some of the essential attitudes of ZIRRCON writ
much larger. The change of which I am speaking is a newfound respect
for indigenous traditions. Bearing out some of what I have described
above as some of the implications of the environmental crisis for religious self-examination and transformation, we find examples of Catholic
leadership speaking respectfully and even favorably of indigenous people's ability to understand and interact with the natural world in a
sustainable way. These statements suggest that this ability is seen as
more than simply a technical competence (Catholic leaders would, for
example, be highly respectful of the people who fix their computers—
but respect in such an instance is not religiously significant). Rather,
indigenous environmental wisdom is viewed as a kind of spiritual and/or
moral gift from which the Catholic world has something to learn.

For example: in 1988 the Bishops of the Philippines (1988)—that is,
the religious leaders of a country with 70 million Catholics—uttered a
heartfelt plea, "What is happening to our beautiful land?" The document described the wide range of disastrous environmental and human
consequences of unplanned and reckless "development" and called for

a profound rethinking and change of direction. So far, so good. But remarkably in this effort the Bishops defined themselves in solidarity with:

> Tribal people all over the Philippines, who have seen the destruction of their world at close range [and] have cried out in anguish. Also men and women who attempt to live harmoniously with nature and those who study ecology have tried to alert people to the magnitude of the destruction taking place in our time. The latter are in a good position to tell us what is happening since they study the web of dynamic relationships which support and sustains all life within the earthly household. This includes human life.

But it is not just that Catholics should have compassion for the suffering of indigenous people, it is also that "For generations the hunting and food gathering techniques of our tribal forefathers showed a sensitivity and respect for the rhythms of nature." And:

> Our forefathers and tribal brothers and sisters today still attempt to live in harmony with nature. They see the Divine Spirit in the living world and show their respect through prayers and offerings. Tribal Filipinos remind us that the exploitative approach to the natural world is foreign to our Filipino culture.

For example: after an extensive process of reflection and consultation, the Bishops from the Columbia River watershed (Washington, Oregon, Idaho, British Columbia) published a lavishly illustrated booklet entitled *The Columbia River Watershed: Caring for Creation and the Common Good* (Columbia River Bishops 2005). Like "What is Happening?" the document included a wide-ranging concern for the ecology of the region, and called on all responsible parties to take in the negative consequences of destructive practices and cooperate in finding ways towards ecological sanity. In a section on regional traditions, the Bishops observe:

> Native religions taught respect for the ways of nature, personified as a nurturing mother for all creatures. They saw the salmon as food from this mother, and the river as the source of their life and the life of the fish. They adapted themselves to the river and to the cycles of the seasons. Among the Wanapum, the River People, some elders

were set apart as dreamers and healers, respected for their visions
and healing powers.

What does it mean that the Catholic Church, which for centuries held
native traditions in contempt and persecuted them, can now speak of
them with respect? The simple answer can only be that great change is
often possible in the face of great threat. And that honest Catholics
cannot help but notice that their own teachings simply had not prepared them to understand the dangers of the forms of life they unwit-
tingly endorsed. Something was missing, and in their honest appraisal
of their predicament they came upon spiritually oriented practical attitudes which contain something they had missed.

This is not to say that western religion is *necessarily* hostile to ecological sanity. As the work of a broad range of ecotheologians has
shown, many (if, in all probability, not all) of the needed metaphysical
and moral resources are there already. From the stewardship reading of
Genesis to the teachings of St. Francis, from the widespread idea that
God speaks to us in Two Books—that of Nature as well as Scripture—to
the kind of spiritual subjectivity attributed to nature in Psalms, the
Judeo-Christian tradition has a plethora of ecological themes and resources.[6]

Yet it was not these motifs that Christianity lived by. And, as far as
we can tell, in recent centuries native peoples did. This difference is the
basis for an openness to and appreciation of (to put it mildly) diverse
spiritual traditions.

V. JUST HOW DIVERSE IS DIVERSITY?

We can only speak of "religious diversity" if we know what religions are
and can count them. To count them we must be able to distinguish
them from each other. While this might seem obvious, in contemporary
religious life it is important to keep in mind. To take a simple example:
is Judaism a religion? Or is it a collection of different religions with
certain historical sources and common practices but which encompass
such radically different beliefs and practices (in, say, modern Chasidism
and Jewish Renewal) that it makes little sense to count it as a unitary
tradition? The answer, surely, is that it depends on the purpose for

which we are counting. To a Nazi a Jew of any kind is a Jew; to an Evangelical who is sure that only belief in Jesus gets you into heaven the distinctions between those who keep kosher and have only male rabbis vs. those who welcome women rabbis and drive on the Sabbath is insignificant. Yet to my brother, who is an ultra-Orthodox rabbi, my own Reform Synagogue is so far from being "really Jewish" that he would not set foot in it (for fear that anyone seeing him enter might get the wrong impression and think that this was really a place for *Jews*).

In a broader context we might wonder what distinguishes a "religion" from other worldviews or forms of life. The Religious Right in the U.S. has argued that secularism is just another religious viewpoint—and they have a point. To the extent that religions are identified not by sacred texts or belief in the supernatural but adherence to certain foundational values and assertions about the meaning of life, this position has some validity. What John Rawls called "comprehensive doctrines" can be based in the Bible or the Communist Manifesto, the Buddha or Ayn Rand. In this sense we face a bewildering variety not just of religions conceived of in the traditional sense of alternative teaching about God or Spiritual Truth, but of worldviews which range over a plethora of moral and metaphysical questions, from the privileged or limited nature of science to the spiritual meaning of sexuality. All of these worldviews share a common inability to justify their essential premises, whether those premises involve, for example, metaphysical claims about God or moral ones about human rights.[7]

What effect does the environmental crisis have on *this* kind of "religious" diversity?

In precisely the same way that it has led some Catholic Bishops to appreciate Native wisdom, it has led in at least some cases to a powerful rapprochement of religion and science and religious and secular environmental activists.

The example of science, coming after centuries of distrust, hostility, and at times direct conflict on both sides, is perhaps the most remarkable. For one thing, virtually every serious ecotheologian, as well as countless pronouncements by religious leadership, contain detailed accounts of the environmental crisis derived from . . . scientific ecology! To take just one example, the United Methodist Church (n/d) includes in its comparatively brief statement on environmental issues the following:

Economic, political, social, and technological developments have increased our human numbers, and lengthened and enriched our lives.
However, these developments have led to regional defoliation, dramatic extinction of species, massive human suffering, overpopula-
tion, and misuse and overconsumption of natural and nonrenewable
resources, particularly by industrialized societies.

That is, familiar uses of scripture or deep moral pieties are not enough,
but must be joined with facts and figures about global warming, toxic
rivers, and desertification. There is a widespread if tacit acknowledgement that the practice of religion now requires ideas (e.g., sustainability) and information (e.g., asthma rates in polluted areas, global climate
feedback loops) which it cannot generate on its own. The closed world
of religion, in which tradition, authority, and abstract theology were
supposed to provide the basis for a religious life, has opened up to
something else.

Second, and even more impressive, there are examples of practical
cooperation between religious leaders and leading scientists over environmental issues. In 1992 for instance, a joint statement signed by 150
scientists and religious leaders in a shared "Mission to Washington,"
proclaimed:

We are people of faith and of science who, for centuries, often have
traveled different roads. In a time of environmental crisis, we find
these roads converging . . . our two ancient, sometimes antagonistic,
traditions now reach out to one another in a common endeavor to
preserve the home we share. . . .We believe that science and religion,
working together, have an essential contribution to make toward any
significant mitigation and resolution of the world environmental crisis. What good are the most fervent moral imperatives if we do not
understand the dangers and how to avoid them? What good is all the
data in the world without a steadfast moral compass? (Joint Appeal
1992: 735)

More recently, in January 2007, at a press conference at the Harvard
Club in Cambridge, MA, a group of Evangelical Christian leaders and
leading scientists addressed the President, Congress, and other leading
political figures, calling for serious action on global warming. Asserting
that defense of life on earth is a "profound moral imperative," the group
cautioned that "reckless human activity has imperiled the Earth—espe-

cially the unsustainable and short-sighted lifestyles and public policies or our own nation" [and] "we share a profound moral obligation to work together to call our nation, and other nations, to the kind of dramatic change urgently required in our day." The group effort had been initiated by Rich Cizik, head of the enormous National Association of Evangelicals—a religious grouping not typically aligned with tolerant, ecumenical Protestantism, progressive Catholicism, or Reform Judaism. Cizik was joined by Eric Chivian of Harvard Medical School, who said, in a statement that crystallizes all these remarkable religious *in the broad sense* changes: "There is no such thing as a Republican or Democrat, a liberal or conservative, a religious or secular environment" (Zaberenko 2007).

This is as remarkable a move for a scientist as it is for a religious leader, for while scientists have not had the social power to oppress religion, the culture of science has often understood itself as being in profound opposition to the irrational, faith-not-reason-based, superstitious, irredeemably old school style of religion. Yet where in scientific theory was Chivian to turn when he wanted to express the shared "profound moral obligation" that he feels so strongly? Is there a scientific way to prove moral obligation? Actually, no. There is only a multi-faceted—religious and secular—tradition of trying to support it, explaining what it means, and arguing over tough cases. In other words, there are only a wide range of comprehensive doctrines, and in this way the barriers between science and religion, in the face of the environmental crisis considered as *moral* as well as instrumental, begin to shatter.

After the watershed of cooperation with science, it is perhaps less impressive but certainly still significant to cite an example of a religious group engaging in direct cooperation with a secular political organization. As the Philippines Bishops observed, those who "study ecology" and seek to live "in harmony with nature" are a religious environmentalist's natural allies. In January of 2002 the Sierra Club and the National Council of Churches cooperated on a television advertisement resisting drilling in the Arctic National Wildlife Sanctuary. The groups had compromised on the language used—leaving out "God" but including "creation"—and the heads of both groups reported near unanimous positive response. In July 2008 a Sierra Club helped recruit for an initiative that took as its goal the training of hundreds of Christian clergy as presenters of the slide show made famous in Al Gore's film *An Inconvenient Truth*. The goal of the training, wrote Sierra Club staffer Lyndsey Moselely, is "to equip faith leaders with the best science available so that you can help educate and inform your communities" (Moselely 2008).[8]

VI. HOW IS THIS POSSIBLE? FMI

The irony of the liberal, tolerant, modern response to religious diversity, the one that celebrates diversity by embracing pluralism, is that differences among religions become minimized and by an ironic turning of concepts, diversity itself if not disappearing, starts to fade out.

For example: Margaret Bullitt-Jonas is an Episcopal priest and a colleague of mine on the Leadership Council of Religious Witness for the Earth—a national, independent, interfaith network dedicated to creating a society in which human beings live in loving, just relationships with one another and with all Creation.[9] As a religious environmentalist Bullitt-Jonas has spoken out and demonstrated, and in 2001 was arrested for a non-violent civil disobedience protesting George W. Bush's energy policy. Bullitt-Jonas has a defined theology. She is a very specific kind of Protestant Christian, and she believes, as Jesus says in the New Testament, that "No one comes to the Father except through [him]." In her interfaith work however, that belief, while not being negated, simply recedes in importance. As she looks around the room at members of the Council—which include other kinds of Christians, Unitarians, Jews, and eclectic spiritual types—another of her beliefs rises in importance: that there are "different ways of imaging the divine and structuring our path to it." This is not anything-goes relativism, she is clear, for all these different ways can be subjected to the same test: Do they lead their respective followers to greater compassion? On this basis Bullitt-Jonas feels that a liberal Jew (with overtones of paganism and Buddhism) like myself, is in a sense *closer* to her religiously than a doctrinaire, intolerant, rigid *Christian* (Bullitt-Jonas 2008).

In a sense, then, calculations of diversity are subject to (at least) two different conceptions of religious identity. For one, religions are distinguished by their formal creed, particular holy books, institutions, and rituals. For a second, the one in terms of which Gottlieb and Bullitt-Jonas are more *religiously* alike than Bullitt-Jonas, and say, Jerry Falwell, vague but real values like compassion (and typically, some kind of ecological consciousness and an acceptance of gender equality) are the key.[10] This sense of religious commonality permeates a good deal of the world's religious culture now and is dramatically furthered by participation in religious environmentalism. For while the struggles of religious environmentalism are clearly practically oriented—cleaning up a river, protecting our infants' blood streams, etc.—they are not *simply* practical. Whether one thinks of the natural world as a place where divinity resides, or simply the Divinity's miraculous gift to humans, there is a sense among the vast majority of religious environmentalists that action on behalf of "all of life" involves an expression of specifically religious values, and has as its object the care of something which itself possesses at least a modicum of holiness. When we all work together on this holy task, then, there is a sense in which we are all part of the "same" religion. We are engaged in a fellowship. We practice together. We support each other's calling. We celebrate life—and defend it—arm in arm. Are there differences? Of course. But as I have observed already, the world's identified religions are filled with differences in any case, and even in the most homogeneous religious community there will be wide variations in the ways in which people imagine or experience the holy.

This result might not please everyone, to say the least. It is not hard to hear a traditionalist argue "Either Jesus is the Son of God or He is not. If He is, and was indeed sent to us to teach us how to get to the Father, then we had better acknowledge Him or we simply won't make real religious progress. The most pedestrian logic tells us that either this kind of claim is true or it is not. No fancy footwork about compassion or ecological concern will change that."

There is much to admire in this position, not the least of which is the idea that religion has boundaries, rules, constraints, and truths. Without those it would seem to fall back into a mish-mash of emotional responses, aesthetic enjoyments, and mildly pleasing socializing.

But while I am aware of that danger, and think that, for example, Bullitt-Jonas' test of religious adequacy would do a good deal to remove its sting, I am more concerned with another religious problem—that the Orthodox believer, the one who is so eager to present me with a clear Either/Or of true belief or false error, has actually mistaken the nature of religious life. That is because we cannot ever unproblematically know what "acknowledging Jesus" consists in. Does it mean simply saying over and over "I acknowledge (believe, have faith, etc.) that Jesus is the Son of God" as if true faith consists in nothing more than verbal repetition? Does it mean quoting scripture—as if we can know what scripture means simply saying it often enough? Can one, perhaps, show more love of Jesus by caring for one's (disagreeable, foreign-looking) neighbor than going to church, or repeating Jesus' name over and over, or even knowing who Jesus is? Or not? Is it a matter of internal, experiential feeling that guarantees the truth of our love of God? Perhaps. But can't we be mistaken about the power of our feelings, or about how important they are for the way we will live in the future? The deep religious problem is that there is no objective way to know who has religious faith, because faith cannot be measured.

In short, whether or not one believes in *any* religion is to some extent a *subjective* question, based in the degree of internal commitment and subject to a variety and not easily applied interpretative criteria of authenticity. As Kierkegaard (1941: 219) puts it "All paganism consists in this, that God is related to man directly. . . ." [11] For just that reason, in a sense Bullitt-Jonas cannot really be sure whether I, who would never say that I believe Jesus to be the Messiah, am as much a follower of Jesus as any of her fellow Episcopal priests. Even if we have to love Jesus to get into heaven, there may be a whole host of ways to do that, some of which might include not knowing that he ever existed! And then the difference between those who embrace diversity and those who reject it, would be that the former, unlike the latter, are not at all sure what that love consists in, *outside* of the chancy, all-encompassing, always questionable, practice of something like compassion.

Now that this compassion extends to all of life, its power for effecting a specifically *religious* transformation of the social world has radically deepened. Since we are beset with a threat to us all, we have the chance to manifest love for us all. If we are all in the same boat, sailing on or going down together, at least we do not have to face the terrors of the storm by ourselves.

NOTES

1. The official account of Harvard's well–funded "Pluralism Project." See Eck 2006.

2. Nuclear war can be seen as the ultimate environmental catastrophe.

3. A great deal could be made of this contradiction, as indeed theologies influenced by feminism's critique of patriarchy have done.

4. My own account, as well as that of other scholars, can be found in Gottlieb 2006a, b, 2003.

5. By comparison, the Kenyan Green Belt movement, the leader of which received the Nobel Peace prize, planted around 30 million.

6. The same can be said of Buddhism, Hinduism, Islam, etc. The passages from key scriptures and theologians are not hard to find, *if* one really wants to find them. Taking them seriously, of course, is another matter entirely.

7. It could certainly be argued that there are to the contrary lots of solid justifications for comprehensive views. Yet the fact that there are so many justifications, for so many different views, and that both the justifications and the views keep on coming, actually reinforces rather than contradicts my point.

8. The Sierra Club has a permanent and significantly funded office to reach out to faith communities. For an account of their work and wide-ranging information on recent faith based environmental initiatives, see Sierra Club 2008.

9. For further information, see the group's website: www.religiouswitness.org.

10. None of this is meant to suggest that there couldn't be a vast amount of real debate on what "compassion" means in any given context.

11. This entire critical line originated with Kierkegaard. See Kierkegaard 1941.

REFERENCES

Bishops of the Philippines, 1988, "What is Happening to Our Beautiful Land?" Marquette University website, July 12, 2008: http://www.marquette.edu/theology/interfacing/ChurchonEcologicalDegradation/documents/WhatisHappeningtoOurBeautifulLand_000.pdf.

Buell, Frederic. 2003. *From Apocalypse to Way of Life: Environmental Crisis in the American Century.* New York: Routledge.

Bullitt-Jonas, Margaret, 2008. Phone interview with author, July 8, 2008.

Columbia River Bishops, 2005, *The Columbia River Watershed: Caring for Creation and the Common Good.* Columbia River Project Website, June 5, 2007: http://www.columbiariver.org/.

Daneel, Martinus L., 2005. "African Earthkeeping Churches," *Encyclopedia of Religion and Nature*, ed. Bron Taylor. London: Continuum.

Daneel, Martinus L., 2001. *African Earthkeepers: Wholistic Interfaith Mission*. Maryknoll, NY: Orbis Books.

Eck, Diana, "What is Pluralism," Pluralism Project Website, July 22, 2008. http://www.pluralism.org/pluralism/what_is_pluralism.php.

Environmental Working Group, 2005. "Body Burden—The Pollution in Newborns," 14 July 2005, Body Burden Website, http://www.ewg.org/reports/bodyburden2/execsumm.php.

Gottlieb, Roger S. 2006a. *The Oxford Handbook of Religion and Ecology*. New York: Oxford University Press.

Gottlieb, Roger S. 2006b. *A Greener Faith: Religious Environmentalism and Our Planet's Future*. New York: Oxford University Press.

Gottlieb, Roger S. 2003. *This Sacred Earth: Religion, Nature, Environment. Second Edition*. New York: Routledge.

Joint Appeal by Religion and Science for the Environment. 1992. "Declaration of the Mission to Washington". In Gottlieb 2003.

Kierkegaard, Søren. 1941. *Concluding Unscientific Postscript*. Translated by David Swenson and Walter Lowrie. Princeton, NJ: Princeton University Press.

Locke, John. 1689. *A Letter Concerning Toleration*. The constitution website, July 22, 2008. http://www.constitution.org/jl/tolerati.htm.

Moselely, Lyndsey. 2008. Email to religious leaders.

Sierra Club 2008. *Faith in Action: Communities of Faith Bring Hope to the Planet*. Sierra Club website, July 22, 2008. http://www.sierraclub.org/partnerships/faith/report2008/report2008.pdf

United Methodist Church General Board, n/d. "Statement on Environmental Racism." United Methodist Church Website, July 1, 2008: http://www.umc-gbcs.org/site/apps/nl/content3.asp?c=frLJK2PKLqF&b=3631781&ct=3986175.

Zabarenko, Deborah. 2007. "US scientists, evangelicals join global warming fight." Reuters new service website, July 1, 2007. http://www.alertnet.org/thenews/newsdesk/N17341633.htm

8

SPIRITUAL DEEP ECOLOGY AND WORLD RELIGIONS

A Shared Fate, a Shared Task

"Deep Ecology—the phrase" originated recently as a stream of academic ethics stressing the intrinsic ethical value of the natural world. However, what we might call "Deep Ecology—the concept" is as old as the worship of the Earth Goddess, as widespread as any seven-year-old girl's fascination with frogs, as fundamental as the way any of us might have our breaths taken away by a brilliant tropical sunset or the startling clarity of a drab December landscape suddenly made white by the season's first snow. "Deep Ecology—the concept" is a sense of reverence and sacredness, insight and inspiration, that is found in (to use David Abram's felicitous phrase) the "more than human" world. Deep Ecology in this sense is not a movement *outside* of world religions, which then might be juxtaposed to these related but essentially different forms of thought and practice. Rather, Deep Ecology occurs within the discursive, emotive, cognitive, and at times even institutional space of world religions themselves. As such, spiritual Deep Ecology shares something of the history, the tasks, and the dangers of the rest of the world's religious traditions.

THE "SPIRIT" IN SPIRITUAL DEEP ECOLOGY

By "religion" I mean organized and overlapping systems of belief, ritual, institutional life, spiritual aspiration, and ethical orientation which are premised on an understanding of human beings as other or more than simply their purely social or physical identities. Teachings can be marked as "religious" in the way they assert (as in Judaism, Christianity, and Islam) that humans are essentially connected to a Supreme Being whose authority is distinct from earthly political and social powers; or by a suggestion (made by Buddhism) that we can achieve a state of consciousness which transcends the attachments, obsessions, and passions or our ordinary social ego; or in the Wiccan celebration of the sexual act as an embodiment of the life-giving force of the Goddess rather than as simply a grasping of moments of purely individual pleasure.

What is crucial is that religion serves as an alternative to understandings of the human identity which center on the social successes of money, fame, political power, career achievement, or community acceptance. Religious perspectives direct us towards what theologian Paul Tillich called "ultimate significance." They seek to orient us to that which is of compelling importance beyond, beneath, or within our day-to-day concerns with making money, getting famous, or having immediate pleasures. At the same time, however, religion also seeks to orient us to the familiar interpersonal world of family, community, and global connections, providing guidance which seeks to root everyday moral teachings in the ultimate nature or significance of a spiritual truth about who we really are. Religions necessarily direct us towards particular ways of living with other people and with the world.

Finally, religions provide rituals—acts of prayer, meditation, collective contrition, or celebration—whose goal is to awaken and reinforce an immediate and personal sense of our connection to the Sacred. These practices aim at a transformation of consciousness, to cultivate within the heart an impassioned clarity of connection to spiritual sensibility.

The celebration and awe for the natural world that are the hallmark of spiritual Deep Ecology match this conception of the essential features of religion. To begin, spiritual Deep Ecology challenges the (now) conventional notion that human beings are essentially different than, separate from, and superior to the natural world. Much of the world's religion, philosophy, law, education, commerce, and common sense have for some time[1] given human beings "dominion" (Genesis) over the earth. People have asserted that the distinctive human capacities for language, "reason," or property ownership signify that we alone have rights, or ultimate moral worth. By contrast, spiritual Deep Ecology prizes our connection to the natural world as vital to who we are. It makes much of our similarities, connections, and interrelations with earth and sky, flowers and fish. In this sense, Deep Ecology is not only a response to questions about whether or not nature has intrinsic value, it is also a distinct perspective about what people are. As other religions tell of that we are a spark of God or a pure awareness, so spiritual Deep Ecology tells us (or wants us to discover) that we are natural beings, tied hand, foot, and heart to a vast web of natural beings that are, in a way, sacred. "World as Lover, World as Self," proclaims Buddhist deep ecologist Joanna Macy, meaning that our essential connection to nature can combine love, identification, and intimacy. "We need wilderness," says Edward Abbey, "Because we are wild animals." It is our sensuous connection to our surroundings, says Abram, which has allowed us to learn, and even to speak. Or, as in Paul Shepard's simple truth: "The Others have made us human."[2]

This sense of connection has at times been recognized in religions that are preponderantly anthropocentric. The Torah ruled that animals, and not just people, were to have the Sabbath for rest. The Buddhist sense of the interconnection of *all* beings was inscribed in children's stories in which the Buddha was reincarnated as an animal. Even in Christianity there were occasional voices which saw the face of God in nature. We might say, therefore, that Deep Ecology at times overlaps with other religious traditions. It expresses, as it were, a "natural" human tendency to respond to with care, love, and awe to nature. (E.O. Wilson dubbed this sentiment "biophilia" and argued that it possibly has genetic roots.[3])

The vitality of our connection to nature is most obviously signaled by the constant realization of our dependence on it. Air, water, and food, the microbes in our gut, the nitrogen-fixing bacterial in the soil—without any of these our illusions of autonomy would crumble mighty fast. Yet there is a more precisely religious element in spiritual Deep Ecology. As Jews or Hindus see themselves as receiving The Truth from scriptures or direct encounters with God—the Deep Ecologist receives sacred truths from the natural world. The Native American sense that each person has a particular animal as a teacher of truths and virtues is thus a kind of "deep ecological" religious sensibility. This attitude appeared likewise when Aldo Leopold beheld a "fierce green fire" in the eyes of the wolf he himself had shot to make the world better for deer and deer hunters, and learned that from the point of view of the wolf, and the mountain it lived on, there were other and better ways to live in the world. Nature for the deep ecologist is not only a kind of spontaneous mall, filled with things to meet our needs and give us pleasure ("And here, some food; there materials for furniture; and, how pleasant, now some lovely bird calls.") It is also a Sacred Teacher—a Torah, Koran, or Gita. While anthropocentric religions have occasionally celebrated the holiness of the natural world, usually as a manifestation of the holiness of its creator, it is only with the most extreme rarity that they see it as a source of wisdom.

For Deep Ecology, further, the teachings of nature, like the Mitzvot of Judaism or the ethical constraints of a traditional Buddhist teaching, direct us back into the social world. Nature's revelations, it is believed, have some very strong implications for social life. For one thing, the interdependence of different parts of an ecosystem, deep ecologists tell us, teaches us about the necessity to curb our personal and collective greed, to exercise the kind of care we seem to have forgotten (or never had), to treasure the multiplicity of species rather than cavalierly eliminate them. In this light, everything that lives is precious, just because it is part of and contributes to, the precious, differentiated whole that is the natural world. A realization of this truth is not simply a pleasant intellectual reflection, but a guide to moral behavior for individuals and groups alike.

Further, an identification with nature can be the source of deep pleasure and deeper calm. Just as people who hear the voice of God may feel a little differently about a flat tire or being passed over for a promotion, so a felt connection with a tree or a bird can soothe the anxieties and relieve the sense of overwhelming pressure to achieve or possess in the social realm. Such a connection might even, if we let it, help us learn not to be quite so (desperately, compulsively) busy. Experiencing ourselves as natural as well as social, part of a cosmos as well as a community, we can find a remedy for the kinds of neurosis that typically are not part of the lives of ants, birches, or elks. Observing how vital all parts of an ecosystem are, we may learn to lessen our desires to succeed at all costs, to triumph over others, or to achieve fame.[4] Seeing how the birth and death of all beings takes places in a cycle of coming forth and returning to the underlying matrix which makes life possible, we can sense our own infinite future as part of what Rachel Carson called a "material immortality."

These are just some of the spiritual lessons deep ecologists have taken from nature. Interpreted through our multiple and varying social contexts, deep ecologists in various historical and social settings have made human sense of the more than human. As other religions have struggled to interpret sacred texts, so those of us who find the divine in the ordinary physical realities have had to decide what meanings they have for our lives. The fact that interpretation has been necessary, that ocean and mountain do not carry transparent spiritual meanings, simply means that spiritual Deep Ecology is in the same situation as any other religious orientation toward Truth.

THE FATE OF RELIGION

One of the great surprises of the second half of the 20th century is the worldwide resurgence of religion. How many people, after all, would have thought that Russian Christianity would outlive the Stalinist secret police, that some of the most powerful post-colonial regimes would define themselves in terms of their religious piety; or that in the last decade before the millennium perhaps the single most powerful unified ideological group in the United States (that bastion of science, democracy, progress, and research grants) would be the fundamentalist Christian right?

What happened to the Enlightenment? (And, whatever happened, it is something that necessarily is happening to spiritual Deep Ecology as well as any other religious or spiritual outlook.)

Quite simply, too many of the promises of Enlightenment did not materialize. If we think of the secular enlightenment as based in the equation "science plus democracy plus the free market equals reason equals freedom plus happiness," we can sense some of the historical and psychological sources of our collective disappointment.

For a start, as the servant of government, business, and careerism, science and technology have proved a mixed blessing. Too many diseases seem impervious to a strictly detached, seemingly objective, medical expertise. "Scientific management" often proves to be an oxymoron. The nifty airplanes drop horrible bombs, the cooled off cars cause skin cancer by eroding the ozone layer, the pesticide is transmuted into a gas to kill people. (Zyklon B, the gas used in concentration camps, was first noticed being used to eradicate insects from old buildings.) Later, we discover that pesticides kill people even when they are aimed at bugs.

As the early Western Marxist Georg Lukacs observed nearly eighty years ago, the modern age is marked by a combination of increasingly sophisticated parts integrated into an increasingly irrational whole.[5] One need only think of the technological prerequisites for—and the real life consequences of—ozone depleting CFCs. Or traffic gridlock; or urban sprawl; or the way the overuse of antibiotics has bred new and virulent strains of bacteria.

On the level of social life, a collection of democratically connected individual producers and consumers seems, for many, to be a poor basis for community. We have the freedom to consume and pollute, to move and to get divorced, but all these seem to promote at least as much loneliness as they do fulfillment. Individually, a rather alarming percentage of the world's richest, most technologically oriented nation are addicted to alcohol, prescribed drugs, illegal drugs, work, sex, adrenaline, caffeine, nicotine, television, psychotherapy, or the Internet.

In the un (less) developed world, secular progress seems to go along with increased class stratification, the decimation of traditional culture, and the rape of the local economy by international corporate interests.

The point of these familiar observations is to locate the current resurgence of personal and collective religious life in a history of the failed promises of the Enlightenment. And, simultaneously, to point out that spiritual Deep Ecology *as anything like a widespread belief and sentiment* is in some ways a product of the same forces. Fundamentalist Christianity is in part a response to the availability of divorce and the presence of pornography. Jewish Renewal, Creation theology, and other progressive/feminist/green/passionate forms of religious renewal are partly responses to the boring modernism of washed out "reform" versions of Christianity and Judaism. Similarly, Deep Ecology is a response to the massive looming presence of the environmental crisis and the

bland deadness of a universe presented as only the object of manipula-
tive science and voracious productivism. In other words, Deep Ecology
is a spiritual answer to the transformation of nature into environment—
in which virtually all our earthly surroundings become stamped with a
human mark, or threaten to become our pets, raw materials, or victims.

Simultaneously, as any religious movement worth its salt contains
occasions for celebration as well as the capacity to warn us against sin,
Deep Ecology offers delights not encapsulated by a vocabulary of individual rights, personal choices, and lots of trips to the mall. A resurgent
Judaism advises us to recover the joys of the Sabbath, and actually turn
off our toys and jobs for twenty-five hours each week. Dorothy Day and
the Catholic Worker movement advised us to recover the freedom of a
freely chosen poverty. Spiritual Deep Ecology, besides warning us of
our mistakes, is also a movement to return to delight in the simple
beauties of land and air. It teaches us to find rapture in a brief staring
contest with a weasel, or to marvel at the interdependence of plants and
insects in a rainforest, or to celebrate the turning of the seasons. Deep
Ecology writing returns us to the magic time of childhood when at least
some of the natural world was *fully* alive. It serves as a kind of magical
regression to the wisdom of childhood. Consider Stephanie Kaza's simple evocation of

> Sycamores! Bright white trunks against the blue horizon! All this
> week I have been seeing you for a distance. Now I am lured closer
> for a conversation, for a chance to glimpse the world between your
> branches. Sweet billowy clouds dance above your arms in the pierc-
> ing equinox light. The bright sun reflects off your tall trunks in the
> crisp, clear air.[6]

This childlike joy can be combined with, as David Barnhill puts it, the
sage's sense that death is integral to life. Just because we see ourselves
as deeply connected to a natural world that is not essentially defined by
a conscious intelligence, the prospect of our own physical death is less
daunting, and we are perhaps more likely to accept that birds, oak trees,
mountains, and even the earth itself are subject to change. As religions
cushion us against the fear of death by promising life in Another Realm,
so spiritual Deep Ecology fulfills the same function by helping us see
this one differently.

More familiar religious movements and spiritual Deep Ecology thus share a kindred origin. It is not surprising, then, that they can be seen as also sharing common dangers, tasks, and temptations.

RELIGIONS AND SPIRITUAL DEEP ECOLOGY

Like it or not, all resurgent religions, even the most hysterically fundamentalist, are post-Enlightenment religions. Unlike the religions before Galileo, Voltaire, Marx, and Freud, any religious tradition today knows that it exists in a social context marked by several new features.

First, there is the obvious growth of technical knowledge that, for all its faults, is essential to the daily personal and institutional lives of the religious devotees themselves. (Every fundamentalist, with the possible exception of the Amish, has his fax machine, Internet address, color TV, and long distance calling card! Or, at least, all of his leaders do.) *Second*, there remain aggressive and self-confident secular philosophies which have tried (with mixed results in practice to be sure—but then how much success has anyone had?) to offer fulfilling visions of human life in nonreligious terms. Secular philosophies and their adherents, despite the excesses of Stalin or Hitler, *The Wall Street Journal* or *Playboy*, still often feel themselves every bit the legitimate equal or superior to religious perspectives. Whatever the rise of religion in recent decades, these secular perspectives are not going to go away. Religions are thus in competition with other perspectives. They are not, and they know it, the only game in town. *Third*, the creation of a world community of language, publishing, travel, and scholarship means that any religion knows—in a way it never did before—that it lives in a world of virtually countless *other* religions as well. While this encourages some fundamentalists to claim, endlessly, that they alone have the Truth, in others it produces an uncharacteristic and refreshing modesty.

This modesty is even more essential to the *fourth* dimension, which is that of knowledge of religions' own past sins. If not particularly widespread among the fundamentalists, this awareness is essential to those progressive elements of the new religiosity, and therefore relevant to spiritual Deep Ecology. Progressive Christians tend to have some awareness of the shameful history of Christian anti-Semitism, of inquisitions and pogroms. Reform, Reconstructionist, and Jewish Renewal groups, even as they may be calling for more traditional forms of observance, take stands against the sexism of traditional Judaism.

One central effect of all these changes is that religion in *our* world lacks innocence of its own history, its own limits, and its own powers. For the new breed of fundamentalists, this means that there is always an Other to be opposed or suppressed. For people with any kind of progressive awareness, to have Religion after Enlightenment is to be faced with the choice of adopting a kind of pre-enlightenment fanaticism or learning how to combine a real religious identity with a kind of postmodern relativism, Kierkegaardian subjectivism, or open-minded ecumenism.

While Deep Ecology is a powerful critic of modernist scientific and economic reductionism, it is, as Michael Zimmerman has argued, always quite difficult to transcend the limitations of the Enlightenment while simultaneously keeping its accomplishments. We see the consequences of the rejection of those accomplishments in religious totalitarianism of all stripes. Political notions of individual rights and a spiritual understanding that mystical knowledge is essentially metaphorical are both foreign to any form of fundamentalism. The mullahs of whatever faith are sure they know what God wants; and they have the whips and chains to put that knowledge into practice. The problem for all contemporary religions is to maintain religious passion—without devolving into pre-Enlightenment tyranny.

What does this mean for spiritual Deep Ecology? Well, as a loose collection of spiritually oriented individuals and groups, the issue of collective power exercised over others is hardly applicable. Deep ecologists are unlikely to be party to inquisitions or schisms. However, Deep Ecology *is* capable of its own kind of fundamentalism, its own blindness to its own moral failings and the possibility of being one-sided, narrow, and dictatorial. In its passion for nature ("No compromise in defense of Mother Earth!" is the slogan of the radical, deep ecologically oriented Earth First!) and its frustration over the way our global civilization is destroying so much of what we need and (should) love, deep ecologists can forget the complexity of contemporary moral life and the dangers which inevitably arise when one identifies oneself as the sole source of value.

In this regard I remember an exchange I once had with a leading animal rights activist and writer. He had just appeared at a panel on animal rights issues at a large academic conference. Many in the audience had been less than sympathetic, raising rather tired complaints about the rights of hunters and whether or not cauliflowers felt as much pain as veal calves and thus ought not to be eaten either. The writer in question, livid at their responses, told me how "They" just "didn't get it." And it seemed, "they never would." In a rare compassionate mood, I was able to put away my own tendencies to self-righteousness and point out that while I disagreed with his critics, we *all* had our faults. For instance, the money we used to fly to this conference, stay at the convention hotel, and have dinners on our academic travel accounts, could have been used for countless other purposes: for instance, to aid animals, people, or ecosystems in distress all over the world. A blank look came over my friend's face, and he drifted away to discuss animal rights with someone else.

In a deeper political vein, *any* politically oriented movement in the late 20th century, whether it has a spiritual orientation or not, must be deeply self-critical. As all religions now exist only after the inquisition, so any political movement—that is, any movement one of whose goals is a fundamental change in social policy and structure—exists "after Stalin." That is, all political aspirations exist after we have seen self-proclaimed revolutionaries who had (or claimed to have) the interests of society as a whole, devolve into brutal tyrants. While communists turned out to be no more hypocritical, inconsistent, or destructive than their counterparts in the world of capitalist politics, their rhetoric was much grander. They defined themselves as the servants of the downtrodden, and became, instead, their new masters.

Spiritual deep ecologists, then, must beware the way Deep Ecology can combine, however inconsistently, or uneasily, with "other" things which are not so pretty. We might remember in this regard Hitler's vegetarianism, and the way some leading members of the Nazi party espoused the inherent values of the natural world, criticized the endless industrial destruction of nature, and sought to protect areas of German wilderness. Sadly, this fascist Deep Ecology was rooted in a nationalistic account of the "special" German relation to "the soil," a relation that necessarily excluded non-Aryans. This Nazi love of nature, and for some Nazis it was quite genuine, combined with a virulent hatred of Jews.[7]

Closer to home, contemporary deep ecologist writers have at times manifested a rather simple-minded misanthropy, seeing population issues as the source of our problems with nature rather than as a complex consequence of poverty, imperialism, and patriarchy. Perhaps more important, deep ecologists have sometimes been blind to the social inequalities that make up the human-nature relationship. It is not—as many have already pointed out—simply a matter of an undifferentiated, and self-centered "humanity" wreaking havoc with other life forms. Humanity is divided up into vastly unequal groups: men and women, North and South, capitalist and worker, World Bank manager and dispossessed peasants, agribusiness and farm laborer. To forget this is to misconceive the forces that are centrally implicated in the destruction we seek to end.[8]

To confront these realities, spiritual Deep Ecology needs *social theory*. It needs systematic theoretical resources to explain, for instance, the expansion of commodity production, the effects of the world market, and the relation between the exploitation of nature and domination of women. The moral posture of spiritual Deep Ecology, without the focused knowledge of critical social theory, will be naive.

This same need arises, I believe, for the moral posture of any religious sensibility. Religions were invented, after all, at a time of comparatively simple, comparatively transparent, social relations. "Love thy neighbor" makes a kind of rough and ready sense when people generally live in tribes and villages. Yet in a world of acid rain and global warming, our neighborhood is the entire earth. Similarly, "Thou shall not kill" becomes a lot harder to follow when "automatically" withheld taxes support a military machine or a simple commute to work damages the world's climate.

On the more personal level, morally oriented religious sensibilities (which include Deep Ecology and all other religions) have need of something like modern psychological theory to help explain and understand "sin." That is, the simple assertion of right and wrong which is characteristic of Western religions, or the simple appeal to ignorance or Karma which tend to arise in Buddhism or Hinduism, need to be deepened by psychological accounts of early trauma, compulsion, addictions, and neurosis. The culture of therapy cannot substitute for moral language. But, for all its faults, excesses, and stupidities that culture cannot be discarded either. To understand *why* people find it hard to stop consuming, for instance, spiritual Deep Ecology had better have some idea about how selfhood in a decentered, mass society is built on consumption. Just railing against our collective "greed" will not do. Social psychologies describing the nexus of personhood, sexuality, human relations, the media, and commodities need to be brought to bear. Similar issues arise when spiritual deep ecologists try to fathom the meaning of our collective powerlessness in the face of ecological madness. Answers (albeit depressing ones) to the despairing "Why can't we change the way we live?" do not arise from within the religious and spiritual traditions, but from accounts of non-violently coercive mechanisms of social control. These accounts are found in, for instance, early Frankfurt School theory, neo-Marxist accounts of ideology, or feminist descriptions of the consequences of patriarchy. In other words, the moral subject matter that is essential for religious life needs to be supplemented by bodies of thought that are themselves not necessarily religious at all.

In short, contemporary religious sensibilities, including spiritual Deep Ecology, are bound by a radically new humility about their own past performance and have a central need to avail themselves of the accomplishments of social and psychological theory. If we are in some way to make a New World or repair this one—which is the dream of any religion that wants to bring the divine to the earth—we had better understand what we are facing.

THE DANGERS OF LIBERALISM

For all its newfound modesty and openness to other theories, it is nevertheless crucial that post-Enlightenment religions not sink into a mild-mannered, anything goes liberalism. Religion that cannot take a stand, that (a little like Bill Clinton) blows with any wind that happens to turn up, is no religion at all. While a new found diffidence about *metaphysical assertions* is one of the hallmarks of progressive post-Enlightenment religion, such a diffidence cannot be extended into the realm of *morality*.

Of course this distinction may well be hotly contested at times. But struggling with it might be one of the hallmarks of a progressive, post-enlightenment religion. Surrounded by competing religious and non-religious perspectives, and knowing that it cannot "prove" its account of God or the Divine, such a religion seeks to combine a commitment to moral value with a strongly—but openly (relativistically, subjectively, etc.)—held view of religious metaphysics. On the one hand, we try to coherently assert that there are many paths to the Truth and many names for God. At the same time, however, we are quite dogmatic about our belief that these paths do not include sexism, exploitation, or selfish violence. To have any relation to the Divine that is not escapist and simply irrelevant to human relations, our image of divinity must commit us to certain moral values—*and thus to certain social relationships*—over others. Our accounts of "God" may be evocative poetry or performative exhortation, but our assertions about right and wrong, good and evil, have to be a little more straightforward.

Many of the particular positive values of spiritual ecology are easily read from its sense of the holy. Sustainability, respect for other species, conservation, celebration of wilderness, etc.—that the deep ecologist is committed to these in the abstract is clear. However, the dangers of wishy-washy liberalism arise for the deep ecologist when the bland images of nature which sometimes emerge from its discussions distort what "nature" really is like. For example, our mystically based love of life may not extend to the AIDS virus; and our wariness at tampering with the sacred character of nature might be suspended when it comes to using genetic engineering to cure cystic fibrosis. Ghetto rats will probably escape the purview that holds all of life as sacred; as might the black flies that cause widespread blindness in Africa. Adopting a deep ecological perspective will not eliminate the hard choices we face—choices about how much to take for ourselves and how much to leave for others; how much to exercise the control we increase day by day, and how much to surrender. And it will not turn the real world into a PBS special on butterflies or dolphins. The love we feel for the more-than-human is not a love that can erase the realities of struggle, conquest and death—of nature as one long and frequently quite painful food chain.

THE DIFFICULT COMBINATION

There is no easy way to describe the struggle of post-Enlightenment religions. Or, rather, this struggle can be stated fairly easily but its accomplishment is another matter! How are we to take a religious sensibility which includes within itself moral demands on both ourselves and the rest of social life and make it socially relevant while at the same time avoiding the perils of dogmatism, sectarianism, and—if it comes to that—violence? The power of religious inspiration can be so over-whelming, yet all too often when it has been translated into social life it has become (in retrospect) so pernicious. On the other hand, the image of a do-nothing, know-nothing religious sensibility, keyed purely to an interior sense of virtue, has itself become dubious.

In fact, a good deal of post-Enlightenment religion, of whatever political persuasion, is socially activist. Just as spiritual life is necessarily affected by the successes—and failures—of modern science, so it has been affected by modern political ideas. Particularly, since the French Revolution there has arisen the notion of an organized, systematic, ideology-driven transformation of social life as a whole. Whatever the fate of political movements led by this idea, a part of it has become central to religious life: the notion that our moral commitments are not seriously held if we do not seek to have them reflected in social life as a whole. The "neighbor" of the golden rule is now the city, the nation, the world. Religion, necessarily concerned with morality, is now necessarily concerned with politics. Yet politics often seems to be a realm of purely strategic maneuvering, a ruthless quest for power, or bureaucratic blindness to the common good. Therefore while religion is attracted to politics—it is also inevitably repelled.

One answer to the dilemmas of these tensions among religion, mo-rality, and politics may be found in the movements led by King and Gandhi. The moral power of non-violent civil disobedience appeals to the heart of the Other, and makes us vulnerable even while we are opposing evil. It seems to avoid the twin dangers of moral arrogance and moral passivity. Of course interfering with the workings of the world might well be experienced *as* violence by people whose jobs (or even toys!) are threatened. Any serious movement of noncooperation with industrial civilization would probably throw a few people out of work, or at least disrupt the morning commute. Yet there is at least *something* mitigating in the way those engaged in civil disobedience are sufficiently respectful of those they oppose to be willing to accept the civic penalties for their acts. This lessens, but hardly eliminates, the degree to which those who would reorient civil life to religious values are experienced as threatening or even assaultive.

Yet it should be remembered that the effects of the movements led by Gandhi and King were mixed. Indian independence was followed by a civil war that led to millions of deaths, and brought into existence two nations that hardly embodied the spiritual values Gandhi espoused. While the U.S. Civil Rights movement integrated public facilities and the voting booth, it did not make the United States a color-blind society. Even the massive federal interventions on behalf of African-Americans (the War on Poverty, AFDC, Affirmative Action) might be said to be a product of ghetto riots more than lunch-counter sit-ins.

Further, we should recognize that the success of non-violent politics in some settings does not guarantee its effectiveness in all settings. And in any case, we should be clear to what extent our endorsement of it as a political method is based on our sense that it works better than its competitors or that it contains a moral correctness which leads us to choose it regardless of the outcome. (Suppose we found out, somehow, that well-timed clandestine assassinations actually worked better than nonviolence—would we make the switch? Is our commitment to nonviolence subject to any kind of empirical test? Or is it just that we refuse to be violent *no matter what the outcome*?)

Perhaps most painfully, a spiritual deep ecologist might well wonder if the severity of ecological issues makes a peaceful, nonviolent, gradualist approach inappropriate to his or her concerns. Gandhi or King could trust that if the present generation of Indians or blacks did not get independence or civil equality, why then the next one would. However: if what we are doing is defending threatened species, protecting at risk ecosystems, preventing massive changes to the global climate, or trying to save the bottom of our common food chain, then the stakes are higher and (possibly) much more immediate. It may be that we are faced with critical problems which, if not dealt with now, preclude any chance that they can be made good "later." To take an extreme example: if, during the height of the Cold war folly, I knew that a launch of nuclear missiles was about to take place, I would not have hesitated to use violence to stop it. In such a case the usual nonviolent argument that "violence only provokes more violence" would carry no weight—for the absence of my violence in this case would simply preclude the possibility of any moral relevance in the future—since we'd pretty much all be dead! The long-term effects of environmental damage may not be as destructive as a nuclear war, but they may be tending (albeit much more slowly) in that direction.

Does this mean that spiritual deep ecologists might well express their values in violent action? That a utilitarian calculus of comparative happiness and pain might justify wrecking bulldozers, assassinating corporate polluters, or at least engaging in ecotage without offering oneself up for punishment? Does it mean that it is more important to try to stop the machine than to provide a moral example?

I do not know the answers to these questions, and in any case this volume is not the place to pursue them at length. I do know, however, that no simple answer about the dangers of "violence" will settle the matter. As the French philosopher Maurice Merleau-Ponty pointed out in response to Arthur Koestler's critique of communist politics in *Darkness at Noon*, the violence is there *already*. The question is not whether there will be violence, but what will we do about the violence that exists? And in the case of environmental violence, it is pervasive, ongoing, and involves us all. Just taking part in our society, even if we recycle and eat organic vegetables, inevitably leads us to be part of it. Each time we drive, pay our taxes, or switch on the electricity, we are contributing.

In any case, I believe it is a mistake to think that "violence" is everywhere and always one thing—and that we therefore can say that it is, or is not, without exception justified or unjustified. There is the violence of war, mass public slaughter initiated by impersonal governments. There are the quiet killings that are part of covert operations. There are back-alley muggings. There is domestic violence, brutality covered by a cloak of family life. There is the daily violence of racism, sexism, and homophobia. And there are all the different ways in which we can be assaulted by poisons in the environment.

Given this range (and surely many more examples could be offered), we can also think of all the different forms which legitimate, spiritually oriented resistance, might develop. There are nonviolent demonstrations against war, pacifist refusals to serve in armies, boycotts of chemicalized foods, individual women who strike back against abusive husbands, or indigenous tribes who try to protect themselves from hired thugs. We do have the shining examples of Gandhi and King—and also the shining examples of Jews who during the Holocaust killed guards in concentration camps and blew up Nazi troop trains.

The meaning, effect, and value of "violence" may be rather different in these different settings. And therefore I believe we must examine each one very carefully before we say, with anything like moral assurance: "These actions in the social world are somehow essentially compatible with the essence of a religious or spiritual approach; and these are not."

CONCLUSION

Spiritual Deep Ecology is at once the oldest and the newest of world religions. Certainly long before anyone prayed to the sky gods, chanted the *Sutras*, or followed a table of commandments, human beings knelt before the splendor of sky and water, and bowed to the mysteries of birth and death. And now that the sky and water bear our mark, and we seek to make ourselves masters of birth and death, it has returned. Spiritual Deep Ecology faces a divinity which is itself under siege. We are called not only to obey the teachings of the more than human, but to save it from ourselves. While in certain versions of Judaism God needed our help to repair or complete His creation, and in Christianity God suffers the flesh and its pains, surely for Deep Ecology the divine is at its most vulnerable. There is no teaching here of a guaranteed outcome, no messiah who will without doubt come riding over the hill at the last minute to stave off the enemy. For spiritual Deep Ecology that which is most dear is right before our eyes—most immediate, most dear, most fragile. (For those who take the Gaia hypothesis seriously, and see the earth as capable of a kind of self-corrective maintenance, human caused ecological damage may soon be corrected by changes that will settle our hash quite nicely. Yet this readjustment will not bring back the slaughtered species or the human cancer victims, both of whose numbers are rising daily. And any cosmic view that "in the end it's all nature anyway" surely misses the point that individual people, beings, and places that we love are being poisoned and destroyed.)

Its task is to make its peace with fragility, and somehow communicate to the other religions of the world the deep truth of how we all share it. As a small sect, Deep Ecology necessarily fails, for all it holds dear will be ravished. It depends for success on our collective will to live (or what's left of that will)—and on the hope that buried in each of us (or enough of us) is that remembered kinship with the divine mystery of all those simple beings that we can touch and see, smell and hear and eat. If we can be brought back to our senses, there is a chance that our sense of the holy can be saved. If we ruin this Creation, I am not sure how any of us—deep ecologist or traditional religionists, secular or spiritual—will be able to look ourselves in the eye. And what will be left of religion, any religion, if that is the point to which we come?

NOTES

1. This period is variously construed as beginning with the fall of the female/nature gods some 4000–6000 years ago, with the rise of monotheism 3000–4000 years ago, or with the emergence of modern science and technology in the 15–17th centuries.

2. Of the vast literature that could be cited, here are four: David Abram, *The Spell of the Sensuous: Language and Perception in a More than Human World* (NY: Pantheon, 1997); Joanna Macy, *World as Lover, World as Self* (Berkeley: Parallax, 1994); Edward Abbey, *The Monkey Wrench Gang* (NY: Fawcett, 1974); Paul Shepard, *Nature and Madness* (San Francisco: Sierra Club, 1982).

3. Stephen R. Kellert and E. O. Wilson, eds., *The Biophilia Hypothesis* (Washington D.C.: Island Press, 1993).

4. See Roger S. Gottlieb, *A Spirituality of Resistance: Finding a Peaceful Heart and Protecting the Earth* (NY: Crossroad: 1999).

5. Georg Lukacs, *History and Class Consciousness* (Cambridge, MA: MIT Press, 1971).

6. Stephanie Kaza, *The Attentive Heart: Conversations with Trees* (New York: Ballantine: 1993), p. 17.

7. See Michael Zimmerman, "Ecofascism: A Threat to American Environmentalism?" in Roger S. Gottlieb, ed., *The Ecological Community* (NY: Routledge, 1997).

8. I have developed this point at length in "Spiritual Deep Ecology and the Left," in Roger S. Gottlieb, ed. *This Sacred Earth: Religion, Nature, Environment* (NY: Routledge, 1996).

9

EARTH 101

We continue to educate the young for the most part as if there were no planetary emergency.
David Orr, *Earth in Mind*[1]

If we can get attached to just one tree from spending 30–45 minutes a week with it, then imagine how attached we could get if we lived in the forest, or visited it every day for work or pleasure. Then we would realize just how important the environment really is and how much magic it holds. If everyone could only see this, then perhaps we wouldn't be in the environmental crisis we are in now.
Ryan D., *Plant Journal*, Philosophy and the Environment

Why are we awash in pesticides, cautious of now dangerous sunlight, frightened for (and of) our breasts and prostates, and lonely for vanished species? Why, that is, do we live in an environmental crisis? Because, say many of us, there is something fundamentally amiss in the depths of our society, our culture, and our civilization. We suffer from a misguided economy, the shortsighted self-interest of governments, our own addiction to consumption, and the deep and destructive flaws that mark how we think about who we are and what it is to be alive on this earth. We have mistakenly taken humanity to be the only species of value, privileged our minds over our bodies, discounted women as "natural" while exalting men as the source of intelligence and religious truth, and assumed that if we had scientific facts we could dispense with spirit. We have separated reason from emotion and all the fields of knowledge (sociology, biology, history, politics, ethics) from each other. We told ourselves (and everyone else who'd listen) that our technological brilliance would produce a safe and happy life, and that we'd progressed far beyond the accumulated wisdom of "primitive tribes" who (how silly can you get?) found wisdom in hawks and mountains.

For those of us who see the environmental crisis as a crisis of our entire civilization, the goal of environmental education is to raise students' awareness of the complexity of the problem, the depth of its causes, and the possibility for personal and collective change. Yet it's one thing to criticize our way of life, and another to figure out how to communicate that criticism in a way that leads anywhere. Sadly, the *manner* in which environmental values are taught may contradict *what* is being taught. Lectures about how mind-body dualism lead us to ignore our physical surroundings are given by an unmoving professor to slumped over, shallowly breathing students. Books are read about the importance of knowing our place in nature while students have no idea what is growing outside the classroom. Ecofeminist messages about empathizing with all of life are taught to students who never spend more than five seconds looking at any particular plant. The factual details of the environmental crisis are learned, while the emotions they arouse are ignored. Deep ecology bemoans our instrumental attitude towards nature and preaches that we cannot be fully human if we do not bond to something outside ourselves. Yet during a course in "Environmental Ethics" students bond only to books, words, papers, and screens.

Consequently, environmental education—not unlike environmental advocacy in the wider society—too often leaves its audiences unmoved. Or they may be struck by the information and the analyses, but without emotional support or positive experiences, they end up with even more despair, cynicism, and numbness than when they began.

Many of us in higher education are seeking a different path.[2] We believe that it is possible to connect our bodies and our minds, our intellects and our emotions, our analytical intelligence and our spiritual hopes, a theoretical account of the crisis with an experience of its meaning. In fact, we don't think students (or anyone else) will learn very much about the environmental challenge until all these dimensions are integrated.

What follows is an account of how I try to do this in a course called "Philosophy and the Environment," taught at an engineering university where virtually none of my students are philosophy majors but most of whom have had at least an "Introduction to Philosophy and Religion" course as background. The course satisfies distribution requirements for engineering and science majors all of whom must do substantial work in some particular area of the Humanities.

✵ ✵ ✵

Before the term starts, I email those registered to let them know that "besides the usual reading, lectures and papers, there will be some rather unusual experiential exercises and meditations in the course." Thus when they come in on the first day, they've been warned.

Standing at the front of the class, I arrange on the small table before me a folder with the class syllabus. Then I take out of my backpack items that seem more fitted to geology or zoology than philosophy: some rocks, a crystal or two, a feather, and a fossilized shell. Then I light a large candle and ring an ornamental Tibetan bell.

From the beginning, then, I invoke two forces. By bringing in actual pieces of the world I announce that our course will not be confined to words. Nature, not just "nature," will be part of the action. The candle and the bell—the students think they're strange, and usually several giggle a bit—invoke a kind of ritualized seriousness which is not only particularly appropriate to a course on the environmental crisis but also taps into cultural images of concentration and self-transcendence. After the initial nervous laughter, I find, students pay close attention. And since each class is started this way, before long the sound of the bell produces a hushed attention that I rarely find in the first moments of other courses.

The class has begun. As it unfolds over the next twenty-eight meetings I am guided by eight premises about the environmental mess we're all in. My goal is not only to explain and discuss these premises, but to help students personally experience them.

Premise 1: *The environmental crisis is so universal and threatening that it inevitably provokes very strong emotions.*

A well-intentioned colleague once told me: "I try to teach environmental material; I have students read the 'World Watch' publications and study a mountain of details. But afterwards they have little or nothing to say. They just seem numb."

Indeed. What happens to our emotional life when we read, for instance, that of the 65,000 chemicals used in the U.S. only around 10% have been tested for their health effects? Or that toxic PCBs have been found in arctic seals (some so affected that their dead bodies have to be disposed of as "hazardous waste")? Or that by age twenty students stand between a 35% and 45% chance of getting cancer?[3] What happens over the long run when students—who now are commonly exposed to something "about the environment" as early as kindergarten—are rarely if ever asked what they *feel* about the situation?

What happens is that people develop some extremely powerful—yet typically unacknowledged—emotional responses. Because they are largely unexpressed, they sap our psychic and intellectual vitality and mark our lives by a joyless numbing out or a frenetic search for stimulation. From the frighteningly high rate of alcohol use to Internet addiction, the consequences of unacknowledged feelings about the environmental crisis are a daily reality on college campuses and in the broader society. Without a shred of empirical proof I believe that the prospects of environmental deterioration simply do darken the horizon of young people—as well as lead them to doubt the competence and wisdom of their elders. All this must take an emotional toll.

My response to this dilemma is not to turn the class into group therapy, but to encourage students to integrate the emotional dimensions of their responses to the situations by offering a view of rationality which does not exclude emotions, and thus does not reproduce the alienation of thought from feeling that is part of the crisis in the first place.

On that first day, after the candle is lit and the bell sounded, I sketch in extremely broad terms what the crisis is all about. (The depth of the problem is also brought home in the first reading assignment, which is to go through all of a mass market environmental magazine, such as *E*, *Sierra*, or *The Ecologist*). I then make it clear that while I try to be objective about our planet, I am not—and have no desire to be—detached. I describe my own fear and grief, share my helpless anger over the threats to my daughters' health, acknowledge despair for the wilderness forever lost. I admit to years of avoiding information about just how bad things are, hoping to introduce the concepts of denial and avoidance and model the possibility of facing them. My goal is to demonstrate to students that awareness of my feelings in this setting is as important as my "expertise" about environmental ethics; and that *their* emotions deserve respectful attention rather than pseudo-rational dismissal. I suggest that the impact of the readings they will be doing may be felt in their emotional lives, and that at the least they should be aware of what is going on for them.

The value of their emotions is, among other things, to remind them that they can still love and grieve; and, as we see throughout the course, the emotions themselves convey information about our world. There are signs of connection to their surroundings and indications that something is deeply wrong.[4] I periodically raise this issue throughout the term, both in the class as a whole and in small discussion groups. Some people report that nothing is happening; others, however, talk about disquieting dreams, increased feelings of grief or anger, alienation from friends or family who think they are making a big deal out of nothing, or serious questions about career choices. The dominant message of the course is that these reactions are perfectly understandable and rational, and that the best response to them is patient, careful attention.

When I ask the students to speak about what they feel on that first day they respond slowly and hesitantly, emboldened by my example but still somewhat unsure that a university classroom is the proper place for emotions. As the hour progresses, however, their statements become increasingly more revealing.

I'm pissed off, one will say, *because the field where I used to hunt for grasshoppers was turned into a parking lot for a mall; and they hardly even use it. What a waste.*

I'm scared, a young woman admits. *Every time I go out in the sun in the summer I think about skin cancer. My aunt died from it.*

Others toss off a kind of irritated shrug. *What does that mean?* I say, letting them know pretty quickly that I won't be satisfied with a mumbled *Nothing.* Usually what surfaces after a few exchanges is that they are very angry, but that they are sure that their anger won't change anything. I ask them whether a deep anger that cannot change the world—and which for the most part cannot even be expressed—can lead anywhere but despair.

And then at times we find something lurking underneath the anger. Several young men tell me they don't see much use in thinking about all these problems. I ask one: *What would happen if you did think about it?*

I don't know, he replies, *I'm not sure I could go on with what I'm supposed to do in this life. If I started to cry, I might never stop.*

Premise 2. *Meeting the emotional challenge of the environmental crisis requires spiritual resources.*

Emotional responses to the environmental crisis are not neurotic feelings that need to be "cured." But we do need direct, intuitive, meditative practices as a source of calm, openness, and connection to enable us to hold them. For want of a better word, I call such practices "spiritual."

To invoke spiritual resources in a college classroom—not unlike asking students to take their emotional lives seriously—is to resist the still dominant paradigms of scientism. (A paradigm widely shared at an engineering college!) In order to make this resistance comprehensible, we have to explore how the rise of science disenchanted the world and the cultural countertrends to that disenchantment that have arisen over the last few decades.[5] In contemporary society many people believe that scientific knowledge is inadequate as a total worldview or a way to respond to crucial personal problems. The seamless integration of scientific research and corporate and military technology has made many of us extremely skeptical about how "objective" or "value free" science is; and technological consequences from nuclear weapons to the hole in the ozone layer have made people suspicious of unmonitored scientific "progress." Further, the boundaries of psychology, biochemistry, and cognitive research have moved towards the notion of a "body-mind" medicine in which physical and emotional health are connected to psychic practices that have deep affinities to traditional meditation exercises.[6]

These and other developments have made people more open to what I am calling (rather broadly) "spiritual" practices: quieting the mind in meditation; using intuitive resources in visualizations; invoking ritualized forms of compassion, repentance, and joy as ways to connect to other people and to the "more than human."[7]

In the first of the course's several lengthy sessions I begin with a full-body relaxation (some students lie on the floor, others lean back in their chairs). I then ask them to imagine some place of complete safety in nature—from their memory or their imagination— and in their mind's eye to see and feel that place in all its details. They are instructed to notice what other beings are there, the climate, the wind, sounds and smells, and the position and appearance of their own body. They will return to this psychic spot a number of times during the course. In the second extended meditation I ask them if this place has a message or gift for them; or if they have something to give or communicate to it.

"Nick" was tall and thin, red-haired and thoughtful. Later I would get to know him well when he did lengthy projects under my direction and became one of "my" students. But this was the first course he took with me, and we were still feeling each other out. After the meditation in which I asked the class to listen to see if their special place had any message or teaching for them there was a long pause. I wasn't surprised, just a little disappointed. My students are smart, but not terribly expressive; a far cry from the "crunchy" types you get at Oberlin or Earlham. And this was the first time I had done this sort of thing in a classroom. Then, slowly and deliberately, Nick stood up and approached the candle in the center of the room. *I got a message*, he said, and paused. I waited; the whole class waited.

Yes, I asked gently, *what did you hear?*

Stop it. Just stop it.

In another exercise students are each given two slices of apple. After going into a relaxation state they munch on the first one. Since this is towards the end of the class, they have already been exposed to the multiple roots of the crisis, from philosophical attitudes to economic structures; as well as the multiple types of beings whom the crisis affects, from plants to indigenous tribes to all of us. I then ask them to visualize the multitude of beings that make the apple possible: sun and water and earth and tree and microorganisms in the soil, and also farm laborers, truckers, supermarket workers, and, yes, pesticide manufacturers. They then eat the second piece of apple—which, some have said, tastes better than the first.

Another exercise focuses on the contrasting of the natural and the commercial environment. I can (and I do) lecture until I'm blue in the face about the effects of consumerism and our loneliness for nature. However, it is one thing to say it, and another to try to provide a context in which the ideas are directly experienced; to provide what Kierkegaard called a "subjective communication" aimed at conveying not a propositional claim but a felt experience.[8] In this exercise I instruct students to spend fifteen minutes in a natural setting doing "nothing"— simply being aware of the sights and smells, sounds and feel of their surroundings. They are then to get themselves as quickly as possible to a mall, a supermarket, a large drugstore—and, once again, to do nothing for fifteen minutes while taking in their surroundings. If they do not learn the lesson by that immediate contrast, they probably will not learn it from my lectures. If they do learn it, than the intellectual critique of consumerism and the urban built environment begins to take on an importance it could never have for them without the experience. In this and in all the other exercises, the experiential does not replace or duplicate the intellectual content of the course, but (when it works) focuses their attention and deepens their understanding.

Premise 3. *Students in classrooms have bodies.*

It seems odd almost to the point of absurdity that the extended critique of Cartesian mind-body dualism, along with extended postmodern discussions of "the body" in feminism and Foucault, are communicated in classrooms that replicate exactly educational settings in which Descartes' premises were accepted. Therefore in "Philosophy and the Environment" certain simple yoga and chi kung postures and breathing exercises are used to promote relaxed and focused attention. Each class begins and ends with one minute of silent attention on the breath. If the energy lags in the middle of a class, I have students do a brief yoga posture to clear their minds. As our bodies are part of nature, and any destruction of nature will harm us, so we learn and think and feel with our bodies. If our bodies are ignored, our ability to learn and think and feel—even about the environment—will be diminished.

Premise 4. *Intuitive experience of the world is essential in helping us understand it.*

How do you teach students that all of nature is connected? That the world is deeply, meaningfully, alive? That not only human beings have value? Or that, at least, these ideas have some basis in intuitive experience as well as formal argument? These basic concepts involved in these questions are the bread and butter of a good deal of environmental philosophy (especially "Deep Ecology") and non-academic naturalism, and are repeatedly stressed in the course reading. And they are

essential to the construction of a world view which opposes our culture's dominant anthropocentrism.

Is there any way to encourage students to experience these ideas
directly?

An essential—and probably my looniest—course requirement is the
"plant journal." Each student must pick some particular "plant"—from
a blade of grass to a tree—and sit with that plant three or four times a
week, recording their experiences. I tell them to study the plant, talk to
it, listen to it, touch it, and smell it. If the plant were to become extinct,
they should be able to tell the world what has been lost. Any (legible!)
record of this experience is acceptable—including writing over and over
that they think the assignment is a waste of time and that their professor
is an idiot.

After years of this assignment, I have seen, time and again, a kind of
magic unfold.

I remember one fellow in particular: tall and muscular, a football
player-fraternity member-beer drinker type who usually dozed or fid-
geted during meditations and clearly wasn't buying much of my deep-
ecology-ecomarxist-ecofeminist-tree-hugger message. At the end of our
seven week term I read his journal. For the first two weeks he did
nothing but record his disdain for the plant, the plant journal, and his
dopey professor. Then he began to notice the details of the small tree
he had chosen. By the fifth week he had named the tree "George" and
looked forward to visiting it. His final entry read: *All the other trees
have their leaves and George doesn't. I'm really worried about him.*

Other students have written:

*I wish to thank nature for giving me peace and perspective in the
middle of the city.*

*I don't think I am contributing to the environmental crisis. No, actu-
ally I am. I always drive my car everywhere when I am home in Boston.
Sorry nature . . .*

*Thank you for listening to my thinking and thoughts, grief and hap-
piness.*

*My tree is actually blooming! And not just one or two buds. Many.
It's like giving birth. I don't know why but it seemed the most dead tree
around. But it has woken up!! It is saved.*

*The tulip is straightening back up. A proud survivor. Her immediate
neighbor has an undignified floppiness. More moss has grown up*

around the base of the rhododendron where my tulip resides. Soon there will be the most fragrant ferns that grow there every summer.

Honestly, I thought this was a dumb, immature assignment. But I'm glad I stuck with it. Having seen the slow process of nature in all its beauty, I will never look at trees the same.

What do students learn from these journals?

- That you can become emotionally attached to a plant. That love, in other words, doesn't stop with humans or even animals. One student began with *I feel kind of silly sitting out here writing about a tree; I don't think I can write much about it other than it's pretty dead looking.* But then a week later she reflected: *Maybe I chose it because it looked lonely.*
- How to be aware of the plant in the details of its existence—roots, bark, leaves, branches. Changes of budding and flowering. To notice the insects at its base, the birds that nest in its crown, the squirrels that jump from branch to branch. That plants are alive, changing, dynamic—and that their growth and change are astonishingly exciting. (Luckily, I've arranged always to teach this course in the spring.)
- To be aware of pollution in a visceral way. Students see the nails in their tree's bark, garbage or broken glass on the roots. They begin to care about how the plant faces acid rain, drought from global warming, threats from construction of new buildings.
- To remember encounters with plants when they were children and to recover a sense of magic pervading the natural world—a sense too easily paved over by "maturity." *I remember picking flowers for the church altar. I won't do that any more. They look better out here.*

  I think about all the things that concern and worry me. Then I look at the tree and it is just so peaceful. Nothing bothers it. I'm jealous!
- To become aware of the guilt and shame they feel about their personal contribution to the environmental crisis. To realize that it is not some abstraction called "nature" that is threatened by our society and our culture, but particular entities: including this one with whom they've made friends. *I stop and think about how we*

as a society have afflicted nature with so many "diseases." And I wonder about the world my children will live in.

How will my future actions—where I work, what I eat, how I live—affect my tree?

- That simply being with a plant can sooth them and make them happy; and therefore that nature has something to offer them that is deeper and more personal than use-values or purely aesthetic pleasure. That, surprisingly, in a communion with nature they can feel their most human. *I have all these deadlines that are to be met and here I am "wasting" my time just sitting by a tree. But it makes me feel so much calmer.*

  My tree symbolizes my life, my growth, my wounds. It's grown as I have and it has been damaged as I have. It has a large broken branch. I have a broken heart.

- That in a world of scientific, technical, and numerical "expertise" and "certainty" there remains special joy in simply asking questions. *Are members of the natural world conscious? Do roaming deer watch their steps so as not to step on ants?*

Premise 5. *No single discipline is adequate to the complexity of the environmental crisis.*

Readings for the course come from philosophy, ecotheology, economics, natural history, and politics. If we are to understand the "causes" of the crisis, we must understand the role of religion and the rise of capitalism, the effects of modern science and the global market. We must learn to see the consequences of the current environmental practices for non-human nature (as in Bill McKibben's *The End of Nature*) and for people (as in our readings on environmental racism). If we are not to be left in despair, we must acquaint ourselves (as we do in the last week of the course) with resistance movements and success stories. This last is critical because even with the rise of campus activism in recent years the vast majority of my students do not relate to political action. When they hear about alliances between native and white activists to prevent destructive mining in northern Wisconsin, or about the sustainable growth of the city of Ciutuba in Brazil, they realize that there are victories to celebrate and work to be done—work in which they, if they choose, can find a place.

Premise 6. *Critical thought—including criticism of environmentalism— is essential to our response to the crisis.*

The point of the course is not to privilege expressing feelings, intuition, or spiritual exercises over intellectual activity, but to integrate all of these together. As both the reading and my lectures are often deeply critical of contemporary society, so it is also necessary to encourage students to voice their own disagreements both to my position and to any particular environmentalist we are reading.

In the context of the environmental crisis, this is a somewhat complicated matter. As a moral being, I cannot (nor do I think I *should*) pretend to neutrality about these matters. Since I really do believe that we are on the civilizational equivalent of the Titanic, it would be unethical of me to pretend that I don't think the situation is dire in the extreme. As a person, a citizen, an educator, I have a responsibility to try to awaken other people to this belief. In doing so I cannot pretend that I believe voices which deny the reality of the crisis have much to support their position. An absence of neutrality on basic questions, we should remember, is often present even in much more conventional courses: few classes on the Holocaust spend much time asking if the Nazis had good reasons to try to kill all the Jews; or on American history if black Africans were better off as slaves; or on physiology whether or not (as medical school textbooks of the late 19th century taught) higher education damages women's reproductive capacity. I do not take the environmental crisis as something about which we can cavalierly and cheerfully examine "competing narratives," since I view it as a practical problem of the greatest significance. This may strike some readers as uncritical and simple-minded. I would only respond that they ask themselves how much they would engage in the search for "competing narratives" after an initial cancer diagnosis were confirmed by a second and third opinion. One could at that point engage in a fascinating study of the history of science, the politics of medicine, and the cultural biases of the western technology. Yet I doubt if such efforts would really be high on the list of someone, even the most sophisticated intellectual, after they received the Bad News. Of course it is a matter of some debate if the environmental crisis is as bad as all that. Support for that belief is offered throughout the course, both in lectures and reading.

At the same time, however, it is necessary for me to make a protected space for students who don't see things my way. Dissenting voices must be encouraged, praised for their willingness to disagree, and dealt with directly and respectfully. This is not always easy, especially when—to my irritation—I hear a student repeating some of the more vicious forms of conservative anti-environmentalist propaganda. Yet human respect can transcend ideological difference, especially since I believe that what is most important is that students come to grips with these issues, not parrot my own views. In my experience most people who seriously engage with the material—intellectually and emotionally—end up heading in (what I think is) the right direction. Serious criticism is itself a kind of engagement, and meets my purposes quite well.

We also spend some time examining tensions within environmentalism itself: notably, over the degree to which the concept of nature is historically constituted and in the relation between deep ecology's stress on the inherent value of nature and social ecology's concern with relations between social structures and ecology. Beyond their intellectual value, these debates have a moral and political one as well, for they reveal that environmentalism—no less than the environmental crisis itself—is a product of human thought and action, not a transcendentally given reality. As a human product the environmental movement is something which these students can take part in shaping. To feel free to do so, they must be able to see that controversies, doubts, and difficulties are part of it.

Premise 7. *The environmental crisis is a desecration of the holy and not only an economic or health problem.*

This premise certainly does not imply that students must believe in God. Rather, I encourage those who wish it to articulate the profound feelings they have for at least some parts of nature; and to express their growing realization that the violation of nature is simultaneously a violation of themselves and of something that is sacred. That sense of the "sacred" can be theistic, pantheistic, or pagan. Or it may simply represent, as in Paul Tillich's phrase, a locus of "ultimate concern." The point is not to impose a view on them, but to allow those who indeed have this experience a place to express it. The key goal is to provide a vocabulary for a sensibility—not to try to convince them that the sensibility exists where it does not. Typically a sizable number of these hard-headed, nonsense young engineers dismiss the notion of finding the sacred in nature altogether. Typically, however, a sizable number of just as hard-headed and no-nonsense types talk about experiences they had when hiking in the mountains, or of swamps they used to visit as kids, or—as happened just this past spring—of an encounter with a squirrel in the park across the street. In describing these experiences, words like mystery, awe, and reverence, once legitimated by me, come easily to their lips.

Premise 8. *Students exist as moral beings in a morally complex world.*

The environmental crisis makes our daily lives morally suspect. I raise the issue of our collective complicity in a crisis we want to alleviate: that all of us, including the tree-hugging professor who does a long commute to work by car, bear some responsibility. Again I do not, and I cannot, pretend to moral neutrality in this issue. In fact, it would be the height of irrationality to do so. And I make moral reflection on their own future choices—all the more significant because most of them will be engineers—an essential part of course discussion. They are confronted—directly but respectfully—with questions about what they would do in concrete situations: for whom will they work, what will they do, what risks and sacrifices will they make? Since morality is not separate from intelligence, I believe it is essential that they rehearse, if only for a few moments, possible responses to future moral dilemmas.

❖ ❖ ❖

All these aspects of the course form (when they work) a synergistic whole. At times, a movement occurs: from the most personal and unspoken (the meditations and visualizations), through an intellectual understanding of the crisis (the readings, lectures, and class discussions), through an "outer" experience of a particular plant, to our concluding studies of environmental resistance movements. The students begin to experience themselves and the entire world as related: by industry and commerce and science and spirituality and governments and political movements; by the way we pollute and the way we conserve; by what we see and what we ignore; by fear and greed, by love and care.[9]

NOTES

1. Orr 1994: 2.

2. As I've learned from conversations with colleagues, many environmental faculty are expanding the sense of what is possible in a college course.

3. See Steingraber and Groopman.

4. Our emotions, as a number of philosophers and psychologists are (finally) teaching, are in many cases rational responses of the human organism. For philosophy, see Nussbaum; for psychology, Greenspan.

5. This is a societal wide phenomenon. See, e.g., Ingelhart, and Ray and Anderson.

6. See Pert and Eisenberg.

7. In David Abram's felicitous phrase.

8. See Kierkegaard.

9. I am grateful to two anonymous reviewers for helpful comments on an earlier version of this paper.

REFERENCES

Abram, David. 1997. *The Spell of the Sensuous*. NY: Vintage Books.

Eisenberg, David. 1985. *Encounters with Qi: Exploring Chinese Medicine*. NY: Norton.

Greenspan, Miriam. 2003. *Healing Through the Dark Emotions: The Wisdom of Grief, Fear, and Despair*. Boston: Shambhala.

Groopman, Jerome. June 4, 2001. "The Thirty Years' War: Have we Been Fighting Cancer the Wrong Way?" *The New Yorker*.

Ingelhart, Ronald. 1990. *Culture Shift: In Advanced Industrial Society*. Princeton: Princeton University Press.

Kierkegaard, Søren. 1992. *Concluding Unscientific Postscript*. Princeton: Princeton University Press.

Nussbaum, Martha C. 2001. *Upheavals of Thought: The Intelligence of Emotions*. NY: Cambridge University Press.

Orr, David W. 1994. *Earth in Mind: On Education, Environment, and the Human Prospect*. Washington, D.C.: Island Press.

Pert, Candace B. 1999. *Molecules of Emotion: The Science Behind Mind-Body Medicine*. NY: Simon and Schuster.

Ray, Paul H. and Sherry Ruth Anderson. 2000. *The Cultural Creatives*. New York: Harmony Books.

Steingraber, Sandra. 1997. *Living Downstream: An Ecologist Looks at Cancer and the Environment*. Reading, MA: Addison-Wesley.

III

Holocaust, Ecocide, Jewish Experience

10

SOME IMPLICATIONS OF THE HOLOCAUST FOR ETHICS AND SOCIAL PHILOSOPHY

The Holocaust is a decisive event for our time, but one of which contemporary philosophers have by and large taken little notice. In this essay, I hope to show that the Holocaust has some decisive implications for both ethics and social philosophy. I will focus on four particular issues: (1) the normative question of the authentic form of remembering the Holocaust; (2) some problems raised by the Holocaust for theories of human nature; (3) the relation of the Holocaust to the positivist conception of rationality; (4) implications of the Holocaust for concerns with social justice, specifically in regard to the creation of the state of Israel and the Israeli-Palestinian conflict.

I. REMEMBERING

The systematic and self-conscious murder of six million innocent and defenseless people is an event of such significance that our relation to it is a matter of moral concern. However, while we possess great knowledge of the factual details of the Holocaust, comparatively little attention has been paid to the distinction between authentic and inauthentic ways of remembering what we know.

Let us begin by considering a familiar form of remembering. We make a list of things we have to do over the weekend. Inscribing each potential act on paper registers, locates, and limits it. Once written, we know the tasks as things which can be handled: so many trips to the store, attics cleaned, floors washed, or phone calls made. If these are capable of being handled, they are in turn capable of being easily forgotten. In fact, we only make the list in order to forget what we have just remembered.

In this remembering-in-order-to-forget, we indicate our mastery over and our unconcern with that which we remember. Remembering the Holocaust in this way implies that we have mastered the meaning of the event for our own subjectivity. By *subjectivity* I mean that aspect of our personal identity which is formed by a confrontation with problems the solutions to which are both of crucial importance and of lifelong duration. These problems cannot be "solved" because part of their solution is our continuing response to them. Kierkegaard, whose usage of the term I have adopted, identifies two such problems: what it means to die and what it means to pray.[1]

A subjective confrontation with the Holocaust can provide serious subjects for reflection. For instance, what does it mean to have to choose—as many Jews did—between saving the life of your sister or your wife, your mother or your husband, your father or your son? What does it mean to resist Nazi power when you know that the Nazi policy of collective reprisal will lead to the torture, starvation, or murder of fellow Jews as punishment for your resistance? Under what conditions, as Simon Wiesenthal asks in "The Sunflower," would we forgive one of the killers? A study of the factual details of the Holocaust reveals moral dilemmas which demand a subjective understanding. Such an understanding requires that we "think ourselves" out of what appears to be our everyday existence and into the Holocaust, rather than try to describe it in familiar terms which would allow us to remember it in a mode of forgetfulness.

Yet the necessity for a subjective understanding of the Holocaust should not lead us to encapsulate the event in a sterile and distorting shroud of mystery. The Holocaust must not be relegated to the realm of the necessarily and ultimately incomprehensible.[2] I believe that Elie Wiesel may be doing this when he states that the victims died with the truth on their lips, a truth we can never know. This approach to the Holocaust is, paradoxically, another form of trivialization. It denies that, in relation to the Holocaust, there exists a truth *for us*. While we may in fact never know the truth which perished with the victims, we have an obligation to discover a truth which exists for those who did not perish. This truth, in turn, requires that we take the Holocaust into ourselves; and therefore that it not remain fundamentally mysterious and endlessly external, like a shrine or an idol. If the Holocaust is essentially incomprehensible, then we cannot, in the deepest sense of the word, think it. But that which cannot be thought cannot be part of ourselves and is, therefore, irrelevant to our identity.

Last in this necessarily incomplete catalog of forms of remembrance is remembering-as-obsession. Here the event is remembered but everything else, including the self, is forgotten. We become immersed in the Holocaust. The gas chambers and barbed wire, burnt buildings and burning bodies become more real than our own lives. Our life becomes the Holocaust—a Holocaust which cannot end because it has occurred already.

Obsession is inauthentic because it attempts to blot out the self who is the subject, the agent, of the act of remembering. We cannot have a relation to the Holocaust if we dissolve ourselves in it, if our own reality is negated by acts of imagination in which we seek to become the past. Further, that seeking is itself a revelation of who we are. Obsession with the Holocaust cannot eliminate the reality of the post-Holocaust self; it can only be that self's pretense at such elimination. But—and here Sartre's account of human identity comes to mind—any attempt to eliminate the self is precisely a project of the self, though one carried out in bad faith. If nothing ever happened but the Holocaust, then neither our present nor our future really exists. And if this is so, then there is need not for action, but only for remembrance. But such remembrance is itself a form of action—one whose partial goal is the obliteration of the moral reality of the self which undertakes it.

In the distorted forms of remembrance I have described, either the Holocaust becomes an event which is essentially unreal or unimportant, or the present itself becomes drained of reality. In either case the significance of the Holocaust for the present and future action of a moral agent is diminished. By contrast, what I take to be the morally appropriate relation of remembering the Holocaust is one in which we remember it as a problematic and continuing event and in which we remember ourselves as moral agents as well. Or, to put the point another way: the Holocaust must be remembered authentically partly *because* it is a problematic and continuing event for us as moral agents. Consider, for instance, the fact that we are faced with the existence of survivors of the Holocaust. What do we who did not directly experience the Holocaust owe to survivors? What does Auschwitz survivor Fanya Fenelon deserve in relation to a television production of her memoirs when someone she believes to be a publicly vocal anti-Semite is chosen to portray *her* life? What do survivors in Skokie, Illinois, deserve when the American Nazi Party proposes to march through their community? How does the reality of the Holocaust alter our usual conceptions of moral obligation and political rights in such situations?

If we have remembered the Holocaust in order to forget it, we will lack the subjectivity necessary to begin to understand that there are problems here. If the Holocaust is mystery or obsession then we will have lost the capacity to act in the present in regard to such problems. In either case, only an authentic remembering makes possible an adequate moral identity.

Finally, the continuing and problematic character of the Holocaust is not limited to our relation to the survivors of the event itself. As we shall see in section IV, the subject of the Holocaust is not simply a large number of individuals, but a single community.

That community has survived the Holocaust and remains a subject of history; yet its fate and those of communities with which it comes in contact have been decisively altered by the Holocaust.

The problematic character of the Holocaust thus includes its continuing historical effects on the nature of relations between Jews and other national groups. What does anti-Semitism mean to the Jews as a people as opposed to the particular Jews who might experience it? What actions taken by Jews in regard to their survival as a people make sense only when understood as actions taking place after the Holocaust? How can the Holocaust itself be used both authentically and inauthentically by Jews and non-Jews alike? And, finally, in what ways are Holocaust-like events happening or near to happening to other groups?

II. HUMAN NATURE

The vast majority of people simply did not believe that the Holocaust was possible. Even Zionist Jews, who denied the possibility of eradicating anti-Semitism within the Diaspora, found it hard to believe eyewitness accounts of the extermination camps. Jews and non-Jews initially interpreted this event in the categories of the past: as yet another pogrom or expulsion.[3] The widespread character of this mistake testifies to the fundamental newness of the Holocaust. This newness does not reside in the facts of mass murder or of the destruction of a particular national community.

Such things had happened before. Rather, the newness had to do with (at least) two other facts. First, the perpetrators intended to destroy an entire community of human beings and to do so without reference to other, ulterior goals. Of course various sectors of German society benefited from the political use of Jews as scapegoats and the economic values of expropriated Jewish property and Jewish slave labor. But there was little benefit to anyone in mass murder. Rather, there is evidence that in the latter part of the war pursuing the Final Solution was at odds with Germany's military goals.[4] By this time, however, mass murder had become an end in itself.

Second, this pursuit of mass murder was no temporary aberration or crazed outburst. It was carried out in a calm, orderly, and scientific manner. Detailed records were kept of it. It was a carefully conceptualized process in which human death became an industry and human body parts served as raw materials. And it was a process conceived and executed by Germany's best administrative, political, and scientific minds.

These facts pose some problems for a number of theories of human nature; that is, theories which purport to explain, in the most general terms possible, why people do and do not act in the ways they do. To be successful, theories of human nature cannot take certain forms of human action as a given. For example, a sociological explanation which shows how German society created a tendency to submit to authority takes for granted the existence and nature of German society. A psychological explanation which explains Fuhrer-worship by reference to German family structure is similarly limited, unless it includes an account of why families necessarily possess the structures they do. The problem I wish to examine, then, is whether encompassing theories of human nature are adequate to the particular features of the Holocaust. I will limit my treatment to two types of such theories: biological and social-environmental.

Biological deterministic theories claim that human beings have a biological structure which produces certain characteristic drives, intentions, instincts, and desires.[5] These are believed to include drives toward aggression and are seen as causing certain characteristic behavior patterns. Despite the unfortunate moral character of the aggressive behavior caused by our biology, claim these theories, such behavior is inevitable. There exist permanent motives for it. The repression of such behavior itself will lead to physiological and psychological imbalances, and thus to a return of the unfortunate behavior in a new form. For biological deterministic theories, the major evidences for the existence of aggressive impulses are the aggressive actions they are said to cause.

However, these impulses are viewed as existing independently of the actions themselves. Otherwise, there would be no way to explain what happens when aggressive behavior is inhibited and aggressive impulses are in some way repressed.

Of course it might be replied that what is repressed is essentially biological in nature, without emotional or moral character, a matter of sheer energy rather than impulses. This claim, however, ignores the fact that it is doubtful that it even makes sense to talk of repressing a biological structure. We may inhibit a physical reaction (the blinking of an eye, for example). We do not, however, repress it, for the term *repression* refers to the alteration of a goal-directed energy—of, in short, an intention. But neither biochemical reactions nor physical movements are, in and of themselves, intentional in this sense. They are not goal-oriented. This can be shown by considering how strange it would sound to talk of heartbeats, the exchange of fluid between bloodstreams and cells, or the reaction of nerves to stimuli as aggressive or peaceful, hostile or loving. Likewise, even if an agent's physical movements cause the death of another person, we cannot necessarily say that the agent acted aggressively. The agent may simply have made a mistake. Biochemical processes and bodily movements have no emotional-moral character unless they express intentions. The familiar point here is that adjectives such as aggressive, hostile, and loving can be applied only to a consciousness—to an awareness and a set of intentions. Only in the presence of a consciousness do we have the kind of human action which biological deterministic theories sought, initially, to explain, such as aggressive action.

This point is of crucial relevance to the Holocaust because many of the people who planned and executed the Final Solution did not do so out of aggression or hostility. They may have disliked or been contemptuous of Jews. But this dislike and contempt did not match the scope of their behavior. For many of these people, Jews were not enemies to be annihilated. Rather, they were objects to be treated in correct administrative fashion. They were not targets of hostility any more than were coal supplies, welfare payments, ammunition, or those other things which the bureaucrats of the Nazi machine were called on to organize and dispose of. This aspect of the Holocaust is described in Arendt's account of Adolph Eichmann. Eichmann's central motivation was not aggression, but devotion to duty.[6] He took no joy in the destruction of the Jews and felt guilty for once striking a Jewish communal leader. His happiness resided in his ability to carry out his duty, to look good in the eyes of his superiors, to obey orders from higher sources effectively and thus fulfill his social role.

Similar attitudes can be found in Himmler's praise of the S.S. for resisting the temptation to spare their particular favorite Jews, thus resisting their own personal wishes. "To have carried this out and . . . to have kept our integrity . . . this is an unwritten . . . page of glory. . . ."[7]

Similarly, historian Raul Hilberg cites complex bureaucratic decisions whose goal was to distinguish political from personal killings and to show that only the former were justified. The basic message was that the destruction of the Jews was in fact legitimate only insofar as it was part of a legal, rationalized, orderly procedure, and not as an expression of rash impulses on the part of individuals.[8]

It could be argued that the surface orderliness and self-control of the Eichmanns was itself a sublimation of aggression, that "duty" was a mask. Yet what evidence is there for such a claim but the existence of the aggressive actions themselves? Why should such actions necessarily counteract the evidence I have just cited? The Nazis' actions can just as well be viewed as evidence of the taking on of intersubjectively created social roles as of biologically based aggression. Or, to cut the point a little finer, a sense of social solidarity may *itself* have been the cause of aggressive impulses. Hatred of the Jews may have been caused in many cases as much by the desire to be a "good German" as by the focusing of biological drives.

Also, an examination of the rise of Nazism shows how much of the Nazis' financial support—and thus their capacity to structure public opinion—derived from the self-conscious desire of Germany's ruling group to manipulate public opinion.

Forgetting the objections already described, a theory which seeks to explain human action solely on the basis of biologically caused aggression can make sense of only one part of the Holocaust.

Such a theory cannot account for the heroism, self-sacrifice, cooperation, and love shown by the victims. Yet their actions require explanation as much as do those of the murderers. In the face of this point biological theories begin multiplying fundamental drives. Human life becomes a battleground between aggressive and cooperative drives, between love and death. To explain the outcome of these struggles in particular cases, however, we will be forced to look beyond the posited drives themselves. We must turn away from the motivational consequences of biology and toward theories which take as their object the social structures shaping individual identity rather than the biological structures supposedly underlying them.

To serve as theories of human nature, social-environmental theories must be theories of history. They must explain not only a particular society, but the range and development of society as such. Since I take classical liberalism and Marxism to be the most widely held theories of history of the past century, I will describe the challenge posed for them by the Holocaust.

Liberalism can be described as follows.[9] The development of rationality will lead to both increased self-knowledge and increased general happiness. As history unfolds, the growth of knowledge will lead to societies increasingly dedicated to individual fulfillment and social justice, since both of these accord with the rational pursuit of self-interest by individuals. The fundamental problems of social life are those of knowledge and democracy.

The movement of history, and thus the scope of human action in any particular society, is determined by the degree to which the rational acquisition and utilization of knowledge fulfill human interest. The more human beings are awakened to the nature of their interests and the rational fulfillment of those interests, the more society as a whole will reflect the values of rationality and justice. Liberalism thus offers a view in which rationality is inherent in human beings, and progress toward increased rationality is the basic movement of history.

Such a view is challenged by the eruption of fascism after the existence of democracy; by the rise of the ideological obscurantism and brutal mysticism of Nazism in one of the most cultured and civilized of modern nations; by the substitution of pseudoscience for rational methodology, for instance, in the use of theories of racial superiority and the rewriting of history to make the Jews the source of Germany's post–World War I problems; and by the creation of a machine for mass murder in the first country to have introduced social welfare legislation.

Nazi Germany rejected rationality and destroyed democracy. For liberalism these developments must be viewed as regressions. But liberalism has little room for regressions, since regressions are caused by rejections of the accomplishments of reason. Such rejections contradict liberalism's picture of a human history structured by the sure advance of our inherent rationality. As a consequence, liberalism is reduced from a theory of history to a political ideology and a set of moral values. Without a faith in the natural human attraction to reason and its accomplishments, the classic liberal theory of historical development cannot be maintained. .

For Marxism, human history is shaped by the dialectic of modes of production. Each such mode is a form of social action within a particular natural and historical setting. Within each the form of action is contradictory: actions performed in the pursuit of fulfilling socially created needs eventually lead to a fundamental transformation of the productive life, class relations, and culture of the entire society. This pattern leads in the general direction of both greater technical power and greater political freedom. The final stage of this process is the transition from capitalism to socialism and, later, communism. Socialism becomes possible because capitalism develops forces of production adequate to guarantee each human being a comfortable life beyond scarcity. Socialism is made necessary because the working class recognizes that these forces of production will not be so used within a society dominated by capitalist social relations. The working class creates various political institutions to express its interest in the overthrow of capitalism; and the inevitable social crises caused by capitalism make it, eventually, possible and necessary for those institutions to take power.[10]

This picture is contradicted by the utter failure of the working class and its organizations to resist the growth of Nazism successfully and, as a consequence, to prevent the Holocaust. The electoral and ideological success of the Nazis took place in a country with a long history of working-class political activity. Yet in the face of a social and economic crisis, the majority of the population of an advanced capitalist country turned away from socialist politics to fascism. Two highly developed Marxist-oriented parties—the Social Democrats and the Communist Party—could neither win over the majority of the population nor effectively resist the power of the Nazis.

It might be replied that Marxism has no trouble explaining the growth of Nazism by reference to the needs of German imperialism and monopoly capitalism, or accounting for the rise of fascist ideology by reference to the monopoly capitalist class's need to justify the growth of the state sector and unify an alienated German population in support of a militaristic foreign policy.

Similarly, one might point out that theories of imperialism account for aggressive and dictatorial policies by the German government.[11]

Whatever their analytic force, these points do not refute the claim that Marxism, as a theory of history, cannot account for the success of fascism as a mass movement in a country with well-developed working-class institutions, political parties, and political consciousness. In traditional Marxism's vision of history, there is no room for the possibility of the ultimate failure of the socialist project. That the working class as a whole, and its political parties in particular, could be defeated by other forces in an advanced industrial society contradicts the basic historical confidence of traditional Marxism.

As a consequence, Marxism, like liberalism, has retreated from its attempts to forge a theory of history. Like liberalism with respect to rationality, Marxism has seen that an analysis of economic development is an insufficient basis for predictions concerning the future of social life in general. Simultaneously, there has developed a tradition of Western Marxism, which is marked in part by the degree of importance it accords to noneconomic social relations and processes and by its refusal to commit itself to a theory of history. Much of this work—especially that on both mass psychology and the consequences of scientistic theory—is a direct response to the rise of Nazism.[12]

The Holocaust is part of a historical regression against which both reason and the working class were helpless. As such, it constitutes a crisis for both liberalism and Marxism. In response to this crisis there has been a reworking of historical schemas into transcendental-moral ones. For example, Jürgen Habermas has recently sought to construct a developmental-logical account of human evolution based on the progressive development of norms of increasing rationality.[13] But though Habermas does show how certain past historical transformations match the developmental order of his schema, he is quite clear to stress that the future may not lead to any progress whatsoever. His schema, at least as far as the future is concerned, is normative rather than predictive. This distinguishes it from both traditional Marxism and classical liberalism, which claimed predictive as well as normative status.

Similar limitations attend the recent high-water mark of liberal political theory, John Rawls's book *A Theory of Justice*. That work constitutes an attempt to provide a rational grounding for norms of justice. It in no way offers arguments to support the claim that such norms will in fact ever be put into practice.

The failure of the three theories just discussed in regard to the Holocaust makes that event an intellectual problem. Or, to put it another way: it is not only for our subjectivity that the Holocaust poses a problem, but for our objectivity as well. An adequate remembering of the Holocaust requires an adequate understanding of it. Yet such an understanding cannot be predicated on theories of human nature which are incompatible with the event. One significant connection between our objectivity and our subjectivity is contained in the fact that believing that we have some general theory of why people act the way they do is central to the conduct of our individual moral and collective political life. Especially in regard to the fundamentally optimistic theories of liberalism and Marxism, the Holocaust poses a fundamental barrier to the regaining of confidence in the future course of human development. Similarly, normative ethics rests partly on the confidence that human beings will follow such principles and rules.

In the face of the prospect that the human race will choose fascism and genocide over other forms of social life, however, normative ethics becomes problematic.

Thus one thing that is lost for both our moral and political lives—or at least drawn disturbingly into question—is the sense of trust that underlay much of our activity in the realms of morality and politics. The belief that the morally correct actions will necessarily create a better world for us, our children, or at least that abstraction "the human race," is lost. We may continue to will the good as moral and political agents, but our expectation that the good will be accomplished in any but the most limited way cannot be supported.

III. POSITIVISM AND RATIONALITY

Rationality was once used to refer to a faculty which enabled persons to identify the highest, most appropriate ends for humans as humans. Since the seventeenth century, however, both this usage and its philosophical underpinnings have come under attack. In the last century an antagonistic position has emerged, in the form of positivism.[14] For positivism, the choice of final ends is not susceptible to rational justification. Rationality is limited to the knowledge of the theoretical laws of the natural sciences or the practical application of such knowledge in the pursuit of arbitrarily chosen ends. For positivism, rationality becomes instrumental rationality—a form of reason to which moral values and political norms are external. These latter are considered to be the outcome of interests, choices, forces, or compromises, not rational justification.

The Holocaust may be the *reductio ad absurdum* of positivism.

For positivism, it is possible to assess the rationality of the Nazis' actions independently of any evaluation of the goal to which those actions were directed. If goals are not susceptible to rational justification, then there is no reason that efficient Nazis are not rational. The only irrationality of the Nazi enterprise, on this view, would be inconsistencies or inefficiencies.

Now this conclusion does not *logically* refute positivism. It is possible for a positivist to say that one can criticize Nazism adequately by using concepts such as evil, immoral, brutal, cruel, without needing to have recourse to "irrational" as well. Yet I believe the prospect of calling people devoted to mass murder "rational" does lead partisans of positivism to reconsider the fundamental validity of their position. Being unable to label certain enterprises as irrational becomes progressively less appealing the more we see the scope of the behavior of which humans are capable—or when we become aware that the Nazis thought of themselves as, and were in the positivist sense, rational.

Designating the Nazi enterprise as rational includes the Nazis within a certain realm of discourse. It makes possible certain kinds of arguments with Nazis and rules out others. We do not argue with a person designated as insane in the same way as we do with someone who is rational but cruel or brutal. Desiring to murder an entire race of people is itself conclusive evidence of irrationality bordering on insanity. Interactions with people who have such desires must take the form of dealing with people who have not merely become morally deficient but who have lost their reason (though these two are not mutually exclusive). Of course, the use of terms such as *irrational* or *insane* in regard to whole societies is itself problematic. However, in a century of the Holocaust, understanding which is meant by "social insanity" is crucially important.

Also, we may consider how integral the concept of rationality is to a host of associated, and highly significant, descriptive and evaluative concepts such as sanity, intelligence, and adulthood.

The application of these predicates depends, in part, on the use of *rationality*. For positivism, a person's commitment to mass murder as an end in itself is irrelevant to that person's sanity, intelligence, or adulthood. This implication of positivism not only drastically limits our use of these concepts, it also seems to violate our normal use of them. We do not, I think, normally assess a person's sanity, intelligence, or adulthood simply on the basis of his or her ability to engage in instrumental rationality, to fulfill the demands of scientific, technical, or administrative reason. Nor should we. For to do so would devastate our capacity to evaluate, teach, and criticize each other.

However, the philosophical problem remains: though we may continue to use the concept of rationality in traditional ways, we are no longer sure of our basis for doing so. We know that the Nazis were not simply morally hideous; they were also irrational, unbalanced, insane. Alas, however, we do not know how we know this. Our moral knowledge is both certain and ungrounded.

Habermas's ambitious attempt to overcome this dilemma is an example of how we remain trapped between a desire to transcend positivism and an inability to do so. Habermas seeks to show that the basic social norms such as truth and justice are presupposed by the use of speech. [15] For Habermas, the use of speech for mutual understanding is the model of communication. Such communication, in turn, is said to require a fundamental reciprocity between speakers, and thus to set a model for free and egalitarian reciprocity in all social relations. To violate this model, argues Habermas, is irrational, for such violation entails violating one of the fundamental features of human life as such: the use of language. The problem with Habermas's argument, as he himself notes, is that speech can be used to deceive and oppress as well as to communicate. In fact, the purpose of some communication is simply or mainly to deceive and oppress. Communication between people who are equal with respect to their mastery of a given language can be embedded in an interpersonal or political context of domination and inequality. The superior partners in such communications thus have interests in the maintenance of unequal social relations. The general interest in reciprocity identified by Habermas thus coexists with particular interests in domination and inequality. [16]

Habermas's failure is symptomatic of the difficulties which will attend any attempt to end the reign of positivism and re-expand the concept of reason. Such a move will depend on the identification of a common interest, the fulfillment of which is necessary or appropriate for humans as humans. In the pre-positivist age, this interest was believed to be derived from a shared and universal metaphysical or religious reality. From Plato to the Middle Ages the ultimate reality of the universe was seen as capable of providing a foundation for identifying rationally justifiable ends for humans as humans. With the replacement of metaphysics and religion by modern science and philosophical ontology, however, such an interest can no longer be derived. Thus, antipositivist theorists are forced to seek some other commonality, as Habermas does in language. These attempts, however, founder on the fact that contemporary social life creates us as persons with significantly different interests; for example, it stratifies us by class, race, sex, and nationality. Also, the absence of a compelling and universal metaphysical or religious myth, and the lack of likelihood of one being generated in a scientific age, mitigate against a return to a pre-positivist framework. It is the claim of Marxism that the ending of the above-mentioned stratification and the creation of a classless society are possible. Such a society would found the universal rationality of ends on the shared interest in an egalitarian and free society, rather than depending on belief in a shared metaphysical or religious reality. The

Marxist claim, however, remains hypothetical until such time as a truly communist society comes into existence.

IV. SOCIAL JUSTICE

The Holocaust, as the precipitating event in the formation of the state of Israel, contributed to the creation of one of the most morally perplexing social conflicts of the modern age. Without the rise of Nazism there would not have been sufficient Jewish immigration to Palestine to create even a potentially independent Jewish community there. Without the Holocaust, the world would have been even less sympathetic to the formation of a Jewish state against the will of more than half the population of Palestine (the Arab citizens) and of all the surrounding countries. Finally, the Holocaust won over the vast majority of world Jewry to the Zionist enterprise.

The Holocaust thus served as motive and justification for the formation of Israel. Yet this formation caused—and, some will claim, required—the creation of a stateless mass of Palestinian Arabs. The satisfaction of the claims of justice of the Jews resulted in a great injustice done to Palestinians.[17]

Situations of this kind, I believe, are not adequately dealt with by existing theories of justice. Such theories usually take as their goal the rational support of norms which guarantee a just treatment of all members of a given community. Rawls, for example, seeks to identify those procedures under which a community can identify social norms as just, or under which injustice works to the benefit of the group as a whole or of the least advantaged members. He is not concerned to study the conditions under which a group must accept an injustice from which other people benefit and it suffers. Similarly, Marx sought a "universal class," the redress of whose wrongs would result in the ending of all forms of oppression. Such universalism does not address a situation in which the redress of wrongs of one group requires wrongs done to another.

Now the notion of an ethical agent facing unavoidable moral conflict will be familiar to readers of Kierkegaard and Sartre. However, these authors focus on individual decisions, not on the fate of communities in history. Also, and equally important, these dilemmas are presented

from the point of view of a particular agent forced to fulfill one obligation at the expense of another. The Israel-Palestinian conflict, however,
is defined by the competing viewpoints of two adversaries, two "moral
agents," the satisfaction of each of whose claims requires the negation
of the other's. Compromise is extremely difficult, perhaps impossible,
here: historically, satisfaction of the minimal demands of each group
excluded satisfaction of those of the other. The Zionist movement demanded at least a bi-national state in which they would have equal
rights and powers with Palestinians. The Palestinians sought national
independence in their homeland, with the Jews as no more than a
national minority. Similarly, noncompromise positions are taken by the
leading adversaries (the Palestine Liberation Organization and the Israeli government) in the present.

The result has been a monstrous injustice for the natives of Palestine. Yet this is an injustice for which they do not have, in the usual
sense of the term, the "right" to seek the full restoration of their land
and the return of the Jews to the European and Middle Eastern countries from which they came. This is so because the injustice done to the
Palestinians is itself part of the process of redressing past, and preventing future, injustices to another group.

The morally perplexing features of this conflict should lead us to
examine its peculiar historical features. When we do so, the morally
relevant agents can be seen to include both the general European tradition of anti-Semitism and the particular expression of that tradition
which was Nazism. We might also include accounts of the machinations
of both the imperialist powers and the Arab governments. When we
situate a question of the redress of injustice within such a broad historical context, the achievement of the kind of abstract justice described in
most philosophical accounts of the subject is impossible. There is no
single, identifiable agent of the "necessary" injustice done to the Palestinians.

How then could redress be possible?

When we see injustices as essentially historically situated, and identify general historical factors as their causes, we find ourselves confronted by morally perplexing situations. The Israeli-Palestinian conflict
may be the most extreme example of this, but it is not the only one.
Moral problems of the justice of affirmative action, for instance, reflect
the difficulty we have in understanding how to redress the history of

injustice done by whites to blacks and by men to women. The present instance is all the more striking because it might be claimed that by establishing Israel the Jews have in fact achieved some measure of recompense for the Holocaust in particular and for historical anti-Semitism in general.

Such a claim, however, would suggest that it makes sense to talk of recompense for an event such as the Holocaust—a suggestion which is highly doubtful. It also leaves unsettled the question of the morality of the relation between Israeli Jews and Palestinian Arabs. To address such issues remains a task for future moral theory.

Though I cannot develop such a theory here, I can mention at least two of its features. First, we may note that our moral perplexity over issues such as the Israeli-Palestinian conflict or affirmative action derives partly from our habit of thinking about morality from the point of view of individual agents. We have given little attention to the fact that communities as well as individuals can be both the subject and the object of moral relationships.

This becomes clear when we remember that what is distinctive about genocide is not that it is the murder of a large number of individuals, but that it attempts to destroy an entire, discrete community. Likewise, the identity with which we function as moral agents is not a purely individual one, but is shaped by our participation in and identification with various collectivities. Ethical theory after the Holocaust must reflect these facts.

Second, such an ethical theory will be shaped by the realization that the world in which morality exists is, in certain essential respects, evil. Ethical theory will no longer presuppose that the accomplishment of moral values is possible. In a post-Holocaust age we need a moral theory which situates human actions within a history which compels us toward evil, where (at times) the meeting of the needs of one group inevitably leads it into conflict with another. For this moral theory, tragic choices are not the exception, but the rule, of moral life. Justice is not a norm to be achieved; rather, injustice is a permanent and perennial fact to be lessened. We will no longer believe that achieving justice in a particular situation is incompatible with simultaneously creating injustice.

The effects of history on communities will be seen to be such that human needs can be met only by a gradual lessening of injustice, not by the complete fulfillment of the demands of justice. This reworking of moral theory, of course, requires as a complement more traditional forms of such theory. Without those forms, there would be no independent analysis of conditions of justice, or injustice, at all. But this new form of moral theory, in situating the pursuit of abstract moral values in a historical context of evil, reflects the values and concerns of a modern age shaped by an awareness of evil. This awareness, in turn, can be derived from no historical event more than from the Holocaust.

NOTES

1. Søren Kierkegaard, *Concluding Unscientific Postscript*, trans. David F. Swenson (Princeton, N.J.: Princeton University Press, 1968), pp. 125–62.

2. For a development of this point, see Miriam Greenspan, "Responses to the Holocaust," *Jewish Currents* (October 1980): 20–26.

3. "That period [of annihilation] struck Jews like a cataclysm of unparalleled proportions, a natural disaster without historical precedent or rational meaning. . . . "(Lucy Davidowicz, *The War against the Jews* [New York: Bantam, 1975], p. 466).

> Locked within their ghettos, under strict surveillance and unrefined terror . . . the Jews . . . tried to assess the possible authenticity of the reports [of extermination camps] in the light of experience and logic. The horror of an enterprise that could deliberately destroy human beings who were innocent of any wrongdoing was inconceivable. The senselessness of the undertaking further undermined the acceptance of the information. . . . These evaluations were for the most part shared by all levels of Jewish leadership and by the masses as well. The information about the death camps was rejected all over Europe, not only by the Jews. . . ." (Raul Hilberg, *The Destruction of the European Jews* [New York: Harper & Row, 1961], pp. 474–75).

4. For the conflict between military objectives and the Final Solution, see Davidowicz, *War against the Jews,* pp. 191–97. For a financial cost-accounting which indicates the strain the Final Solution placed on the German economy, see Hilberg, *Destruction of the European Jews,* pp. 644–46.

5. For example, theories of Nietzsche, Freud, Lorenz, and Ardrey.

6. See Hannah Arendt, *Eichmann in Jerusalem* (New York: Viking Press, 1963).

7. Davidowicz, *War against the Jews*, p. 200.

8. Hilberg, *Destruction of the European Jews*, pp. 646–49.

9. For classic liberalism, see the works of John Stuart Mill and James Mill. For an opponent's summing up of liberalism as a theory of history, see Fyodor Mikhailovich Dostoevsky, *Notes from Underground*, trans. Serge Shishkoff, ed. Robert G. Durgy (New York: T. Y. Crowell, 1969).

10. See, for instance: Karl Marx and Friedrich Engels, *The Communist Manifesto*, trans. Samuel Moore (New York: Washington Square Press, 1964); Rosa Luxemburg, "Social Reform or Revolution," in Rosa Luxemburg, *Selected Political Writings*, ed. Dick Howard (New York: Monthly Review, 1971); and the 1891 *Erfurt* Program of the German Social Democratic Party, the most powerful and influential party of the Second International, described in Carl E. Schorske, *German Social Democracy* (New York: John Wiley Press, 1955), pp. 5–7.

11. Rudolf Hilferding, *Das Finanzkapital* (Vienna: Wiener, 1910); Vladimir Il'ich Lenin, *Imperialism, the Highest Stage of Capitalism*, vol. 19 of *Collected Works* (London: Lawrence & Wishart, 1942); Rosa Luxemburg, *The Accumulation of Capital* (London: Routledge & Kegan Paul, 1951).

12. For a survey of Western Marxism, see Dick Howard and Karl Klare, eds., *The Unknown Dimension* (New York: Basic Books, 1972).

13. Jürgen Habermas, *Communication and the Evolution of Society*, trans. Thomas McCarthy (Boston: Beacon Press, 1979), pp. 69–177.

14. The sources of positivism range from Hume's denial of the logical relations between *ought* and *is* to Karl Popper's claim that rationalism in science and social life can only be founded on a species of faith or personal decision.

15. Jürgen Habermas, *Knowledge and Human Interests*, trans. Jeremy J. Shapiro (Boston: Beacon Press, 1971); *Theory and Practice*, trans. John Viertel (Boston: Beacon Press, 1973); and *Communication and the Evolution of Society*.

16. For a development of this point, see my "Habermas and Critical Reflective Emancipation," in *Rationality Today*, ed. Theodore F. Geraets (Ottawa: University of Ottawa Press, 1979), pp. 434–40; and "The Contemporary Critical Theory of Jürgen Habermas," *Ethics* 91 (January 1981): 280–95.

17. For surveys of the history involved, see Walter Laqueur, *A History of Zionism* (New York: Schocken Books, 1976); and Maxine Rodinson, *Israel: Colonial-Settler State?* trans. David Thorstad (New York: Monad Press, 1973).

11

"THE HUMAN MATERIAL IS TOO WEAK"

My father-in-law Jacob Greenspan (of blessed memory) was a diminutive, energetic Polish Jew who survived the Holocaust by fleeing, along with his wife and approximately 800,000 other Jews, into Soviet Russia after Germany invaded Poland in 1939. All Jews who indicated that they wanted to return to Poland after the war were considered potential enemies of the state and sent to labor camps near the Arctic to cut trees. After two and half years in such a camp, the Greenspans were freed, and they made their way to Uzbekistan, where they managed to eke out a living for two years. After the war, they returned to Poland and then to a Displaced Persons camp in Germany from where they emigrated to the U.S. in 1951.

Jacob told me this story in bits and pieces over the years, always reminding me that before the war he had been a communist. "But after I saw Soviet Russia . . . that was the end for me. We used to say, 'Stalin is the Father of the World.' And you know what? they were terrible in that Soviet Russia. Just terrible." Then he would put his hand on my arm, his son-in-law, whom he knew quite well as a leftist, a self-proclaimed Marxist, and say: "Roger, socialism is a great ideal, but the human material is too weak."

It was, I am sure, the particular combination of the Holocaust and what he saw of the Soviet Union that made Jacob doubt our collective human strength. For, after all, the Soviet system had been proclaimed as the antidote to fascism, the hope of humanity's future. With the fascists on one side and the communists on the other, where would there be hope? One need not have a particularly ideological bent to be struck by Jacob's words, for in his mind "socialism" was less about some particular economic and political arrangement than about a society of justice and care: where people, including but not only Jews, would be respected and allowed to live. Jacob's conclusion was that such a society was simply not possible. We could try to be decent as individuals, care for our families and our restricted communities, but the dreams of full-scale change in social life were simply not going to come true.

Though very intelligent, Jacob had practically no formal education, having stopped school at fourth grade to work to help support his family. Yet his piercing blue eyes, his passionate conviction, and above all his experience of life meant more to me than piles of academic books about the possibility or impossibility of social change. He had lost his grandparents, parents, and seven of his ten siblings to the Nazis, and he had lost his faith in socialism to Stalin. He had been a believer, as I was, in the dream of a truly better world. Now he no longer was. I could not ignore what he said, just because it was *he* who was saying it.

Is the human material too weak for a decent society? Certainly there is not a great deal of recent history that would contradict Jacob's truth. If you are not depressed about the state of the world, a friend of mine is fond of saying, you haven't been listening to NPR. Or, as Elie Wiesel put it, "Has mankind learned the lessons of Auschwitz? No. For details consult your daily newspaper."[1]

❊ ❊ ❊

A classic response to Jacob's truth, offered by social theorists as disparate as Max Weber, Karl Popper, and George Bush, is to invoke the virtues of capitalist democracy as opposed to both fascism and communism.[2] At least, these theorists tell us, capitalist democracy is structured around competing social powers: the state is checked by the corporations, and both can at times be confronted by quasi-popular movements. At best, eschewing unrealistic and therefore necessarily totalitarian systems, capitalist democracy allows for the unfolding of the individual and community in a way that is particularly fitting to human nature and objective moral truth. Social problems can be rationally assessed and remedied one by one, an ultimately much more rational and feasible method than trying to impose, all at once and at gunpoint, some self-proclaimed elite's vision of social perfection.

Still the unregenerate socialist despite Jacob's cautionary tales of the Soviet Union, I cannot be a believer in the saving powers of the current system. For one thing, we could (at length) ask whether or not "capitalist democracy" really is a coherent social category, bringing to mind the ways in which capitalist democracy can give way to totalitarianism (as in Germany) or provide extensive support for it (the U.S. giving aid to fascist Chile, or Saddam Hussein, or Al-Qaeda). Alternatively, we might focus on the mass destruction perpetrated directly by the U.S. in Vietnam and Cambodia, as evidence that capitalist democracy is fully capable of mass murder in pursuit of what it takes to be its national interests.

Rather than pursue those lines of argument, however, I wish to bring to mind a form of contemporary mass murder which if it does not stem exclusively from capitalist democracy, has capitalist democracy as its leading cause.

I refer to the environmental crisis. This crisis—which has become more like a long slow decline than a single apocalyptic event[3]—is in some ways a Holocaust writ large, a slow tightening of a human-made noose around all of humanity. Climate change, suddenly more dangerous sunlight, poisoned water, soil turning to desert, a cancer epidemic as much as 80% of which is shaped by environmental factors—these and other aspects of the crisis are responsible for untold deaths, illnesses, social dislocations, and cultural devastations.[4] While environmental destruction is not new in human history, nothing remotely like this scale of devastation has occurred before. That capitalism is central to this process has been shown by many theorists. The relevant factors include: capitalism's built-in necessity for endless expansion, the commodification of all aspects of life, the push to develop technology, the externalization of pollution from the costs of production, and ideology of competitive individualism over community concern, and the development of mass consumerism.[5]

Why invoke the environmental crisis in a book on the Holocaust? After all, the differences between the two events are numerous.[6] The Holocaust involved the centralized, strategically planned annihilation of a particular group, but ecocide stems from a myriad of sources and is not anyone's self-proclaimed goal. Rather, it happens because corporations pursue profit, governments develop military power, ordinary citizens seek a "better lifestyle," and peasants deforest hillsides so they can cook dinner. It is these varying strategies for profit, power, pleasure, or simple survival—and not the grand plan of a 1000 year Reich—which will ruin the world.[7]

Yet if the environmental crisis is not "like" the Holocaust, the latter certainly has some important lessons to teach us about the former. For a start, the Holocaust reveals just how devastating modern states, bureaucracies, and technologies can be; and thus how carefully "ordinary men and women" must be about what they take for granted, how they fit in, and what they accept in their social order.[8] This lesson carries into the present, teaching us that while environmentalists' direst predictions must always be evaluated in detail, they cannot be dismissed out of hand due to a mistaken confidence that governments and corporations would not commit mass murder; or that intelligent citizens might not just sit back and let it all happen. After Auschwitz, such confidence makes little sense. In a way, the Holocaust "prepares" us to take in the fact of ecocide, teaching that there is virtually no limit to human folly, lust for power, and bureaucratic complicity in mass murder. The slaughter of six million Jews and five million other victims, carried out coldly and "rationally" by civil servants and professionals as well as politicians and soldiers, by a "legitimate" government and with the sanction or passive acceptance of much of the rest of the world, is an omen for the environmental ruin we are creating now. This time, however, the catastrophe spreads far beyond the borders of any particular community, region, or nation.

As the Jews, Gypsies, homosexuals, and communists were singled out by the Nazis, so we now hear about the countless indigenous peoples with monstrous cancer rates because of uranium mining on their land, or victims of cultural genocide because their forest homes were turned into so many board feet of lumber, their villages dispossessed in the name of some mindless "development" scheme. Also, when we see the full force of our own denial of the ecological dangers surrounding us, we may remember that it was thought impossible—especially by the victims!—that a modern, industrialized state could systematically slaughter millions of unarmed civilians.

Finally, and of great importance, we must remember the sheer irrationality of part of the Nazi enterprise. Alongside the ideological and financial benefits of the Holocaust, there was a kind of madness when the German government made transporting the Jews to the death camps their first priority, even when that priority interfered with their own military goals. Does this not remind us of how the assault on the rainforest eliminates dozens of species of trees that have been evaluated as having potential for cancer treatment (even for the cancers that may afflict those who direct the assault)?

So if the evils of fascism and communism taught Jacob the weakness of the human material, now it is industrialized capitalism (democratic or non-democratic) that carries the message. Its banners are pesticide-spraying airplanes, dioxin-spewing industrial chimneys, chemical food contaminants, and leaking landfills.

✿ ✿ ✿

Does philosophy have anything to say in response to Jacob's truth, a truth which we keep learning from generation to generation? An initial answer might well be that philosophy is an academic discipline conducted by professionally trained scholars whose goal is the analysis of concepts and the study of worldviews. If some of its practitioners wrestle with the problem of evil, the validity of norms guiding social systems, or the relation between personal and institutional responsibility, others are legitimately engaged in asking questions about the semantics of "truth" or the mind-body problem. Some philosophers, just like some historians, sociologists, or social psychologists, will concern themselves with Jacob's problem, but others will not.

On the other hand, there are at least some thinkers among us who believe that philosophy is deeply affected, perhaps to the point of impossibility, by Jacob's truth. If the rise of science had unavoidable consequences for epistemology, and the French Revolution taught Hegel (and through him Marx) that human communities and norms always exist in history, then the Holocaust and ecocide teach us of the collective human capacity for madness and evil of such magnitude that the very purpose, the very *raison d'etre* of philosophy gets called into question.

To explain this point we could adapt Adorno's bitter quip that "After Auschwitz it is barbaric to write poetry" (Although he did later acknowledge that "perennial suffering has as much right to expression as a tortured man has to scream")[9] and say that after the Holocaust it is barbaric to write philosophy.

What would we mean by that? For one thing, that it is barbaric to write philosophy *as if the Holocaust had never happened.* It would be barbaric to think philosophically, that is, without taking the human capacity for this kind of horrific action as a permanent possibility; and to ask whether one's own philosophical activity contributes in any way to understanding how such an event could take place and how it could be prevented from being repeated. Why would philosophy which ignored these issues be "barbaric"? For a start, it would be (or "is") purely academic in the worst sense of the term, for it would be concerning itself with rationality, truth, moral norms, and philosophical anthropology without ever asking if any of its conclusions could ever have any practical effect. If philosophical practice unfolds in a world shaped by the Holocaust, other forms of genocide, and our actual practice of ecocide; if, that is, "the human material is too weak," then of what possible value are the general principles—from epistemology to ethics—that we seek to analyze, criticize, and create? If the human material is too weak, then for the most part truth will be obscured by error, rationality by madness, virtue and morality by folly, greed, and violence. Why work to find out what rational norms are if science is to be practiced by experimenters in Auschwitz, or to be bought and paid for by corporations, or controlled by an American political administration that can forbid its own scientists from saying what they know to be the case?[10] What is the point of arguing, as Richard Rorty does, that the goal of public philosophy is to find ways for us to be less cruel to each other,[11] if human moral weakness means that cruelty will only continue and (given our increase in technological and bureaucratic power) increase? We cannot do philosophy as if the Holocaust and ecocide are not our primary realities, for if they are, then perhaps philosophy has no point.

To put this point another way: philosophy, no matter how abstruse its subject matter, takes as a kind of transcendental horizon the idea that the truths it produces can be used by human beings. When philosophy is not practiced under that horizon, it becomes no more relevant to the human condition than chess or stamp collecting: interesting or amusing to a certain type of person, but of no use to anyone else. In the face of a Holocaust, or of ecocide, it is barbaric—or perhaps immorally decadent might be a better way to put it—to spend one's life in socially irrelevant pastimes. And this is especially true of an activity with the pretensions to universal truth and human significance of philosophy.

The alternative to this kind of barbaric decadence is a discipline for which certain historical truths, rather than simply a certain method or tradition of texts, is essential. One cannot, after all, do philosophy without the presuppositions that humans are rational, live in societies, and engage in action guided by norms. Similarly, philosophy in the present needs to take for granted the knowledge that human beings can commit genocide and are now engaged in ecocide. In this last process "the whole world will become Jewish,"[12] as ecological damage comes to define the final phase of our existence as a species. The Holocaust and ecocide (along with many other events that could be added to the list) cast doubt on the value of the entire enterprise of philosophy. To ignore them is to surrender in advance to their implication that philosophy is pointless.

Please note that I am not arguing that philosophers should stop philosophizing and simply engage in political action: go to demonstrations, support the Green Party, or picket the local polluting factory. I do not think that we have answered all the questions philosophers should ask. The Holocaust prompts authentic philosophical inquiry, I believe, because to some extent human beings function philosophically. Philosophers—if we have any social value at all—make critically conscious what others take for granted without questioning. It is philosophy's task to ask, for example, if the instrumental concept of rationality which emerged from the Enlightenment made it harder for Germans to distinguish between efficiency (killing the most Jews at the least cost) and morality. Or if the widespread notion of the fit between modernity and progress is undermined by Germany's all too fatal technologically powered moral regression. Or to what extent "ordinary" Germans who perhaps were not themselves particularly anti-Semitic but did nothing to oppose Nazism bear responsibility for genocide. These and many other philosophical questions have been asked already.[13] My point is that if philosophy wishes not to be barbaric or immoral it is no longer free *not* to raise them and others like them.

In contemporary terms, the environmental crisis raises its own philosophical questions. For instance, how is it possible that humanity is engaged in an industrial, economic, and cultural system which is undermining its own conditions of survival? (If this question seems in some ways sociological or psychological as much as philosophical, that should tell us that not only philosophy's subject matter, but also the very idea of its disciplinary boundary, can be called into question by history.) Theoreticians of ecocide must also ask what the history of pesticides, the moral structure of consumerism, and the marriage of empirical research and large profits tell us about our conceptions of and norms concerning science, technology, selfhood, and justice. They must inquire whether after the last century "nature" still exists; and, if it does not, on what we will be able to base norms to guide us towards a rational and sustainable society.

The morally compelling character of the Holocaust and the environmental crisis, the fact that as academics or intellectuals we are not morally free to think as if they do not exist, can be explained in another way. After the Holocaust we cannot responsibly or morally "do" philosophy (or law, or science) without asking ourselves the question of whether or not we are practicing the contemporary, and in particular the environmental, analog of *Nazi* ethics, science, or law. Each of these disciplines, after all, contributed to the Nazi effort. Professors of law designed ways to distinguish degrees of Aryanness or Jewishness; philosophers justified the superiority of Aryan nation; scientists presented anti-Semitism as rational and did vicious experiments on concentration camp inmates. If we are not to repeat these patterns in our own time, we cannot turn aside the kinds of questions I have been raising here by saying "This isn't my area, I'm more interested in the relation between epistemology and philosophy of mind."

Facing the question of complicity is no easy matter. The dominant institutions of Germany— the universities, churches, corporations, and professional associations—went along. In their professional roles they supported or ignored Nazism. And for the most part individuals did not resist in their personal lives.[14] What they did and failed to do is therefore a source of enduring shame for them as individuals and of deep questioning about professional life in general.

The same holds true, I believe, in the present. Therefore we may not avoid thinking about the Holocaust and ecocide because we may be reproducing now what was done then. Since the dominant institutions of our culture are contributing, each in their own way, to ecocide (just as the dominant institutions of Nazi Germany each had their role in the Holocaust), examining our lives in this respect will not be easy. Especially, it will be difficult because many of our society's dominant institutions—*including the ones in which philosophers are employed*—are engaged in a kind of systematic and lunatic denial of what is actually happening. It is as if passengers on the Titanic, when there might have been some hope of saving the ship, were to say: "We cannot interrupt our usual pursuits—dressing for dinner, dancing the night away—for any reason." Thus most universities hold to the same old distribution requirements, the tried and true disciplinary arrangements, the familiar rules that English Composition is necessary but ecological literacy, God help us, is an "elective." Many philosophy departments, and to a great extent the American Philosophical Association, treat environmental issues as peripheral at best: an intriguing, but certainly minor, sub-field.

To go against this grain requires courage. We risk alienating our employers, compromising our standing in the profession, affronting people who think we are overstating the case in an overly emotional way, and—the ultimate threat—not getting tenure. Resisting the mass, lemming-like movement of modern industrial society requires us to put our energy against a seemingly unstoppable mass going in the opposite—and mistaken—direction. Further, like the Holocaust, the environmental crisis evokes overwhelming emotions: fear, anger, guilt, and despair. But unlike the Holocaust, the environmental crisis is happening *now*. There is all the more reason for avoidance and denial, all the more reason to isolate by emotional distance, ridicule, or passive aggressive silence the colleague who stands up at a department or faculty meeting and says: "Something is happening that will not allow us to continue as usual. We need to make some changes."

❁ ❁ ❁

And here, paradoxically, study of the Holocaust offers a resource of support, encouragement, and even inspiration. Here the Holocaust, certainly a confirmation of Jacob's truth, is *also* a challenge to it.

I have in mind the amazing story of Jewish resistance. From smuggling food into ghettos to resist starvation to an uprising which closed the death camp Sobibor, from organizing (against widespread local anti-Semitism) armed partisan groups in the forests to sabotage in the slave labor camps, Jews fought back.[15] While the historical information about the extent of this resistance activity is well known, its reality (apart from the Warsaw Ghetto uprising) is still largely hidden in the public presentation of the Holocaust, as well as in philosophical assessments of the meaning of the event. (I remember hearing on the car radio an NPR special on the anniversary of the closing of Auschwitz, and helplessly yelling at the reporters for not mentioning the revolt which took place in the camp. More seriously, for many years comparable omissions marred the Holocaust Memorial Museum in Washington, D. C.).

For the Holocaust, while it *is* the story of the piles of Jewish bodies from horrific pictures we watch over and over, is not *only* that story. It is also a story of Jews with guns, Jews making birthday cakes of crumbs in concentration camps to keep their spirits up, Jews retaining dignity against more than overwhelming odds. It is the story of suffering and victimization but also of courage and even occasional victory. If we fail to recognize the complexity of this story, we will not have confronted the event in its moral fullness.

❋ ❋ ❋

Philosophy is, if it is anything at all, an attempt to answer the question of what things mean: for instance, what does it mean that humans speak, respond to reasoned argument, believe (or don't believe) in a God, or pursue scientific knowledge? And the importance of philosophy, such as it is, resides in the fact that what we think things mean shapes what we think is right and how we act. Jacob's truth is above all a philosophical truth, for it was uttered by him, in the wisdom of his years, as a reasoned assessment of the meaning of human existence. But Jacob, who spent the war in a labor camp and returned to find his family and community decimated, did not experience Jewish resistance first hand. Though the struggle to survive formed the core of his experience, resistance did not.

That more people killed Jews than Jews resisted, that many times more Jews died than fought back, is surely a terrible truth. But it is not absolutely clear that this numerical difference should obscure what the resistors accomplished and what their resistance signifies for our lives. Quantifying human behavior as the meaning of human existence reveals a particular theoretical commitment that must be argued for. It may be that the remarkable courage and perseverance shown by resistors, even if it is only a small fraction of Holocaust history, represents a human possibility that defines what our species can become as much as what the perpetrators did. The same partiality affects any attempt to make sense out of the environmental crisis. The main engine of modern industrial civilization may be hell bent on self-destruction, but there are many people who are trying stop the machine, or at least slow it down so that the drivers can come to their senses.

How significant human resistance is to our assessment of the "human material" is in part up to us to determine. Are resistors a tiny and insignificant minority or are they an indication that the human material can be much stronger than it usually is? Are they a footnote to an otherwise bleak history or an inspiration for the rest of us, so that we expend our strength to prove that human material is better than Jacob thought? Can we reverse the forces which now govern the world? If Jacob's truth stands, I have been suggesting, philosophy as an enterprise simply loses all but the most minimal of value. But if Jacob's truth must be squared somehow with the truth of resistance, then it is at least possible that philosophy can become part of the resistance movement that Jacob's truth does not include. Since the very transcendental horizon under which philosophy functions requires that Jacob be wrong, it is up to us who claim to be philosophers to prove him so—or give up philosophy. Our resistance to ecocide signals our belief that humans are capable of a decent society. To sustain ourselves in that effort we need to remember that as dark as things seem now, they are certainly no darker than they were for the Jews who resisted during the Holocaust. If they could fight back, so can we.

Rejecting the traditional Marxist notion that socialism was inevitable, Leon Trotsky said that humanity had a choice, "between socialism and barbarism."[16] We who come after Jacob, living in the midst of humanity's self-caused plagues, have a choice as well: between confirming Jacob's truth or trying, with or without rational hope, to show that the human material is stronger than he thought. To do so we must believe that resistance, since it has been practiced by others, is possible; and then we must make that belief the basis of our philosophy and our lives.

NOTES

1. Elie Wiesel, *A Jew Today* (NY: Vintage, 1979), p. 12.
2. Max Weber, *From Max Weber: Essays in Sociology* (NY: Oxford University Press, 1958); Karl Popper, *The Open Society and Its Enemies*, (Princeton: Princeton University Press, 1971).
3. Frederic Buell, *From Apocalypse to Way of Life* (NY: Routledge, 2003).
4. Along with Buell's painfully effective summary of recent material, one might consult Sandra Steingraber, *Living Downstream: An Ecologist Looks at*

Cancer and the Environment (Reading, MA: Addison-Wesley, 1997); and Mark Jerome Walters, *Six Modern Plagues and How We Are Causing Them* (Washington, D.C.: Island Press, 2004). Updates can be found in a variety of environmental magazines and websites, including those of the Sierra Club, Greenpeace, National Resource Defense Council, Worldwatch, etc.

5. See for example Martin O'Connor, ed., *Is Capitalism Sustainable? Political Economy and the Politics of Ecology* (NY: Guildford, 1994); as well as the journal *Capitalism, Nature, Socialism: A Journal of Socialist Ecology.*

6. Historical claims about the Holocaust which follow here are based on a wide variety of sources, including: Francois Furet, ed., *Unanswered Questions: Nazi Germany and the Genocide of the Jews* (NY: Schocken, 1989); and Daniel Goldhagen, *Hitler's Willing Executioners: Ordinary Germans and the Holocaust* (NY: Knopf, 1996); Raoul Hilberg, *The Destruction of the European Jews* (NY: Harper, 1961); Leni Yahil, *The Holocaust: The Fate of European Jewry* (NY: Oxford, 1990).

7. I have developed this comparison in much greater length in *A Spirituality of Resistance*: *Finding a Peaceful Heart and Protecting the Earth* (Lanham, MD: Rowman & Littlefield, 2003).

8. Christopher R. Browning, "Bureaucracy and Mass Murder: The German Administrator's Comprehension of the Final Solution." in Asher Cohen, Jav Gelver, Charlotte Wardi, ed. *Comprehending the Holocaust: Historical and Literary Research* (Frankfurt, Verlang Peter Lang: 1988).

9. Theodor W. Adorno, "Cultural Criticism and Society," in *Prisms* 34, 1981; and *Negative Dialectics* (NY: Continuum, 1973), pp. 362-63: "Perennial suffering has as much right to expression as a tortured man has to scream, hence it may have been wrong to say that after Auschwitz you could no longer write poems. But it is not wrong to raise the less cultural question whether after Auschwitz you can go on living."

10. For these claims in the current context, see Jed Greer and Kenny Bruno, *GREENWASH: The Reality Behind Corporate Environmentalism* (NY: The Apex Press and Third World Network, 1999). There have been numerous reports of the politicization of science in the Bush administration. See, for example: "Ranking Scientists Warn Bush Science Policy Lacks Integrity," Environment News Service, 20 February 2004, http://www.oneworld.net/article/view/79763/1/.

11. Richard Rorty, *Contingency, Irony, Solidarity* (NY: Cambridge University Press, 1989).

12. In response to a TV series on the effects of nuclear war Elie Wiesel said that it seemed "the whole world has become Jewish."

13. By the editor and many of the authors in this book, for example.

14. The most conspicuous collective exception to this was the German church's response to the Nazi euthanasia program, which was instrumental in stopping it.

15. There is an enormous literature on resistance. Besides the overall Holocaust surveys mentioned in note 6, one might begin with Lucien Steinberg, *Jews Against Hitler* (Glasgow: University Press, 1974), and Hermann Langbein, *Against All Hope: Resistance in the Nazi Concentration Camps 1938–1945* (NY: Paragon House, 1994). I have offered a philosophical analysis of the concept of resistance in "The Concept of Resistance: Jewish Resistance to the Holocaust," *Social Theory and Practice*, Vol. 9, No. 1, April 1983, reprinted in Roger S. Gottlieb, ed., *Thinking the Unthinkable: Meanings of the Holocaust* (Totowa, NJ: Paulist Press, 1990).

16. Leon Trotsky, quoted in Jim Higgins, "The Ideas of Leon Trotsky," *Revolutionary History*, Vol.6 No.2/3, Summer 1996.

12

JUSTICE IN A TIME OF MADNESS

Righteousness Ain't As Easy As It Looks

To call for justice is at the same time to rail against its opposite. From Old Testament prophets to contemporary public interest groups, from democracy seeking citizens of Greek city-states to national liberation movements, those who pursue the creation of a more just way of life necessarily seek to remove *injustice*. In their call for better treatment of themselves or others, in their fearless critique of (in Marx's bold phrase) "everything existing,"[1] they align themselves with good and oppose the bad; they support a change for the better while resisting forces that make things go from bad to worse.

How are they able to think their claims and commitments? And how easy—or indeed possible—is it to do so when the source of undeserved pain and loss is not only calculated strategies for power, wealth, or prestige, but a kind of sweeping madness which afflicts us all, even the best of the prophets among us?

* * *

The conceptual structure of "justice" involves, at least, the following: identifying an action or type of action, whether of a person, a group, or an institution; and describing the action in terms of its moral character-istics—i.e., in terms of familiar moral concepts like right/wrong, fair/unfair, just/unjust, proper/improper, decent/indecent, honest/dishon-est, and the like. Also, while the variety of contexts in which injustice arise will make the assignment of responsibility more or less easy, it is also necessary to decide who is responsible for these actions.

Finally, along with identifying, describing, and ascribing responsibility, we need to be able to distinguish the reciprocal positions of profit and loss. Who benefits from injustice and who suffers from it? And what is gained and what taken away?

This conceptual structure is equally present in ancient biblical criticisms of a self-satisfied and corrupt elite as in modern accounts of exploitation or gender discrimination. In Leviticus we are told that the laborer must be paid at the end of the workday. If you hold his wages, he will suffer (19:13). We are also cautioned against favoring any class of people in law courts (19:15). The prophet Isaiah denounced the McMansions of his day: "Those who join house to house, until there is room for no one but you" (5:18).

Similarly, Marx's classic theory of economic exploitation held that the working class created the wealth taken from them by capitalist owners of productive forces. This wealth gave the ruling class personal pleasure and, more important, social power. As a consequence the workers were degraded at work and rendered vulnerable to political powers based in wealth they themselves had created.

As the many authors of this book make clear, the Jewish tradition is filled with clarion calls for justice. These echo in all our sacred texts, and have been equally present in secular Jews' abundant presence in a very wide variety of progressive political movements.

What is perhaps less clear, not only to the Jewish tradition but to all of us, is how to understand justice in the face of madness.

* * *

For example: the Holocaust. Now it is certainly true that if ever there was a paradigm case of injustice, the Shoah is it. The actions involved? Legal and social degradation, theft of property, consignment to slave labor, and mass murder. The injustice involved? That the Jews were innocent. The victims? The Jews. The perpetrators? The Nazis and the collaborators. The benefits to the perpetrators? Among other things, billions of dollars of Jewish property and political power from scapegoating.

The Holocaust, in other words, can be properly seen as a context in which one group unjustly (to say the least) benefits from what it does to another.

But what about that aspect of the Holocaust in which the perpetrators did *not* benefit? What about actions which, while devastating to the Jews, were also damaging to the Nazis? What happens when injustice is bad for those committing it?

To take two cases in point[2] : The death camp complex Auschwitz-Birkenau was not only a site of mass murder, but also a number of factories, some which made essential war material such as ammunition. The factory workers were Jews, condemned to produce the weapons for their own killers. The situation of these workers approached the ideal of capitalism—it cost virtually nothing to keep them alive; and if they died, no one would be held responsible. The cost of producing their labor was virtually nil and there were plenty more where they came from. Yet even in this context some workers were better than others, and it would be more efficient—and thus better for the German war effort—to have experienced workers who knew what needed to be done rather than have to train an endless supply of new ones because the old ones had dropped dead from starvation or been killed.

That is why a number of times the commandant of Birkenau protested the extreme starvation and frequent random selections and killing of his workers. It simply did not make economic or *military* sense. Yet it went on. The goal of genocide, that is, had become an end in itself. It was no longer solely about killing Jews to get their property, or their slave labor; or even to scapegoat the Jews in the pursuit of political power. Death of the Jews had become its own reward.

If this is not madness, what is?

Another case: by 1944 the German Army was struggling in a two-front war. To the east, the Russians had proved surprisingly resistant to a final collapse. In the West the American entry to the continent placed extreme demands on German resources. It was necessary, in the face of this extremity, to be able to move German troops and material as quickly and efficiently as possible. Yet several times trains were not available—they were occupied carrying Jews to the gas chambers. Complaints, demands, and beseeching by army commanders accomplished nothing. From the highest circles of the Party, from Hitler himself, a stark and simple directive appeared: nothing, *nothing*, was to take precedence over the Final Solution. Nothing—not even the attempt to win the war.

To sacrifice one's most needed goal—military victory—in order to kill: is this not madness?

When madness sweeps a social setting, at least one of the typical structures of claims of injustice are removed. We can no longer say "You are oppressing us in order to get . . . " for in this bizarre setting oppression is its own reward.

Of course it might be argued that the Nazi world view was so distorted that eliminating the Jews was in itself a good: a moral imperative, a goal worth sacrificing for. That is to say, from *their* perspective it made sense. Clearly, however, from the standpoint of military commanders and munitions makers, it did not. Moreover, to the crazy person his or her madness always seems reasonable. That is part of the very definition of madness.

In the case of the environmental crisis, the situation is even more strained and morally difficult. For however much we've lost the sense of *benefit* in the last extremities of the Holocaust, the distinction between perpetrators and victims remains all too clear. Mad or not, all the Nazis were killers, and all the Jews, victims.

Now, as in Elie Wiesel's prophetic observation that "The whole world has become Jewish," even that distinction is at time strained to the breaking point.[3]

❊ ❊ ❊

This is not to say that the environmental crisis is not a situation from which some people benefit. Clearly there is a great deal of money to be gotten from selling pesticides, even if they are carcinogens and degrade the soil. Building weapons may lead to enormous pollution, from waste products of building nuclear weapons to the toxic chemicals used to protect tanks and airplanes from rust; but weapons provide power. On a more individual level, non-organic produce is cheaper, non-hybrid cars have more storage space, and some people really do like their thermostats set to toasty in the winter and chilling in the summer. There are a lot of short-term, self-interested reasons to contribute to our non-sustainable form of life.

This is also not to say that everyone's responsibility for the environmental crisis is equal. The peasants who deforest hillsides to cook dinner are not the same as executives of oil companies who obstruct governmental action on global warming. The woman who has to commute many miles to work to support her children is not the same as the lobbyists who convince legislators to keep car fuel efficiency standards pathetically low. The migrant workers who die from pesticide poisons are not the same as their manufacturers.

So, not unlike the way the Holocaust provided enormous amounts of stolen money and served political ends, the environmental crisis—with its attendant unjust effect on human beings and other life forms—does as well.

And yet, there is also an element of madness in all this as well.

When we learn, for instance, that of ten randomly selected newborns the average number of toxic chemicals in their placental blood was *one hundred and ninety*, might we not wonder if the manufacturers of those chemicals, or the people who sell them, or the lobbyists who seek to keep them legal, or those of us who buy them—if all these do not themselves want as desperately as the rest of us to have children born with bloodstreams free of chemicals which cause cancer, neurological defects, and lowered immune systems? Why would we poison our own children if we were not at least a little crazy?[4]

When the government of China refuses to cap its global warming emissions until the average income of their country reaches $10,500, and this despite the fact that with its generally low technological resources and lengthy coastline it is extremely vulnerable to the effects of global warming, might we not wonder why these powerful men think that more cars, TVs, and meat-based diets will make up for floods, droughts, and searing temperatures?[5]

When all of us, the author of this essay no less than any of its readers, more or less continue more or less as usual, turning our minds to all the other Very Important Things we have to do, and allow governments, schools, businesses, TV weathermen, universities, churches and synagogues and mosques, the PTA, and the Knights of Columbus to act as if this isn't happening, or as if enough is being done about it, or as if some mystical "They" (the EPA, the U.N., clever engineers, brilliant scientists, and—God help us—"the market") will take care of it—might we not reflect and see that we, no less than any junkie on the corner, have been led by addiction to our "way of life" into a kind of madness?

⁕ ⁕ ⁕

And so we must ask: What is justice in an age of madness? How are we to call for justice when along with a fully authentic moral critique of the powerful we must turn an accusing finger at our own selves? If

Isaiah also oppressed the worker, if Marx had been a rich capitalist, what then?

Moreover, given the present context: is there anything specifically *Jewish* to be said about all this? We have, as the essays in this book attest, a long and honorable history of moral outrage, of standing up to The People Who Are To Blame. Are we equally good at self-awareness, humility, and seeing our own faults?

To this last point it can with some justification be replied that actually we are. The prophets, after all, were Jews criticizing other Jews (if not themselves). Collectively, at least, the Jewish religion has a long history of moral self-examination. What is the month-long period of Tshuvah [repentance] preceding Yom Kippur, after all, but a time to look closely at our own failings? If the practice has been ignored or trivialized, that does not mean it cannot take on a new and vital meaning tomorrow. Surely environmental tshuvah is called for. Similarly, we are not without our self-critiquing prophets today. From Arthur Waskow and Art Green to Michael Lerner and the staff of the Coalition on the Environment and Jewish Life (COEJL) Jews are telling *other Jews* (as well as the population at large) to repent of their sins and change their ways.

Yet this prophetic call bears a distinct and disturbing mark. Even Arthur Waskow plugs his computer into the same greenhouse gas emitting, power grid as everyone else. Even Michael Lerner damages the ozone layer by flying around the country to promote his vision of a sustainable society in which we heal our relations to the earth. Even Roger Gottlieb uses countless pages of paper in rough drafts to craft his eloquent environmental manifestos.

To the extent that we participate, we are all (at least) a little guilty. To the extent that we are guilty, we are also (at least) a little crazy. As a nation, as a civilization, we may well be on the equivalent of the Titanic, spending an awful lot of time rearranging the deck chairs rather than watching the ocean get closer and closer.

✻ ✻ ✻

Again, we may ask, what specifically Jewish resources do we have to face the crisis—and to face at the same time our complicity in it?

First, there is the capacity to learn from history. If all religions have this, it is important that ours does as well. What was the Talmud, after all, but a drastic shift when history demanded that we abandon a Temple cult in favor of the Near East's first portable religion? What are

Reform Judaism, Conservative Judaism, Reconstructionism, and even in some ways the Modern Orthodox, but shifts in our understanding of Judaism in response to our liberation from the Ghetto, our achievement of equal civil rights in modernized societies, and our realization that most of us will not live in Israel? What is Israel itself but a response to the historically unprecedented reality of the Holocaust?

It is in this spirit that we can note the position of Rabbi Ismar Schorsch, who helped create the National Religious Partnership for the Environment, an interfaith coalition with a wide range of educational programs for faith groups and society as a whole. Schorsch, for many years the chancellor of Conservative Judaism's leading educational institution the Jewish Theological Seminary, is not hesitant to take Jewish tradition to task and advocate a fundamental transformation. It is a mistake, he argues, to use Judaism's rejection of paganism to propel Judaism into an "adversarial relationship with the natural world." When that is done "the modern Jew is saddled with a reading of his tradition that is one-dimensional. Judaism has been made to dull our sensitivity to the awe inspiring power of nature. Preoccupied with the ghost of paganism, it appears indifferent and unresponsive to the supreme challenge of our age: man's degradation of the environment. Our planet is under siege and we as Jews are transfixed in silence."[6] This statement is all the more significant because Conservative Judaism was, as much as any other form of Judaism, a longstanding adherent of the very "one-dimensional reading" of tradition that Schorsch is criticizing. His claim, then, suggests that Jews have been theologically and ethically misguided. We have been participants in injustice, and not known it.

In a considerably milder example, but one which is still in a self-reflective mode, there are suggestions by the Vancouver chapter of COEJL as to environmentally sensible gifts for the eight nights of Hanukah. For example, "turn down the thermostat," "skip a car trip," "recycle your paper," etc.[7] These have a certain cuteness about them, but they also have a deeper meaning. For how many Jews, after all, has Hanukah been a celebration of consumerism; or at least a way to make their own kids feel less left out for not getting all the stuff other kids get at Christmas. The implicit import of the Vancouver COEJL list is, then, a challenge to consumerism—and a reminder that Jews, despite our admirable history of commitment to social justice, may be just as much participants in this addictive displacement of human energy and hope as anyone else.

✵ ✵ ✵

Even deeper than our attachment to consumerism, there is perhaps an equally pernicious attachment that honest self-assessment must prompt us to challenge: our venerable addiction to self-righteousness. After 2000 years of conscienceless victimization by the non-Jewish world, and even more after the horrors of the Holocaust, we may be more than a little entitled to this addiction. We have been brutalized for no fault of our own, all the while teaching a powerful and influential set of moral values. And so we tend to believe that we are (with a few exceptions, such as those "other Jews" who after all aren't being Jewish in the right way) godly, chosen, special, good—the others are, well, "goyim": a term whose literal meaning of simply "nations" should not obscure its usually at least slightly pejorative overtones.

By this time the Jewish self-image of (inherent?) moral superiority has been for many of us weakened by Israel. The Occupation has raised all sorts of ethical questions, and has proven to some that a Jewish state can be as self-interested, aggressive, punitive, and downright mean as a gentile one.

But the Israel-Palestinian and Israel-Arab conflicts are fraught with enormous moral complexity (the cause, some say, of the Death of God—who seems to have collapsed while trying to find an equitable solution).[8] Issues of survival, national identity, continuing and often psychotic anti-Semitism—all these make it reasonable (if not correct) for many to see anti-Zionism as just another round of unjustified Jew-hatred.

When it comes to the environmental crisis, however, there is no defense. Our free and easy participation in the environmental practices of our society implicates us as much as anyone else in its environmental crimes: its astronomical cancer rates, ferocious eradication of species and indigenous peoples, and vastly disproportionate production of greenhouse gases and consumption of energy. No appeal to the saintly values of Chasidic masters or the bold calls for justice of Amos can save us from the realization that we are as mad, and as harmful, as everyone else.

What then should we do?

For one thing, it is necessary to bring awareness of our part in these crimes to our own community as well as to the world at large. Self-congratulating synagogues must be asked about their environmental practices. How is the shul heated and cleaned? Are paper goods used as if they come from and go to nowhere? What environmental values are taught in religious school and stressed in sermons? Thankfully, resources both theological and practical have been created to enable us to give positive, helpful answers to these questions. We can do energy audits, use organic cleaners, and refer to Jewishly authentic ecotheology. And we can commit our institutions to environmental politics with at least as much fervor as we have to racial equality or the struggle against anti-Semitism.

Second, the way the Jewish environmentalist raises these questions must reflect that the Jewish environmentalist, probably not all that much less than the unawakened Rabbi or religious school teacher, is part of the problem as well as part of the solution. There is therefore a *way* to be an environmentalist that is morally appropriate to the issues at hand. It is with deep humility, with compassion for the weaknesses of others as well as our own complicity, with a large dose of self-deprecating humor and no dose at all of thundering denunciations of all those sinners out there. Doubtless there are sources for this attitude in the tradition. Just as Jewish ecotheologians have created Green readings of Torah and Talmud, so Jews much more knowledgeable than myself must find those sources. We have countless examples of Jewish wisdom, courage, self-sacrifice, intelligence, and (often biting) wit—doubtless we can find some examples of humility, moral self-awareness, and compassion for shared limitations as well.

This does not mean that we should stop calling a spade a spade. Pollution, anti-green lobbying, and covering up environmental crimes are what they are—and all the humility and self-effacement in the world should not keep us from saying so. Indeed, we might even think of considering the environmental record of the Big Givers who have enormous power in our communities. Would we welcome a millionaire, no matter how generous, who also funds Hamas or the American Nazi Party? It would, to say the least, be a contentious issue. Why then should we allow a polluter to be on the board of trustees? (Someone might say that Hamas and the Nazis specifically target Jews, and therefore supporting them is much worse than polluting the air and water which, after all, affect everyone. Perhaps—but to the Jewish women dying in droves of breast cancer, an affliction caused or worsened in great measure by pollution, that distinction might not seem so relevant. Which, after all, has killed more Jews—breast cancer or terrorism?)

No doubt all of these moves, especially questioning the Big Givers, will cost money. We environmentalists will be told that we just can't afford to go Green in any meaningful way.

My simple and intolerant response to this is "nonsense." It is *never* an excuse not to do something "because it costs money." Doesn't it cost money to teach Hebrew, support Israel, and counsel the bereaved? Of course, we will be told, but those things we *have* to do, they are what we are.

And if we are not equally, and at times more, about no longer being in full and unchallenged complicity with an environmental structure that is murderous to non-human and human alike, what are we?

Are we not party to a monstrous injustice? And are we not more than a little mad?

NOTES

1. Karl Marx, "For a ruthless criticism of everything existing," in Robert Tucker, ed., *The Marx-Engels Reader* (NY: Norton, 1975).

2. See Lucy Davidowicz, *The War Against the Jews* (NY: Bantam, 1975), p. 466; Raul Hilberg, *The Destruction of the European Jews* (NY: Harper, 1961), pp. 474–75.

3. He made this comment many years ago in response to a TV series about the after effects of nuclear war.

4. "Body Burden: The Pollution in Newborns," Environmental Working Group website:http://www.ewg.org/research/body-burden-pollution-newborns.

5. "China Rejects Caps, Aims to Cut 'Carbon Intensity,'" Planet Ark Website: http://www.planetark.com/dailynewsstory.cfm/newsid/41411/story.htm.

6. Ismar Schorsch, "Tending to our Cosmic Oasis," *Melton Journal* (Spring, 1991); online at Luminaries website: http://learn.jtsa.edu/topics/luminaries/monograph/tendingto.shtml.

7. COEJL website: http://www.coejl.org.

8. An observation attributed to I.F. Stone.

13

WHAT DIFFERENCE DOES IT MAKE THAT WE'RE JEWISH?

Global Climate Change and Transformations in Jewish Self-Understanding

What difference does it make that we're Jewish? As the glaciers melt, the storms increase in power, the weird weather freaks us out, the species go extinct, and hundreds of threatening changes—from tropical diseases moving north to drought crippled agriculture—darken our future, maybe it is just our sheer physicality that matters. Perhaps global climate change is such an overwhelmingly chemical and biological event that all this stuff about God, history, culture, and moral values dwindles into insignificance. To the extent that this is true it is instructive that in some cases the business of being Jewish, about which we make such a fuss, is really not important at all.

On the other hand, the full catastrophe is clearly not yet upon us. Despite everything that has happened already, we still have time to evaluate, plan, and if nothing else take steps to shape how we will respond to the disasters and what the distribution of pain will look like. We may yet be able to mitigate the degree of the calamity, though (admittedly) our chances of doing so in a significant way are speedily diminishing.

And in this process, to the extent that it shapes our moral character and our social ties, our Jewishness is essential.

So what are Jews to make of global warming? And in particular, what are we to make of the fact that as citizens of highly industrialized countries we freely engage in environmentally lethal processes which are already having lethal effects on countries which benefited much less from breakneck "development" and will suffer much more from its consequences.

To begin, even to face the specter of global warming, we will have to overcome our avoidance and denial, our false confidence in technology and bureaucracy, our blind assurance that "*they* just won't let it happen." To do so we should have recourse to our own darkest hour and history's greatest preparation for the perils of modernity. As victims of the Holocaust it is incumbent upon us to remember that "the unimaginable" is often right around the corner. Besides being an exercise in insane ethnic hatred and self-delusion, the Holocaust was also a carefully planned bureaucratic and engineered *program*. The belief that technology cannot be used for insane ends or with catastrophic effects should have died with the trench warfare of WWI, but its purest refutation did not appear until Auschwitz. Witnesses and victims of the Shoah, can we not apply that lesson to the devastations—of climate change but also surely of the poisoning of air, water, earth, and our own bloodstreams—caused by our own bureaucratic and technological regimes? It thus makes a difference that we are Jewish, because this has already been done to us.

Second, and perhaps more difficult, our participation in the creation of climate change poses a profound challenge to our collective self-image. We have described ourselves as a "kingdom of priests and a holy nation," and prayed that the peoples of the earth would acknowledge our God and (by implication) learn God's will from us. We have (justly) celebrated our vastly disproportionate contributions to world culture, and publicly proclaimed our victimization by the world to which we have given so much. We have told everyone else and even more each other how morally special we are.

Yet in the face of global warming, it turns out, we are not really different than any of the "goyim." We too want our big cars, our endlessly expanding economy, our energy-wasting appliances, our jet travel to Israel and Miami. No matter how singular our religious services, cultural style, or average level of advanced degrees may be, we have been and continue to be as short-sighted and selfish as everyone else.

While there are Jewish environmentalists and Jewish environmental organizations, they do not represent a collective accomplishment that sets us apart from any other religious group, which also have theirs. In terms of our collective environmental practice we are (in a phrase guaranteed to horrify most Jewish parents if applied to their children) about average.

There are many lessons to be drawn from all this. Here is one. As Jews, it is now our task to rethink, and act anew, our relations with the several billion non-Jews, as well as countless non-humans, with which we share this planet. Our task now is solidarity. Not to be a moral example as the group who knows better because God gave us a special message God hid from everyone else. Not to be victims in need of special aid. Not even to be a separate but equal community which will take care of itself as other communities take care of themselves. If our resources—from the Talmud to Elie Wiesel, from what we've learned from the Holocaust to what we learned from being part of progressive political movements for 150 years—are distinct, our focus should not be on that distinctness but on our similarity and on the depth of our connections. Just like everyone else, we have sinned and need to change our ways. Just like everyone else we share the earth as our only home and depend on other humans to face this threat. Just like everyone else we are scared of the future, scared to change, and scared to look at the truth. Just like everyone else our present responsibility is to face a daunting future and our own stubbornness and despair, to prove that we are truly made in God's image, and that we—when faced with this desperate choice between business-as-usual and living up to the truth—can indeed choose life.

14

THE OCCUPATION

One Fable, Three Commentaries

Once upon a time there was a people who moved around a lot. They lived here, and then they lived there. They lived all over the place, because whenever they settled anywhere people would scream at them, "You're not like us, get lost!" and they would have to move.

Eventually the people got really tired of having to move and came to a beautiful land filled with peaceful people. There they grabbed up a lot of the land and made the peaceful people live in tents in the desert. Some of the people they let stay but they were cruel to them, and really nice to each other. And as time went on they took more and more of the land, because they were greedy.

The peaceful people never forgot the beautiful land, and fought to be let back in. And they fought harder and harder and harder, until finally the ones who'd stolen it had to let them back. And then they all shared the land and lived in peace.

Soon something wonderful happened. Everyone in the lands around this beautiful land started being kind and good to each other. They shared all the money they had with poor people, and didn't try to hurt their neighbors or people who disagreed with them any more.

And so everyone lived happily ever after.

"What was *that*?" demanded Joel, looking up from the video game that he was playing on his laptop.

"It's a fable," said Sarah.

"It's stupid," said Joel, "it doesn't make sense. Why would the other people get kind just because the first one did?"

"I don't know," Sarah replied, "But isn't that what mom says will happen with the Israelis and the Arabs."

"Quite right, Sarah," said their mother, Rebecca, efficiently scrolling through the "Electronic Intifadah" website, checking on the latest violent Israeli assaults in Gaza and the West Bank. "As we say, 'The road to Baghdad goes through Jerusalem.'"

"I don't get it," grumbled Joel. "Why don't people just go straight to Baghdad?"

"What it means," explained Rebecca patiently, "is that the troubles in this region will be solved only *after* Israel stops oppressing the Palestinians, and gets out of Gaza and the West Bank, and gives them their freedom to live like other nations. My friends in the Palestine/Israel Working Group make it clear: the Occupation is the central factor blocking a just and lasting peace. Once it's ended everyone who wants peace and justice will work harder. And they'll get more support for their work because people will see something good can happen."

"So," said Joel, looking closely at the huge map of the world which covered one wall of the room, "if these people here," pointing at Nablus, "and here," Gaza City, "get better off, then people here and here," Cairo, Damascus, Beirut, "will be better off too?"

"Absolutely," said Rebecca.

"*Why?*"

"Oh this is just something you'll understand when you're older. Everybody who is not a Zionist imperialist knows that Israel is the focal point of the region's problems. Poverty, lack of development, oppressive dictatorship, religious fanaticism—all these would improve if Israel gave back the land."

"How much land?"

"All the land."

"All?"

"Well, all the land they took in 1967."

"So they get to keep some of the land? Will all these people," he pointed to Syria, Iran, Egypt, Hebron, "be happy with that?"

"Well . . . yes."

"And that's what they all say?"

"Well, no. Some do say that the Jewish state must be 'obliterated'—that means completely destroyed. And you see Joel, that's why it's so important for the Palestinians to get their freedom. Because what Israel is doing to them, with our government's help, is just so much worse than anything else going on there. That's the key. And if Israel doesn't get it right, it will destroy itself."

"So how bad is what Israel is doing, Mom?"

"It's like South Africa."

"That's awful," Sarah chimed in. "What about women? Do women have it a lot better in the countries around Israel?"

"Not exactly," murmured Rebecca, so low Sarah didn't hear her.

"But you and Ma would be okay there, right?"

"It's . . . uh . . . complicated," Rebecca answered, imagining herself and her lesbian partner living openly in Cairo, Damascus, or Tehran.

"And do these people get along with each other when Israel doesn't interfere?" asked Joel.

"Not all the time," Rebecca said vaguely, trying not to think of Syria in Lebanon, the latest deaths from Fatah's budding war with Hamas, or yesterday's bomb in an Iraqi marketplace.

"But all the other countries let people vote and have open newspapers and stuff, not like what Israel does to the Palestinians. At least that, right?"

"Not exactly. But if the Palestinians get their justice then the bad rulers of these other countries wouldn't be able to distract their own people by talking about the problems of the Palestinians."

"That sounds good," Sarah agreed. "And then they wouldn't have anything else to distract them with, right?"

Silence.

Joel persisted: "So if Israel gets defeated, or limited, or destroyed, all the other countries will do better? How will that work, actually?"

"Actually," said Faye, Rebecca's partner and the other mother in the home, as she entered the room, "we really don't know. The Occupation is awful, but so are a lot of other things in those countries: lack of freedom, terrible sexism, habitual violence, hoarded wealth, deep ethnic hatred. And anti-Semitism."

"There you go with that 'anti-Semitism' thing again," groaned Rebecca. "That's always used to stop us from criticizing Israel. The Palestinians just want their freedom."

"The Palestinians," hissed Faye, "elected a party whose covenant quotes from the *Protocols of the Elders of Zion* and says Israel wants to rule the world. Does that mean anything to you?"

"Oh, they just say that," Rebecca answered breezily. "They don't really mean any of it. Once the Occupation ends all that propaganda will just stop."

"Besides, you're avoiding the real point," she was almost shouting now, "Israel is racist, and colonialist! It takes all that support our government gives and uses it to control these poor people. They just won't let the Palestinians live."

"And," Faye responded with deadly calm, "if the Palestinians get what they want, or at least what some of them want, what do you think will happen to Israel? If Israel goes back to the 1967 borders, the rulers of other countries won't be able to 'distract' with the Occupation anymore, but what of Israel's very existence—which Hezbollah and Hamas say they will never accept? You think the Islamic movements that won't have non-Muslims controlling one inch of 'Muslim land' will be happy when Israel goes back to where it was in 1967?"

"Just sounds like a war to me," said Joel. "Israel's on top now. And later somebody else might be. War, war, and more war." He folded an old United for Peace and Justice flyer into a paper airplane and sailed it across the room.

"But if peace is made somewhere, it helps other people to be peaceful. Right Mom?" asked Sarah.

"Maybe," said Faye. "Maybe if there were real democracy in Iran, or peace and security and two states for Israelis and Palestinians, or if our government didn't prop up dictatorships in the area to control the oil, or if religious leaders on both sides were truly religious instead of murderous, or if people really tried to understand each other's pain. Maybe one good thing *would* lead to another. And maybe it wouldn't. We can *hope* that a Palestinian state wouldn't be a springboard for more war against Israel, but we can't be *sure*."

"When did you get so cynical?" demanded Rebecca. "Didn't the whole civil rights movement start with a few sparks in Montgomery and Nashville? Didn't feminism start with these tiny little groups of women in New York and Boston? We've seen it, over and over again—when the force for transformation rises up it can change the world!"

"True," sighed Faye. "But it's hard not to despair. I look at the uncontrolled violence of Fatah and Hamas, and the controlled brutal power of Israel. I see all these men with guns acting like, well, *men*! And on the other side the non-violent Arabs and peacenik Israelis and even groups of Palestinians and Israelis working together. I'd like to think 'Yes, even a little hope could turn the tide.'

"And," fiercely, "even if I'm not sure anything will work, I won't stop trying to work for peace.

"All that I'm saying now is that there are a *lot* of things that could turn the tide. It's not *just* the Occupation. The Occupation is not the center of everything wrong in the Middle East. There is no center."

"The Palestinians are starving, while the Israelis live like Europeans," said Rebecca quietly, "and build and build and build until the Palestinians have no water, no land, no crops, no economy, nothing. Are we just supposed to watch and keep silent?"

"Look, even with the dangers of withdrawing, you know I've been against the Occupation forever. It's devastating for the victims and morally and politically degrading for the Israelis. And I do think that there won't be peace until it ends. But I also know that all this talk about how Israel's mistreatment of the Palestinians is the main problem, the issue on which everything else hinges, is just another of way of saying that what Jews do is worse than what anybody else does. There's a name for that kind of thinking and you," long hard pause, "should know what it is."

Rebecca glared back. They would never agree on this, never.

* * *

"Just what the world needs," brooded Ahmed, tapping the ashes from his pipe into an ashtray made from the casing of a tank shell, "another American Jew with another clever justification of the Occupation." Outside his window the Gaza city darkened swiftly as night approached. There had been no Israeli incursions today, and no rockets fired at the Jewish settlements. Yet tomorrow there probably would be more killing, committed by God knows who, for God knows what reason. In the meantime, everyone went around screaming about "Zionism" and "anti-Semitism" and "terrorism" and "imperialism" and, Allah help us, "jihad." And when they weren't just screaming, they were shooting. Israel and Hamas, Fatah and the Syrians, Iran and the Hezbollah and, oh yes, the Americans, they all had their opinions and positions and interests and principles. And they all had their guns and bombs.

But his eight-year-old nephew had just died from complications of a bullet wound, complications that weren't treated because there were no medical supplies, and no one seemed to have enough to eat. His sister hadn't left her bedroom for two weeks, sunk in a depression so deep she could barely look at her own children, the ones still left alive. Outside his window a group of nine and ten-year-olds played at being martyrs, imitating the sounds of explosions with their high-pitched voices.

Ahmed wished he could sit around writing about politics, and be upset because people had the wrong opinions. He'd write something to show that Gottlieb had missed the point, that he didn't get it—that Ahmed, and his family, and everyone he knew were all dying. Some quickly from the bullets and bombs, and the rest slowly from hunger and fear and despair, a twisted knot that was being pulled ever tighter by Israel and America. He'd let Gottlieb and all the rest of them know that he didn't want to kill anyone; he just wanted a life, and a tiny little country of his own to live it in. But in this short time before dark he had to try to get some food for his sister's kids. Then he would go to the mosque for evening prayers, and try to get the words out without crying too loudly.

❋ ❋ ❋

"Sure, end the Occupation . . . brilliant, just brilliant," thought Ari. "Sounds easy. I wouldn't have to be morally degraded anymore. I could go back to Haifa instead of putting my ass on the line protecting these stupid settlements. The ones the government keeps promising to get rid of. And then maybe they'd stop trying to kill us in Jerusalem and Netanya." And maybe there wouldn't be any more children like his niece Leah, who would never walk or see again because she'd been on the wrong bus. Or women like his Grandmother Rose, who'd survived Bergen-Belsen but died in Jerusalem after she ordered a slice of pizza at the wrong time.

Doubtful . . . but maybe.

"But the people who know for *certain* are the ones who don't know anything."

He picked up his rifle and went off to the checkpoint, knowing that he'd probably vote for the peace candidate in the next election, just as he had the last time. Even though the candidate who claimed to be for peace had spent more time showing how tough he was than actually negotiating for peace. He'd go to the next demonstration against the Occupation as well, whether he could muster any hope or not.

IV

Disability and Humanity

15

THE TASKS OF EMBODIED LOVE

Ethics, Religion, Disability

My younger daughter, Esther, is 14. She is developmentally "delayed"—though I think her train is really on another track rather than simply slow to arrive at this one. She also has multiple physical problems, the most serious of which is a generalized muscular weakness leading to a severe scoliosis. Her other disabilities include a seizure disorder, an anxiety disorder, leg braces for the world's most pronated feet, easily dislocatable joints, bad knees, allergic asthma, mild to moderate hearing loss, and digestive problems. On a given day she takes six medications and 10–12 supplements. On a given week she has six therapy appointments. In a given year she might have 40 doctor appointments. However, she also loves pop music and Julia Roberts movies, will talk your ear off if you give her half a chance, had a Bat Mitzvah, and is often the most emotionally direct and spiritually advanced soul I know. Forgetting the precise word, she once called marshmallows "fire ice cream" and she is the only person I've ever met who has totally mastered the Buddhist virtue of sympathetic joy, of really taking complete delight in the happiness of others.

On the scale of special needs Esther fits somewhere in the middle. She is not in a wheelchair, she can talk, and she can relate to others, she continues to develop intellectually. Other cases are easier; and others are much, much harder.

I am describing Esther because I think that her life, and that of her parents as her primary caretakers, constitutes a challenge to many of the ways we have thought about justice, morality, and spiritual life.

Rooted in the concept of the autonomous individual, secular moral theory has little place for persons in need of constant physical help and cognitive support, nor for those who provide care for them. Religious ethics, on the other hand, while much more keyed to the natural frailty and interdependence of all human beings, has had comparatively little to say about the *particular* situation of the disabled and their caretakers. Judaism in particular has rich resources in Moses' speech impediment ("I am slow of speech," he tells God, trying to evade God's command to confront Pharaoh); and in the way Jacob had to wrestle with an Angel and become lame before he could carry on the covenant. Yet despite the occasional lovely folk tale about people praying to God by playing the flute because they are unable to read, disabilities are not given much attention or concern in the Jewish community. And the culturally Jewish emphasis on conventional forms of intelligence is particularly hard on individuals or families facing developmental issues.

As Esther's father—and someone who has spent his professional life writing and teaching about modern social theory, ethics, and spiritual life—I have found these gaping holes intellectually embarrassing and personally alienating.

This essay will continue recent efforts to redress this inadequacy by exploring some of the theoretically and personally vexing problems that come from the condition of serious disability, both from the point of view of the disabled child and from that of the child's caretakers. I will offer many more questions than answers. Indeed if there is any certainty in what I say, it is that the life *of* and life *with* a special needs child is centered on questions which are both inescapable and unanswerable.

As a preface however to what I have to say, I invite the reader to reflect on why it has taken so long for moral, political, and spiritual thinkers—who have written so much about so many things—to think deeply about disability issues.

Here are two reasons I think are important:

First, those who do the thinking and writing about moral life are not the people who take care of children or the dependent. Thus they are not aware of the effects on our lives of having severe disabilities, nor of caring for those who do.

Even when those who care for the dependent—i.e., women—are socially liberated enough to take their place among those who write about ethics, they do comparatively little thinking about the disabled and those who care for them. This may be because insofar as they are able to write about ethics, other people are taking care of their children.

It is, I suspect, only when those who do the caretaking can also do the writing that this issue seriously comes to the fore. Further, it is under the pressure of a disability rights movement that the ethical issues involved are taken seriously by a widening circle. (This is, parenthetically, another example of the dependence of abstract normative thought on historical and political change.)

JUSTICE AND DISABILITY

Who is the typical moral subject? Western philosophy possesses, at least, five dominant moral traditions, each with a distinctive answer. There is the Greek emphasis on natural development and fulfillment, the rights tradition based on rational autonomy, the Marxist tradition based on the collective liberation and fulfillment of the working class, the feminist emphasis on mutuality and empathic connection, and the Judeo-Christian tradition based on submission to God stemming from a free moral choice.

These traditions, as different as they are in many respects, share two premises:

They first presuppose that all moral subjects are *capable* of entering into moral life: that they are healthy, or rational, or capable of empathic mutuality, or possess the ability for committed moral choice, or for participating in democratic processes.

Second, they agree that all moral subjects are equally *free* to enter into moral life. That is, that people's life responsibilities are roughly equal, or, at least, apportioned to their abilities and station. If they are not equally free, then it is our historical task to make them so. Those who are not allowed to own property, vote, receive an education, or become the head of philosophy departments only fail to do so because they are unfairly prevented. Only history holds them back.

Why are disability issues a problem for these moral theories? Because for the disabled, and their caretakers, it may be too physically or intellectually demanding to take part in the processes of deliberation, self-representation, emotional connection, or ethical self-development that these models require.

Consider first the problem of political participation. As Eva Kittay argues brilliantly in *Love's Labor*, formal political equality will not produce a just society as long as the labor of dependency, itself requiring a unique blend of personal involvement and moral commitment, is *culturally* assigned to women; and *economically* assigned to poor and non-white women. Will women who can vote, own property, and become brain surgeons be truly equal if they are expected to take primary responsibility for caring for their own children, their aging parents, their paraplegic sister?

In a society in which political rights are assigned to—and lived out by—autonomous individuals, caring for a disabled child puts caretakers at an extreme disadvantage. One comes to public affairs with half a mind, unable often to think beyond the next doctor's appointment, medical crisis, or need to deal with some caregiver who is not doing a good job. This dilemma is similar to the more widespread phenomenon of women taking a disproportionate amount of responsibility for childrearing and housework. However, in the small nuclear family the period of childhood dependence is contracting, and a good deal of it can be commodified. The much more extreme dependence of those with disabilities goes on forever, cannot be commodified to anything like the extent to that of normal children, and is much more extreme in any case.

Similar problems arise for other moral frameworks. For instance, access to the collective processes of workplace democracy or community control of local economic affairs in socialist or Marxist schemas, is restricted by a life of care. If socialism is impossible because, as someone once said, it requires too many meetings, the caregivers of the disabled are typically too physically, emotionally, and intellectually drained to take part in those meetings.[1]

In feminist models of morality, which often invoke mutually empathic relationships rather than the collective administration of justice, as the key to moral life, there are also problems. The ability to have a truly mutual friendship when you are devoting so much time, energy, and emotion to a child is seriously compromised. At the end of a day filled with anxiety and frustration, I often find myself emotionally drained, too filled with my own feelings to listen very well to those of another, or to reach out across a divide in which I literally feel like I live in another country. Our family has often lived at the edge of emotional and physical (not to mention financial) collapse. (As one acquaintance put it: "You remind me of Job." Why was I not comforted by the remark?) Those friends who have stuck with my family have been people who find it rewarding *despite* a frequent lack of full mutuality.

Similarly, at times my marriage has seemed more like one long exercise in collective medical management than romance or emotional bonding. For a while, as my wife put it, it seemed I had married Esther, so much of myself was given to her care. And my wife, for her part, seemed married to the telephone, through which she engaged in an endless round of making, rescheduling, canceling, and checking on appointments, finding new healers, instructing old ones, getting more information, dealing with teachers and therapists—many of whom *themselves* had to be taught, handled, instructed, coddled, or challenged. Also many of the disabled themselves, for instance those with Autism, are moral subjects but cannot enter into mutual relations to a full degree. They do not give back as they are given to.

As to the Greek model, the melancholy truth is that disability and the care for disability limit our capacity to understand and to act in the world. Simply, disability constitutes a kind of ill health. It can often keep us from fulfilling the model good of our species; and from reaching a characteristically human fulfillment. Caretakers often cannot develop many virtues that we should. At other times we are called on to develop others—like looking on the bright side of things or putting up with endless rounds of frustration—to an extreme degree. If the disabled are to be included as full subjects in this framework, a radically different model of health will need to be presupposed.

How then will the disabled and those who care for them even be thought of as having moral worth, since they cannot take part equally in the activities that define one as a moral subject?

INFINITE WORTH AND FINITE TRIAGE

One answer to this problem of the exclusion or second-rate status of the disabled and their caretakers is to rework our conception of moral life in spiritual terms. I actually have great hope for this framework, and I believe that you cannot confront disability without spiritual resources, not if you are to avoid slipping into bitterness, despair, envy, or numbness.

In a spiritual perspective we concentrate on gratitude instead of entitlement, on devotion rather than publicly measurable achievements, on serving without limit rather than making sure we get full value for every bit we do. Instead of secular moralities based in (individual or collective) self-representation or personal fulfillment, on strict calculations of justice where (God forbid) we never fail to get the least thing we deserve, we offer submission to the will of God and the recognition of the infinite worth of each soul. Like Arjuna in the *Bagavat Gita*, we learn to act without expecting to control the outcome. Like the characters in the Elijah folk tales of Jewish tradition, we think that our child might be a great prophet whose every gesture carries a hidden meaning. Or as Mother Teresa said, when asked how she could get so close to a leper: "He's just Christ in one of his more distressing disguises." We make the best of what we have. And try to find its hidden treasure.

However. Let us keep in mind that disabled children require a disproportionate amount of time, energy, and money. Conventional ethical and religious platitudes about the "infinite worth of the soul" (just like the secular version of "to each according to his or her needs") are not particularly helpful when a child needs one hundred doctor visits a year, three to four hours of direct help for activities of daily living, and between fifteen and twenty hours of indirect help per week for phone calls to doctors, therapists, HMOs, schools, etc. and for strategizing by parents.

Of course if we presuppose a spiritual calculation of the infinite value of each soul, then the enormous care given to the child who has disabilities could be justified—but *only if* that child were the only thing the parents had to do in their lives. However, typically, or at least often, this is not the case. There are other children; and there is the rest of our lives. Given the level of care some children with disabilities require, what are to become of the parents' *other* ethical obligations?

For a start, how are parents of the disabled to fulfill their responsibilities to the disabled child's siblings? When your emotional resources are drained with the disabled child, when you want the "normal" child to make up for what the child with disabilities cannot, when you want *something* not to be difficult? Many answers are offered here: try to find some "special" time to be with the "normal" sibling; explain to them what's going on; give them space to express their feelings; generate resources from extended family, friends, community; remember that love is all that matters. All these are true. But they do not eliminate the haunting sense of guilt, confusion, and self-doubt which arises—bit by bit or all at once—as you see the effects on the other sibling(s) of what you've given to the disabled one. There is a permanent sense of inadequacy: a sense that requires—certainly—therapeutic intervention; but which is *moral* as well as *emotional*.

It is in fact a *moral* question to ask: How much should I give, as a father, to each of my children? When do I say: "I've done enough for Esther, now it's Anna's turn?" Is the fact that Esther's problems are more serious and that her disappointments are less capable of being assuaged by some substitute gratification mean that I can at times turn my back on Anna's needs? Is Anna's heartbreak, even if only of the normal adolescent type, but one made worse by our "special family" status, always to be less pressing than Esther's? And if it is not, then when does the normal child get precedence?

As I've suggested, I wouldn't for a moment deny that there is a strong undercurrent of neurotic angst in these questions; but I would insist that there is something of interest to moral theory as well. Who receives, in this emergency room of family life, the benefits of triage? This is a moral as well as a psychological question. As someone who makes a living responding to moral questions, I ask myself: to which moral theorists—secular or religious—would I turn for help in answering these questions. Consider these stellar names from the canon. Plato, Aristotle, John Locke, Immanual Kant, Moses, Buddha, Jean-Paul Sartre, John Stuart Mill, Karl Marx, John Rawls, Richard Rorty, Carol Gilligan, Iris Young, Michael Walzer, Cornel West, Michel Foucault, Jacques Derrida, Jurgen Habermas. Who among them have directly addressed such matters?[2]

Let's draw the circle wider still. Does the "proximity" of the disabled child necessitate or justify the parents' abandonment of their ethical obligations in the wider society? Is their moral horizon to be contracted to one person? Talking about "infinite" worth is comforting in some respects. As the Talmud teaches, to save one life is like saving the whole world. But how should we respond when we face a whole range of "infinitely worthy" lives, and find that we're equipped with considerably less than infinite resources. If there are philosophical resources here, they must come from Søren Kierkegaard's account of the Tragic Hero, caught between the pincers of conflicting ethical obligations. Or, perhaps, from Job.

People will say, and it is comforting when they do: "You've done wonders for her. You should really feel proud." And at times I do feel that way, marveling at what one acquaintance called our "masterpiece child." But when I think of how I have pretty much abandoned the activist, in the street politics of my youth and early middle age, let countless opportunities to enrich the university where I teach pass by (or even learn most of my students' names), and failed to reach out to friends, that sense of pride can wither somewhat.

Finally, under what conditions—and in what ways—may parents simply give up the struggle to sustain their disabled child's quality of life? This question is usually cast as the quandary of euthanasia: do we abort the damaged fetus, disconnect the feeding tubes, refuse "extraordinary" measures, avoid another "necessary" yet excruciating surgery? Such dilemmas, as important as they are, do not exhaust the range of personal and moral difficulties. Few special needs parents choose death for their children. From my own experience, and that of other special needs parents I know, the questions are at once less dramatic but more—much more—persistent.

Consider Esther again. There is, for instance, a renowned expert of cranio-sacral therapy in Hartford, Connecticut, a two hour drive from my house. Sometimes extraordinary healers give extraordinary results—often it's time and money and effort down the drain. We're already taking Esther an hour away for a once a week treatment by a leading physical therapy office, hoping to handle her potentially life-threatening scoliosis without potentially life-threatening surgery. This takes about four hours of driving and treatment, and costs $100 out of pocket. But perhaps the CS person is worth it. Or perhaps the CS plus the physical therapy would have spectacular results, enabling Esther to develop that sense of her body's position in space to straighten her own spine. Can we afford the extra $120 a week, the extra five hours of driving and treatment? If we can't afford it now, should we make enough changes so that we can? How about a new supplement that will cost, say fifteen dollars a week, but which (some people say) really makes a difference in terms of energy and resistance to colds? We already spend around $1500 a year for supplements, but is that enough? And what will happen to our budget for other things, not to mention our ability to donate to environmental or feminist or human rights causes, if we do so?

A life of triage is morally demanding because there always seems to be so much at stake. So much dependent on the instrumental and moral correctness of what one does. The spiritual view of infinite worth does not solve these questions. There is simply too much infinite worth to go around.

THE RESPONSIVE COMMUNITY

One thing that has been established in writing about disability is that the concept is to some extent socially constructed. Whether or not someone is disabled is partly a function of what resources are available at a given time, what conveniences are "standard" in a society, and how we expect people to behave. Those of us who wear eyeglasses, suffer from asthma, couldn't survive a New England winter without central heating, or use orthotics will have some idea what I mean. The nature of paraplegia will be changed when wheelchair ramps are as standard as elevators.

Similarly, the question arises: what changes are to be made—the institutional equivalents of wheelchair ramps—in equalizing the participation of caretakers of the disabled to make our society more just?

The most important single move here would be to socialize the care of the dependent, with a collective realization that the disabled, their caretakers, the caretaker's extended family, friends, colleagues, and the larger community are all practically and morally connected. This sounds fine in the abstract. (Actually, it sounds pretty good in the concrete as well.) However, we should realize that making the requisite institutional changes so that dependency needs could be met without destroying or crippling the caregiver's own life would require massive alterations in our social priorities.

For instance, before my department criticizes me for missing committee meetings, I could be asked whether my absence has something to do with the hundred or so medical appointments to which I take

Esther each year. Once this fact (and several others) registers, it might be necessary to alter my workload accordingly. If extra help is needed to educate a delayed or hyperactive child in a religious school, perhaps what's necessary is for the budget, curriculum, and structure of the entire school to be rethought, rather than to be told: "We're short of funds for an aide this year; you'd better go somewhere else; or perhaps you could help out in the classroom."

Responding inclusively to such situations would require a massive rethinking of social goals. Am I to be excused from faculty meetings and departmental committees because of my responsibilities for Esther's care? If I am not, is my workplace—unjustly—relegating issues of dependent care to the private sphere with the negative and unjust consequences? If my workload is to be adjusted, then to compensate for my limited participation others will have to take up the slack. The department, and the university, might have to state (and mean) that equitable caring for my disabled daughter is one of their central goods, and that satisfied students, lots of publications, and top rankings in *U.S. News and World Report* do not always outweigh what Eva Kittay calls the "nested dependencies" presented by Esther, myself, and the surrounding community. Institutional and personal "success" would have to be redefined. This would be hard enough at my non-profit university. Imagine a similar situation arising in a law firm, a software company, or the military.

In the modern world, where money, power, commodities, and pleasure have substituted for community, it seems hard to see how this transition might come about. Supporting the disabled and their caretakers in a loving and equitable way may well be the just and virtuous thing to do, but in our present society it seems a very distant goal.

Many of us offer as an alternative a society organized around need rather than autonomous individuality and the marketplace. As much as I long for such a society; and as much as I feel healed when I'm in a setting where even a little of it takes places, there is a problem here. And this problem links my particular situation to what may be the critical question for contemporary social philosophy.

It is this:

Traditional communities governed by ties of need and connection rather than autonomous individualism and commodities not only integrated their members and cared for them in the way modern society does not, they were *also* rooted in hierarchy and tradition. Everyone felt at home, but as in most homes authority and privilege were neither equally shared nor democratically allocated. If you think of gender relations among orthodox Jews or the Amish, for instance, communities where the dependent are typically quite well cared for, you get some idea of what I mean. The questions therefore arise: What would social morality *be* if it were not based on equality, reciprocity, and autonomy? How can a need based social morality function in a modern society? How can we have community without hierarchy defined by rigid tradition? How can we have the freedom and equality of modernity and still respond to people's dependency?

Further, in a modern society in which needs are created by strategic social engineering, how are we to define what real needs are? Could we even envision a society in which people are able to distinguish between real needs and false needs, needs and wants, healthy desires, unhealthy desires, and plain old addiction? And this question necessarily leads to the question of what people deserve. The family triage questions get writ large. How much should we spend on special education, on aides in the classroom, on special exams or curriculum, on helping the disabled work or live like other people? Are we willing to cut the military budget in half to take care of our disabled children? To give retarded adults a decent place in the community? To love our senile elders?

At the very least: when will moral philosophers and theologians bring such questions into the center of what they write and teach?

SELF-REPRESENTATION

While Esther can express her feelings and preferences, she cannot fully comprehend the consequences of life choices, nor assess the effects of her actions on her own future experience. A good deal of the time, when she is allowed to choose her decisions are greatly affected by how choices are presented to her. At other times, my wife and I must straight out speak *for* her.

How do we know when we're doing it right? What norms and virtues are called into play in determining when the way we speak for her is legitimate?

There are no fixed answers here, and certainly no talk of Esther's "rights" will solve the myriad complicated questions. Do we, for instance, allow her to play on the basketball team at her special needs school, knowing that even in this setting of the disabled she is at serious risk to fall and break a bone, throwing off months of work to strengthen her spine? Esther has seen her sister play varsity basketball for years. Now, she thought, it would finally be her turn. Do we let her know why we are forbidding it, in the hope that she will mature in her understanding of her own bodily needs? Or do we simply lie and say that she is too young and could play, perhaps, next year? Or that the coach—who actually left the decision to us—said she would not be safe?

No ethic of rights or justice or greatest happiness can begin to touch such questions. Rather, what is needed is close attention to a range of virtues that must be developed. I have had to work very hard to develop two of these. The first is the ability to look without flinching, denial, avoidance, or false hope, at exactly what my child's disabilities are. What can she do, what can't she do? Where is she safe and where is she in too much danger? When is *my* emotional need to see her have some fun to be put aside in favor of *her* need to be safe? The point is that I will not be able to judge what needs to be forbidden (even though trying it would give her great pleasure) and know what is worth the risk *unless* I first have the courage and honesty to see who she actually is.

The second virtue may be the emotional foundation of the first. It is a kind of acceptance that says, "Yes, my child is disabled. And may die from it. And will certainly be limited by it. And my life, and hers, can still be of value nevertheless." This might have been harder for us then for some others, just because Esther has never had a diagnosis, and thus for many years lacked any clear prognosis as well. It requires a kind of surrender in the midst of never-ending labor. A kind of realization that the desperate effort to fix is both a great virtue and a great vice; that it can accomplish what look like miracles, and also cause us to ignore the beauties that we do have. Combining dedicated effort with detachment is, I believe, something we all need to help us face the vicissitudes of life. In this, my situation is no different from that of someone not caring for a child with disabilities, except that perhaps in mine the issues stand out more clearly.

RAGE, ACCEPTANCE, LOVE

However, while there is a kind of psychological acceptance that is necessary if we are to see our children clearly and hear them even if they cannot speak, spiritual acceptance is a different matter. As I witness my child's undeserved pain, when is rage at God a justified spiritual response? Are familiar spiritual values of submission to God's will or acceptance of our lack of control over life always the preferred response?

Further, when disability is socially caused—for example, traceable to environmental pollution or poverty—what do religious ethics have to tell us about the proper mix of anger and acceptance as I confront my child's fate?

I do not think there is much of value about this in most religious traditions, though perhaps that is only because I haven't looked very hard. I have been told by folks much more knowledgeable than myself that traditional Judaism has spoken very little about the issue. And in *The Art of Happiness*, the Dalai Lama, when asked about the moral choice between abortion and raising a profoundly disabled child, had remarkably little to offer. This might take us back to a point made earlier. Religions, just like political philosophy, are typically created by people who do not care for the disabled.

My own thoughts here are scattered and incomplete, a work in progress.

One thing I'm sure of is that it is a mistake to personalize a social problem. Environmental pollution is responsible, I'm sure, for a significant percentage of genetic problems that cause disabilities. Esther's mysterious neuro-motor problem may well be the result of some environmental toxin that affected my wife during pregnancy. In this way, many disabilities are *social* problems, not personal tragedies. To those readers who have, or know someone who has, breast cancer, the same lesson applies. The disabled need their rights not only after they are born with problems. We also need to exercise the right to an environment that does not damage us to begin with.

As for God? I know that for a start anger at God is a legitimate aspect of spiritual life. To be angry at God is just as much a part of prayer as is love or devotion, awe or repentance.[3] In all those states of mind, feeling and soul, we are confirming that moral laws bind the universe as a whole, just as they bind us as moral agents within it.

That's why I think I'm entitled to rage at God when I witness Esther's pain, her limitations and disappointments. When I think that "normal" love relationships and opportunities will simply never be hers. As she herself said, when I told her that because of her special needs she could not return to her beloved day camp as a counselor: "Now's the time to scream at God."

Yet I also believe that spiritual life need not be bound by any one moral posture—neither anger at the unfairness of life nor gratitude for the blessings we do enjoy. I believe I can thank God for the simple purity of Esther's soul, for the emotional support she gives to our family and her friends, for the glinting light of pure happiness she finds in simple pleasures—other people's as well as her own. I am, like others who suffer unjustly in this life, entitled to rage at God for the unjust pain I feel or witness—if I *also* praise Her for the beauties and joys I've received: gifts that I deserve, really, no more than I deserve the pain.

And Esther, what of her rage, acceptance, and love? Despite her pain, Esther knows that life is beautiful. And when asked, at age twelve, what the meaning of life was, she answered without hesitation: "to love people." (Later she added, "and dogs and cats!")

At her Bat Mitzvah she commented on a passage in Numbers 20, about yet another time when the Jews lost confidence in their journey. "I think this story basically means that you should not complain because it only makes the journey harder. You should just keep going and try hard and not complain. Just do what you have to do to get where you're going. When the Jews were losing confidence, I think they should have breathed and said to themselves 'It's okay, we'll make it.'" Her own life, she went on to say, is that way too.

Another time, as part of a talk she gave to five hundred people at a Friday night service to mark our Temple's commitment to inclusion, she said:

> To parents that have kids with special needs: You need to learn to be patient because it's not your fault that your kid was born like this. If your child is having a hard time, you can give them a hug and say "Everything's going to be okay," and put your arms around them and be loving to them . . . . Having special needs, I have been able to deal

with it in a way that has been calming most of the time. For me, I have been able to be closer to God because of having special needs.

On the other hand, Esther is perceptive enough to see the differences between herself and her able-bodied sister, the other kids on the street, the teenagers in the sitcoms she watches. And, amazingly, she is wise enough to know how to voice her disappointments not only to her parents or friends but to God as well. "God, why did you give me this body, why did you give me special needs?" she will cry out, sometimes in the middle of shooting baskets in our driveway. And then, having demanded an accounting from the Source of Meaning, she will shoot another lay-up.

In her wisdom there lies a great lesson for ethicists and spiritual teachers alike: to acknowledge the pain, to love and care for each other as best we can, and to carry on. But this task will evade us unless we make sure that our moral insights, political struggles, and prayers include the Esthers of the world along with everyone else.

In the end I can say, with Job, "Man is born to trouble as the sparks fly upward." Or as the medieval Catholic priest Thomas à Kempis put it:

> God has furnished us with constant occasions of bearing one another's burdens. For there is no one living without failing; no person that is so happy as never to give offense; no person without a load of trouble; no person so sufficient as never to need assistance . . . therefore, we should think ourselves under the strongest engagements to comfort, and relieve, and instruct, and admonish and bear with one another. (1952, 23)

NOTES

1. I have developed this point as a criticism of Antonio Gramsci in Gottlieb (1987).

2. Ruddick's (1989) exploration of how mothers think about their children would be a good place to start. Ruddick does not examine cases of nonstandard dependence, however.

3. For a long version of my perspective on this, applied to environmental issues and the Holocaust, see Gottlieb (1999).

REFERENCES

Dalai Lama and Howard C. Cutler. 1999. *The Art of Happiness: A Handbook for Living.* N.Y.: Riverhead Books.

Gottlieb, Roger S. 1987. *History and Subjectivity: The Transformation of Marxist Theory.* Philadelphia: Temple University Press.

———. 1999. *A Spirituality of Resistance: Finding a Peaceful Heart and Protecting the Earth.* New York: Crossroads Publishing.

Kempis, Thomas à. 1952. *The Imitation of Christ.* Harmondsworth, UK: Penguin.

Kittay, Eva. 1999. *Love's Labor: Essays on Women, Equality, and Dependence.* New York: Routledge.

MacIntyre, Alasdair. 1999. *Dependent Rational Animals: Why Human Beings Need the Virtues.* Chicago: Open Court.

Ruddick, Sara. 1989. *Maternal Thinking: Towards a Politics of Peace.* Boston: Beacon Press.

16

DISABILITY AND THE TASKS OF SOCIAL JUSTICE

Like all great social justice movements, the full entry of people with disabilities into social life requires that we examine society as a whole and our own individual experience and beliefs, as well as take a new look at the group in question. Given the comparative newness of the disability rights movement, as well as its many unique features, these tasks pose remarkable theoretical challenges and offer rich opportunities for teaching.

1. *What is a "disability"? Who is "disabled"? Who decides?* Is "being disabled" a simple, natural fact about a person, comparable to their height or eye color? Or is it more socially constructed, like "being a resident of Michigan"? Some have argued for the distinction between an "impairment" and a "disability." An *impairment* is some restriction on the normal functioning of a limb, organ, or mechanism of the body. A *disability*, by contrast, is a kind of disadvantage or restriction based in social structure and/or technological development. Five hundred years ago I, with poor vision bordering on legal blindness, would have been seriously disabled. In our society, I need merely put on my glasses to see almost perfectly. My *impaired* vision is, in contemporary America, no *disability* at all. Severe dyslexia causing an inability to read is a big deal today; but in a peasant village in which almost no one was literate, the concept of "having trouble learning to read" would not even exist. If new technology were devised that would compensate for quadriplegia

the way my glasses compensate for my nearsightedness, would people with severe spinal cord injuries cease to be disabled?

Notice also how key the concept of "normality" is here. We generally do not think of babies as "disabled," even though they cannot walk, talk, or feed themselves, yet a twenty-year-old who could not do those things would be. As people approach old age, they generally become progressively less physically able, and often less mentally so. Are all old people disabled? What of conditions such as chronic fatigue syndrome, which can ebb and flow over the course of a week or month? Do people with such syndromes go in and out of the disabled group? Are seven-year-olds who cannot tolerate sitting at desks for extended periods "disabled" with ADD or are they the victims of an educational system which stigmatizes a natural and widespread need for physical movement? If a young woman with developmental delay cannot go into public alone because she lacks the social skills to know whom to trust, is the real disability hers or that of a society in which so many people are predators?

2. *What is autonomy? What is intelligence?* Clearly people with certain disabilities are highly dependent, and this, many feel, is the defining mark of their difference. Yet while people without classic disabilities may not need Seeing Eye dogs or wheelchairs virtually all of us in modernized societies are dependent on other people for food, electricity, housing, information, and medical care (for a start!). We also need the energy provided by the sun, the action of nitrogen-fixing bacteria in the soil, food, and water. Further, at different points in our lives our own needs may vary greatly. Break a leg or pop an eardrum and you find yourself in a radically different position than you were. At other times it may not be us who changes, but the "normality" of our surroundings. A twenty-year-old will do fine if the elevators are out of whack, but someone in their seventies might not be able to walk up fourteen floors. Given the universal fact of human dependence and the way the extent and nature of that dependence can vary over a lifetime, why is it so critically important to distinguish between the disabled and the rest of society? What is gained by making some kind of categorical separation between the two?

As for intelligence: it is true that my daughter, who has a variety of distinct physical and mental special needs, cannot read the *Times*, do long division, or understand the nature of representative government.

On the other hand, societies controlled by people of "normal" (or even "superior") intelligence have created a world in which enormously clever technical accomplishments combine with monumental failures of efficiency, morality, and simple common sense. (One need only think of nuclear weapons and nuclear waste, gridlock, the hole in the ozone layer, or the fact that 29,000 children die *each day* from malnutrition or preventable diseases to see what I'm referring to.)

Again, could it be that focusing on what my daughter lacks is a distraction from our own limitations? Could it be that "normal" society is riddled with such monumental obtuseness that singling out the developmentally delayed as being the ones who are deficient in intelligence is itself an act of monumental *chutzpah*? And perhaps a reflection of our accommodation to the social and political status quo?

3. *How does "disability" relate to issues of justice and politics of identity?* Like other social issues, disability can be thought in terms of justice and recognition; both the protection of rights and the granting of respect and care. Like other groups, from peasants, workers, and women to homosexuals and the colonized, those with disabilities have been marginalized, stigmatized, denied equality, and literally not seen. Because of this shared experience both the condition of and the resistance by the disability community can be explored by applying the familiar vocabulary of democracy, rights, freedom, and respect. In this investigation it must be remembered that human identities are multiple: no one is simply a woman, a Hispanic, or blind. Each person's identity is formed by several social identities: class and race, gender and nationality, sexuality and forms of ability/disability. Further, as white and black women have racialized experiences of patriarchy, so within the disability community there is a hierarchy in which those with only physical impairments have more status and presence than those with mental or emotional ones.

There are also (at least) two ways in which disability issues are unique, and therefore require radically new concepts and policies. First, unlike being female, African American, or gay, having an impairment is a real loss: the impairment makes for an inability where there might have been an ability. This fact should never lead to a global devaluation of the person with the impairment, but neither can Down's syndrome or paralysis be glossed over as simply a "difference," like being of a different race, culture, or gender. A person who cannot walk simply should not be treated exactly like someone who can, at least when it comes to the design of a building.

Second, the need of people with disabilities for extensive forms of personal care creates political issues for their caregivers as well as those with disabilities themselves. The intense physical and emotional nature of caregiving labor, as well as its devaluation in our society, creates a socially and morally problematic situation. Those who care for the extremely dependent carry a burden far in excess of the normal subjects of political life. In many cases they do not have the time, energy, or money to organize, represent themselves in the public sphere, or reshape social life in terms of their interests. Because the labor of dependency is poorly paid and assigned to racial minorities, and doing it well requires a unique blend of personal involvement and moral commitment, dependency workers often lack the time, energy, or resources to represent their personal interests in a public sphere designed for autonomous individuals. Even political reforms based in other struggles may well not be adequate to this one. For instance, although women can vote, own property, and become brain surgeons they will lack real social equality if they are expected to take primary responsibility in the care of their own children, their father with Alzheimer's, or their paraplegic sister.

4. *How do we teach this stuff?* Along with historical and theoretical writings on disability and justice, it is essential for students to get a sense of the actual life experience of those who have faced these challenges. Memoirs, biographies, and films can provide some insight into particular lives.

Also, there are forms of developing awareness that are at least as important as reading books and writing papers. Here are some possibilities: 1. Keeping a journal in which the student pays attention to the way these issues surface in daily life, around campus, in the news—in everything from "retard" used as a putdown to the presence or absence of wheelchair ramps. 2. Having students reflect on their own experiences of difference—how they felt "different," "unable," "less than," when they were bad at sports, late to learn how to read, or lacked friends. Students might write paragraphs on this topic and then read them aloud anonymously in class. 3. Having students share experiences of disability from their own lives or their families: who has a brother with Down's syndrome, a mother with chronic fatigue, or their own unusual condition? 4. Having students "become disabled" for a day or a week. Use a wheelchair, have a scarf over their eyes, tie all the fingers of their right hand together. 5. Having students connect to someone with a serious disability and interview them; or have the person lecture to the class.

In short: make it real.

REFERENCES

Some books you might find useful. There are countless others.

Charlton, James. *Nothing About Us Without Us: Disability, Oppression, and Empowerment.* Berkeley: University of California Press, 1998.

Gottlieb, Roger S. *Joining Hands: Religion and Politics Together for Social Change.* Cambridge, MA: Westview, 2002, Chapter 8.

Kittay, Eva. *Love's Labor: Essays on Women, Equality, and Dependence.* NY: Routledge: 1999.

MacIntyre, Alasdair. *Dependent Rational Animals: Why Human Beings Need the Virtues.* Chicago: Open Court, 1999.

Mair, Nancy. *Waist-High in the World: A Life Among the Nondisabled.* Boston: Beacon Press, 1996.

Meyer, Donald J. *Uncommon Fathers: Reflections on Raising a Child with a Disability.* Bethesda, MD: Woodbine House, 1995, p. 190.

O'Brien, Ruth. *Voices from the Edge: Narratives About the Americans With Disabilities Act.* NY: Oxford University Press, 2003.

Scotch, Richard K. *From Good Will to Civil Rights: Transforming Federal Disability Policy.* Philadelphia: Temple University Press, 2001.

Shapiro, Joseph P. *No Pity: People with Disabilities Forging a New Civil Rights Movement.* NY: Random House, 1994.

Wendell, Susan. *The Rejected Body.* NY: Routledge, 1996.

17

ONE TRUE FAITH

Bill J. Leonard, coauthor

Roger:

He was a smallish, dapper, well-dressed academic. Very accomplished, I found out later, in the history of the Baptists. He had an open, intelligent face, a slight drawl indicating he'd spent a lot of time in the South, and an easy confidence that told me we'd both spent a lot of time giving talks at academic meetings. The references to experiences in church and his explicit Christianity, the carefully pressed jacket and tie, the fact that his academic area was far from my own mix of radical politics, environmentalism, Judaism, and eclectic spirituality—all these really didn't make much difference as I listened to him deliver his paper. And I suspect the same was true for him as he heard me begin my comment, his eyes widening first in shock and then in delighted recognition. For despite my casual clothes, my obviously culturally Jewish mannerisms, and (now not so new anymore) New Left politics, there was a profound fact that joined us together: we were both fathers of seriously handicapped daughters, and both heavily involved in their care.

Soon after we had lunch, talked two hours nonstop, often finishing each other's sentences as we shared our experiences about doctor's appointments, unusual treatments that don't work, the effects of our daughters on our marriages, and how we feel about other people's more or less normal children. Acquaintances who knew us both could never figure out what two such different people were doing together, having dinner in some conference hotel and laughing like hell at a joke about how we handled our daughters' menstrual cycles.

And that is how I got to know Bill Leonard. We very rarely discussed religion, though I do remember once asking him why he was a Christian and he began an answer by saying he was fascinated by the spiritual character of Jesus. But the conversation got interrupted and we never pursued it. He did send me two of his sermons to read—eloquent, morally clear, emotionally powerful, and filled with love. Were the insights necessarily *Christian* more than they might have been Jewish, Islamic, or Buddhist? I'm not sure.

So what have I learned about Christianity, about "interfaith" relations, from my American (not Southern!) Baptist friend?

It is, perhaps ironically, that we have the same religion. Well, neither of us has converted, of course. He still goes to church, I to Temple (and to the yoga mat, the meditation cushion, and places where I can talk to the trees). It is that the religious differences between us are really far less important than what we have in common. We each have our own names for God, religious holidays, precious spiritual teachers, and particular hymns or nigguns that move our hearts. But all these things, while important, are not the heart of the matter. For me, and I believe for him as well, the heart of the matter is a life of love, a sacrifice of public accomplishment to the slow, repetitive, often painful, occasionally delightful, life-long task of parenting our daughters, and a hope that somehow global society can turn toward a modicum of care and reason and away from cruelty, collective greed, and environmental lunacy.

I suppose one could say that we have different religions but similar moral, perhaps even political, outlooks. But I think it is more than that. It is that the very *meaning* of our religious beliefs—his in the Gospels, mine in the moral ideas of the Prophets and biblical injunctions to justice and care—center on the degree to which two highly imperfect men can realize these commands to love our neighbors, see all people as made in the image of God, and replace secular injustice with a moral community. If that is the essential meaning of faith, if the differences in metaphysics or choice of holy book are real but comparatively unimportant—comparable, for instance, to the particular melody to which the words of a psalm might be put—then in just that sense we are co-religionists. There is no interfaith learning here, for there is just one faith.

There are Buddhists and Hindus, Sikhs and Native Americans, Evangelicals and Catholics with whom we share this faith. But we do not share it with the fundamentalists on either (or any) side who are attached to their metaphysics, their particular religious script, their moral arrogance and exclusivity. Religiously I have more in common with Leonard than with the Orthodox Jews who have no sense of the rights of Palestinians; and he has with me far more than with Christians who would cheerfully shoot abortion providers or think that 9/11 is a punishment for homosexuality.

In the end, perhaps, there are only two religions in the world. Ours, and the one which makes creed more important than love, being right more crucial than staying in touch with other people.

Bill:

"Roger Gottlieb understands." That's what I have said almost from the first moment we met years ago at a session of the Religion and Disability group at the American Academy of Religion. We started talking to each other that day and we have not stopped, gathering at each November's AAR for an uncommon meal, part Passover, part Eucharist, part Bacchanal—conversations at once disarmingly cynical and unashamedly spiritual. The process of parenting persons with special needs requires responses (it would be premature to say skills) that no one anticipates acquiring until that moment when a medical professional says something like: "I'm afraid we'll need to keep your newborn for a few days, there are some problems."

And your life is changed forever.

There are multiple stages related to physicians, therapists, teachers, schools, friends, schedules, family life, personhood, and medication, medication, medication. Friends and extended family are at once helpful, frustrating, frustrated, and often easily exhausted. To find someone who understands as Roger understands is simply a gift of grace. He is correct. Each November I say to colleagues: "I'm going to the AAR where I will have dinner with Roger Gottlieb, and once again we will finish each other's sentences." In those moments, as we debrief I know I can whine, rant, confess, weep, laugh, live, and die a little—and Roger will understand. I hope I can do the same for him.

Our journeys are profoundly distinct, yet hauntingly parallel. We both came of age in the 1960s, Roger with a strong engagement in the counter culture, I with a strong engagement in Southern culture, contexts that were strangely radicalizing for each of us. Our professional and personal identities are shaped by academia, research, writing, students, and a love for the classroom. We are married to two brilliant and fiercely independent women, creative intellectuals in their own right, who carry us with patience and wonder into the intense realities of parenting our beloved daughters. Our daughters are delightful and demanding individuals who continue to discover themselves as they move through the stages of their own lives, with us and apart from us. Turns out we are also both people of faith, at times coloring outside the canons of our respective Jewish and Christian traditions, but stuck with and in them nonetheless. As one of us (I can't remember which one) remarked after a particularly impassioned conversation: "We still believe some of this stuff, damn it!"

The traditions, at least pieces of them, still galvanize and energize. I remember the day Roger described his daughter's bat mitzvah, noting that he especially loved being Jewish at those moments when a bunch of adults have to sit down and listen to a thirteen year old teach them something about God. After years of quoting his comment in sermons and lectures it finally dawned on me that Roger Gottlieb knows something of Jesus' context and tradition—who he was and where he came from—that I may never know. They are both Jewish, aren't they? (Studies show!)

At its best, I hope our friendship mirrors Roger's superb phrase (and book) the "spirituality of resistance," a sense of the Sacred that centers us separately and together while freeing us to explore the margins of our own traditions and the world we inhabit. Enlightened and ornery, by grace.

Roger:

It's not hard to say what one loses by having a severely handicapped child. The least important include time, money, and sleep. More deeply, sometimes so deep that (as Bill once said) one cannot even think about it, are personal freedom, dreams of watching a child move into a normally fulfilling life, grandchildren, and a marriage that is not shaped by endless care for a child that never grows up.

But there are also gifts. I sometimes say that with my first child, who was born brain damaged and died after two months, God picked me up by the scruff of the neck and tossed me into a very different room. With

Esther, who thankfully is alive and flourishing, God slammed the door, ensuring that my life would be forever and continuously different.

As difficult as it is, there are also precious lessons to be learned here.

The first is about Esther. She embodies the power of Spirit in a way I have never encountered in another human being. Physically fragile, cognitively impaired, riddled with anxieties, she remains the bravest person I know. She taught herself to shoot baskets by shooting—and missing—her first thousand shots. She gives talks about her life at local elementary schools, even though she is very nervous beforehand. She sits and meditates at a local peace center, goes to Torah study at the Temple with me, and in both contexts shares her often insightful thoughts even though she understands perhaps one word out of three of what the "adults" are discussing—but is still willing to share the truth as she knows it. For her work she socializes with residents at a nursing home—watching them age and age and then drop from sight into death. She sings to them, helps with the board games and the snacks, even though she will have nightmares when she sees them hooked up to oxygen machines or taken away in an ambulance.

"Hear O Israel, the Lord our God, the Lord is One," says the single most important Jewish prayer. And what is it to believe that God is One? For me, it is to believe that One is God—that this life, with all its sorrows and cruelties and imperfections, is a mystery and a miracle. Faith for me is not a confidence that Something Really Nice will happen later, because Someone I can't see is taking care of things. It is about finding the ability to give love now, in this life, no matter how much darkness there is and how much it all hurts. To the extent that I have faith, much of it I've learned from Esther.

And then there is a lesson about myself. For as I come to love, and cherish, and see the wondrous beauty of my handicapped child I have also learned (at least sometimes, and usually with great difficulty) to see the same thing in myself. For am not I, like the rest of us, slow to learn? Don't I forget what I've said I should always remember? Don't my petty, and not so petty, foibles prove that I, no less that Esther, have a basic cognitive impairment?

And yet . . . if Esther is worthy of love, well then so am I. If Esther can be insightful, courageous, and compassionate despite her disability, then I too don't have to be perfect or blameless to do the same. Realizing this has been deeply healing for my own particular brand of neurotic masculinity, which took as its goal always being the best and smartest and most in control person in the room. It has made me, I believe, not only happier and more peaceful but also a lot more fun to be around. This is a gift from Esther's heart to mine. It makes me more able to treasure the One, to care for the widow, the stranger, the orphan, and the earth, and to accept the disabilities that mark the life of every human being I will ever encounter.

In that religion that Bill Leonard and I share, it has brought me closer to God.

Is that not a precious gift?

Bill:

"Nobody works a room like Stephanie." "She never meets a stranger." "Were it not for her special needs, she would surely be running for office!" Across the years, more friends than I can count have offered such descriptions of our daughter after observing her in multiple social settings. Indeed, Stephanie's social skills and networking abilities are truly amazing. They reflect both her determination and her vulnerability, signs of life that at once energize and exhaust, form and inform her way in the world. In a sense Stephanie's social abilities represent a powerful coping mechanism, allowing her to respond to situations familiar and unfamiliar; claim a setting as her own even as she fears it. Even daily transitions do not come easily for her. At the same time, her response to others lies at the heart of her personhood and spirituality, a way of declaring who she is and where she fits in the society around her. Sometimes religious communities have nurtured those skills; sometimes they have inadvertently inhibited them.

Preparing her for those moments takes great energy from us as parents as well as from other formal and informal teachers and caregivers who have known and worked with Stephanie throughout her life. Sometimes she "takes a room by storm" in order to deal with the storm that surely rages within her in almost every new or transitional situation. And therein lies the vulnerability, solid moments when she recognizes what she wants to do even as she is continuously forced to come to terms with inevitable boundaries.

Celebration comes readily, from Advent through Pentecost in the church year, with elves, bunnies, bears, and leprechauns thrown in for good measure. Festivities for her late April birthday begin shortly after

Christmas and are so all-encompassing that one friends calls April "the festival of Stephanie," a description she appropriates gladly.

All this is to say that Stephanie helps me confront my own determination and vulnerability, qualities I can more readily nuance, indeed disguise, but which are no less present in my own social coping mechanisms and fragile spirituality. And perhaps I should stop right there, since Stephanie's life is a constant reminder of the dangers and difficulties of generalizing about who she is and what she means in the church, the world, and of course to God. Her life demands ways of parenting that we could never have anticipated thirty-six years ago. But isn't that the case with all parenting? As time passes and mortality looms large, the thought of someday leaving Stephanie alone in the world may be the greatest reality I have ever confronted. Determination and vulnerability endures to the end.

So in the religion that Roger and I share, we are at once sustained by and gambling on hope.

V

Technology and Death

18

WHAT ARE WE DOING HERE?

I have seen the future, it is murder.
Leonard Cohen, "The Future"

When Apple Computers resident genius Steve Jobs died in 2011 there was a remarkable spasm of media hype about who he was and what he had done for the rest of us. From pundits to the ordinary he was hailed as our Edison, our Disney, and as important as JFK. We were told that he had shaped our lives, changed our lives, and made our lives so much better. This outpouring seemed to me then and still seems to me now to represent a fundamental—and gravely danger-ous—misunderstanding of what in general it means to be human, and what in particular humanity is most in need of right now.[1]

I have nothing against Jobs, who brilliantly combined incredible business sense with an intuitive grasp of how people relate to gadgets. I have nothing against computers, of which I've owned several and in front of which I spend far too much time; or against, for that matter, gadgets. I'm on my seventh mp3 player, which is packed to the gills with my favorite music.

I also say this, let me be clear, as someone who uses the web exten-sively and has played more than a few video games himself (and not the wholesome ones, either). I like my computer, and I like to play games. (There is a no doubt immoral pleasure in going online and beating some no doubt younger people at a game like Halo, and then letting them know they've just lost to a 67 year old.)

But I also like sweets, and eat more than I should. So the fact that I enjoy the kind of things that Jobs made possible doesn't make them good or good for me. I see computers, the internet, and smart phones as a bit like vampires: compelling, charismatic, sexy. But soon after you start to make love to them you realize they are sucking your blood. Indeed, who is not familiar with sitting down to a computer or their phone "for just a few minutes" and later realizing with a start that a sequence of email, web surfing, Facebook, tweets, Instagram, a game, or just messing around has lasted hours?

If it's all so wonderful, why do so many of us get up from sessions like those with a mildly depressed, neurologically hung over feeling? A slightly confused, slightly guilty sense of lost time combined with fatigue, anxiety (there's so much out there, did I miss something good?), and a hard to describe unnatural, electrified numbness, as if the brain has been plugged into something it shouldn't. It may well be that the neurological experience of screens, quick mouse clicks, finger swipes, instantaneous changes, and an endless beckoning world is not good for our brains or bodies. As for the content: a near infinite mall raising consumerism to dizzying heights; a trillion websites and blogs of uninformed raucous opinion; games many of which submerge players in virtual mayhem and fantasy; endless rounds of superficial socializing. All of these are the very opposite of self-knowledge, gratitude, or restraint.

But it is a sign of the incredible spiritual poverty of our time that gadgets like an iPhone or an iPad can be thought of as things which *fundamentally* change our lives, for they do not. They make for some conveniences and some pleasures, certainly, but conveniences and pleasures are not really the center of our lives; or if they are, that tells us something deeply sad in and of itself.

For example: now that I can carry four hundred hours of music on a device smaller than a matchbook, do I understand the music any better? Do I appreciate it more than when I had to take an old LP out of a cardboard sleeve, put it on the turntable, and place the needle on the grooves? Having all that glorious sound at my disposal, in three seconds to be able to choose from thousands of tracks of classical, jazz, new age, pop, or folk—does it make me love it more? Or does it just trivialize the experience so that I take it all for granted?

More important, far more important: now that I have a cell phone and can "reach out and touch" any of my contacts with a quick call or quicker text, do I care about any of them more deeply? Am I any better at keeping in touch with people I haven't talked to for a while, healing wounds from the past, or dealing with differences that arise within my family? Am I more honest about what I feel? More compassionate about other people's suffering? Any less likely to show off when I get an article published or to gossip about some third party whom both my phone pal and I dislike? These are some of the crucial spiritual tasks which I face and I don't see the gadgets making them any easier.

If you have a cell phone which takes videos, plays games, reads bar codes, provides instant maps to anywhere, and can use the half million or so apps available, are you a better person than you were before you got it? Are you more able to handle questions of life and death, to face aging or illness, pain or disappointment? Is a world of terrorism and imperialism, environmental blight and staggering debt, hunger and poverty and sexual violence less awful because you can close your garage door from twenty miles away and access YouTube's twenty-five million videos while you are stuck in traffic or waiting for your coffee at Starbucks?

I've heard all about "there's an app for that." Is there one for wisdom? Let alone justice?

The answer, it seems to me, to just about every one of these questions is a resounding "No." And in just that sense our lives have been barely touched by anything done by Steve Jobs in particular or by the computer-cell phone-iPod-iPad-Android "revolution" in general. And they will still be untouched when nanotechnology puts computer chips in our bloodstream or programs bacteria to serve as sources of information. The essential human tasks remain. And these are, I believe, very easily stated but enormously difficult to accomplish. They are tasks for a lifetime, and ones that cannot be automated, done better by a computer chip, or "improved" out of existence. For individuals they are the spiritual virtues, the practice of which is the only way to get close to long-lasting and non-destructive contentment: mindfulness, self-understanding, acceptance, gratitude, compassion, and love.[2]

The need to develop these virtues is the same as it has always been. "Progress"—especially technological (as opposed to moral or political) progress—is simply irrelevant. As Kierkegaard put it: "No generation has learned to love from another, no generation is able to begin at any other point than the beginning . . . no generation learns the essentially human from a previous one."[3]

It might even be the case that this brave new technology, despite all its convenience, is actually making these spiritual tasks harder. It is already a commonplace that the little magic screens are making us more distracted and less able to connect as members of families or in intimate romantic relationships. Parents complain about how difficult it is to reach their kids at dinnertime or on family outings; and, perhaps surprisingly, kids are complaining about comparable problems in reaching their parents. (Pseudo) connection is breathtakingly easy: dash off a thought on your computer or phone, click "send" and your thoughts can reach an old friend, a near stranger, everyone on your contacts list; or can be posted on a website for all the world to see. Does this make our communications more heartfelt, the result of more care and attention to the words we use and their emotional and moral effects? As we sift through the dozens or hundreds of emails and texts we get each day, do we read them carefully, seriously consider what they have to say, even—outlandish thought—have the time and attention to read them twice?

If the amount of information on the internet is not infinite, it is pretty close. Certainly this can be a real convenience to a writer who is in need of a fact, an image, a quotation. It's a lot easier to just google it than schlep to a library, or even look through my own book collection. Yet could it be that connection to a virtually (!) endless supply of information, products, reviews of products, and spectacle cultivates in us a corresponding endlessness of desire? A sense that no matter how much I've read or seen, there is so much more out there that I'm missing. To the point where no amount of time is enough, and no matter how strained our eyes or our back we still have left so much undone, so many wants, curiosities, and greeds unsatisfied. Having so much, we have too much. Having so much to do, we do too little that matters.

Is life "easier" with all these "conveniences"? In many ways, again, the answer is not at all clear. Wireless email means that there is virtually no place and certainly no time when we can't be "at work." Gee, that's . . . really . . . great. Except now "time off" is virtually impossible. How great is that? The beckoning convenience returns to a vampire face as we start to see that with all these breathtaking technological advances, people have never been so tired, as if some hidden force were draining our energy. Because I use my phone anywhere, people can be pissed off if I don't answer their calls or texts. And I can feel socially constrained never to turn the damn thing off. Because I have so much music available on my satellite radio (slogan: *Everything, all the time!*) I can switch stations until I find something I already like instead of actually listening to something new and developing my taste. The machines replace our memories, our capacity to amuse ourselves if there are no batteries around, and our face to face engagements with other humans.

Some convenience!

Someone could reasonably reply that the web puts at our disposal an incredible range of useful information, from explanations of legal and medical matters that we'd otherwise have to pay a small fortune for to consumer reviews of products and services. From a political point of view, the propaganda and organizing power of social media has proven to be a surprisingly powerful decentralizing force that allows for communication and coordination among the oppressed. And we certainly should not forget the role of the new technologies in the lives of people with disabilities. My daughter, who has multiple physical and cognitive handicaps, surfs the web, began a fledgling blog reviewing films she likes, can check up on her Temple, her old school, her favorite celebrities—all without leaving her room. And there are computerized devices that surely make life significantly easier or at least more tolerable for many afflicted with a host of ailments.

Yet for all its convenience, we can still wonder what there is here that is really of value. In itself, the mass of information is not fundamentally new, just a vastly greater quantity of books, magazines, catalogs, and advertisements on a screen. The shoot-'em-up games and pornographic webcams *are* new, but can we say they are great contributions to human culture? Do smart phones make it easier for people to relate to my daughter—to find out just how much she has to offer despite how much she lacks? Are people more open to the truth of disability—their own personal vulnerability, the inevitability of aging and decline—then they were before we could text each other? The role of social media in the Arab Spring was much celebrated. A few years later, however, we see that all the Facebook pages in the world can't create a society in which democracy, human rights, religious diversity, and environmental responsibility are the norm. With or without millions of smart phones, all these things take a long, slow, immensely difficult process of human emotional and moral development. There can be no shortcut.

Like printed books (which, the bards quite properly warned, would cripple people's memories), the internal combustion engine, and antibiotics, the jury is likely to be out on computers, the web, and cell phones for some time.

The essential tasks of life—how to be kind, good, and wise; how to control one's mind and order one's emotions and desires; how to connect to other people and other species with compassion; how to create a just, caring, and rational society—no machine will take away the essential difficulty of such things. In a time when we are constantly offered things to "make life easier" it might do us good to remember, as Kierkegaard was fond of saying, that sometimes what's needed is a little more difficulty.

Rest in peace, Steve Jobs, and thanks a lot for the toys. And now let's get back to the essential task of being decent human beings.

NOTES

1. Elements of this chapter were published on the web as "Steve Jobs—Rest in Peace, But Let's Not Overdo It," Huffington Post website: http://www.huffingtonpost.com/roger-s-gottlieb/steve-jobs-rest-in-peace_b_1003491.html; and "Video Games: Vampire or Teacher?" Tikkun Daily Website: http://www.tikkun.org/article.php/20090327094600689.

2. This perspective is developed in Roger S. Gottlieb, *Spirituality: What It Is and Why It Matters* (New York: Oxford University Press, 2013).

3. *Fear and Trembling* (Princeton, NJ: Princeton University Press, 1983), pp. 121–123.

19

A SONG SUNG BY THE UNIVERSE

That was the day of the white chrysanthemums, so magnificent I was almost fearful. . . . And then, then you came to take my soul. . . .
Rainer Maria Rilke, "Crowned in Dreams"

If there were no eternal consciousness in a man, if at the bottom of everything there were only a wild ferment, a power that twisting in dark passions produced everything great or inconsequential; if an unfathomable, insatiable emptiness lay hid beneath everything, what would life be but despair?
Søren Kierkegaard, *Fear and Trembling*

Rejoice, rejoice, we have no choice but to carry on. . . . Carry on, love is coming, Love is coming to us all.
Crosby Stills and Nash, "Carry On"

One can think about death for any reason. For me, the following thoughts were occasioned by viewing the French movie *Amour*.[1] For someone way beyond middle age watching the film was, as we used to say, quite a trip. Here you witness the illness, degeneration, and death of an aging French piano teacher, who is cared for by her loving, stoic husband. The acting is superb, the writing spare and focused, the pacing almost in "real time" as the camera lingers on the woman's first stroke, being bathed by an attendant, the husband's excruciating attempts to get her to eat some oatmeal. In the end the husband, overwhelmed with grief for his wife's guttural cries of pain, her loss of even a shred of autonomy or dignity, and perhaps also his own exhaustion, frustration, and anger, takes matters into his own hands.

This is the kind of last weeks, months, or years many of us may well expect. The very great majority of those who read these words will not die of war, starvation, or lack of medical care. Although some, sadly, may be taken early by cancer, auto accidents, or murder, most will die from age: with dementia or Alzheimer's, after strokes or heart attacks or some other slow, debilitating condition reduces us to pale, burdened, endlessly needy shadows of our former selves.

There is an easy way out of the fear and grief this reality generates: to believe that pretty much the way we are now we go "somewhere else." For me, notions of heaven were never what William James called a "live option." The thought that I could be "myself" without a body does not connect to anything I've experienced in life.

How could I be *me* without *my body*? Without emotions—which as we now know are physical phenomena in the brain, glands, and cells as well as psychological responses to thoughts and experiences. Without a specific location—for isn't that part of what it means to have a body: that we are *here* and not somewhere else? How could we be "in heaven" without a body to put us there? And if we have a body, don't we have to eat and drink and breathe and (pardon the indelicacy) excrete? Are there toilets in heaven? And what happens after you flush them?

Similar problems attend notions of reincarnation. What would it mean to be "me again" when I am actually starting another life from scratch, knowing nothing of, never connected to, an earlier "me"? If I do not remember anything of my former life, in what sense is it mine? True, it could possibly have some unknown and probably unknowable effect on who I am now. But that is just as true of the history of evolution, or of the atoms that make up my body. And none of these are generally considered part of my *personal* identity.

It is surely true that some people effectively imagine ways to connect their sense of themselves in this life to an image of immortality; and it is possible that life after death might exist in some way far beyond my current capacity to conceive. All that I can be sure of is that right now *my* comfort must take another form.

A less faith-based, non-metaphysical alternative to heaven and reincarnation is the suggestion that people "live on in the memories of those whose lives they have touched." While in *Amour* the couple had a daughter and one of the woman's students was a successful pianist, it was clear that after the old folks' death both of them would fade from people's consciousness pretty quickly. Outside of the extremely few who are Very Great or at least Very Famous (Plato, Buddha, Stalin) none of us are thought of very much after a few years, or at most a few decades: when the people who knew us for who we were—as opposed to our books or political acts, say—themselves pass away. A faded photo, a passing memory—and then nothing. How often do any of us think of our great grandparents—if we knew them at all? And these were people just as capable of sexual pleasure, boredom, and hope as we are.

Which leaves us—or at least me—with the unshakable belief that I face a future of continually becoming less than I am now: less intelligent, active, and industrious, with worse hearing, eyesight, and ability to concentrate. To whatever extent my family, students, friends, and readers think of me in the present, that awareness will before too long diminish to nothing. There will be a gradual turning down of the volume of my reality until the player, one way or another, just shuts off.

I can still remember lying in bed, perhaps seven years old, crying about all this, terrified at the thought of the annihilation of my budding self-consciousness, of the nothingness to which I would sooner or later be condemned. I kept trying, and failing, to understand—rather, to experience—what it would be like if I were dead; what my mind, my self, would be like if *I* were no longer here. (Needless to say, I didn't get very far in this endeavor.) My mother stroked my cheek and did her best to be reassuring, "Don't worry, this won't happen for such a very, very long time." For some reason that was good enough then. Today Mom's words carry, shall we say, a bit less weight.

What makes aging and death tolerable? Perhaps nothing. Perhaps we must all, as Dylan Thomas put it, "rage against the dying of the light." And really there is nothing wrong with such a response. Surely it is just because the juice of the cherry, spilling out of your mouth onto your shirt and you don't care because it is so wondrously sweet—that it must be bitter to know one day all you'll have in your mouth is dust.

And now there is something vastly more important in the air (and the water, the earth, and our bloodstreams): it is the mass death of all the other species our current environmental practices are causing. A sixth great extinction; the worst, scientists estimate, in the last seventy million years. As I diminish and approach death I cannot be comforted by the thought of how so much that I love will continue, because so much of it will not.

Anne Frank believed:

> The best remedy for those who are afraid, lonely, or unhappy is to go outside, somewhere where they can be quite alone with the heavens, nature and God. Because only then does one feel that all is as it should be and that God wishes to see people happy, amidst the simple beauty of nature. As long as this exists, and it certainly always will, I know that then there will always be comfort for every sorrow.

But what place is there for Anne's remedy for unhappiness when we go outside and find a clear cut forest, a fished out ocean, a river carrying untold tons of plastic waste, or songbirds dying from pesticide poisoning? Will we find comfort? Or will our anger at death simply increase a thousand fold?

But besides anger (and its cousins grief, fear, and regret) there are other (non-heaven, non-reincarnation) ways to face death.

The first is simple and seems almost unarguable. Think of life—and I mean not just our own allotted time but the whole system which makes it possible: planets and seasons, microbes in our gut and nitrogen-fixing bacteria in the soil, the way plants make food from sunlight and water and oxygen and DNA brings the past into the present and the future. If we truly love life then we must love death as well. Without death things would be unbearably crowded, all sorts of folks (in the broad sense) would have nobody to eat, and there would be little room for innovation, growth, and evolution. There would be no way to weed out the maladaptive types, and no way to cultivate improvement, development, and innovation. We would all be fixated in some vastly earlier stage of existence. And 99.99999% of what we get to taste and see in this life, including our own alternately glorious, dopey, confused, and insightful selves, could never have come into being.

Hold onto that thought and join it with another: if I stop thinking of myself like a mountain, or a stone cathedral, or some other item which seems built to last and instead think of myself, my *self*, as something radically different, maybe death would seem less threatening. Maybe I'm not an entity, a thing, a meant-to-endure presence the end of which is some kind of noble, heart-rending tragedy. Maybe I'm just a whole different type of stuff altogether.

Does a song regret ending? As the last notes of the symphony crash into the air and slowly fade, is there some regret from the melody and harmonies whose echoes will soon turn to silence?

Perhaps that is all we are: just a song sung by the universe. Does a song—does my ego—really want to last forever? Thankfully I've grown a bit since I was seven, and now I think not. We—I—will end, and if the song is as sweet as ripe cherries there might be a faint wish from us or others that there be a little more. But if we live with awareness and gratitude, compassion and love, we will face the end of the song with grace, knowing that the composer and performer is not us, but forces vastly larger, more creative, and (almost) infinitely more enduring.

What are these 'forces'? How are they larger and more creative and enduring?

We can start small. Walking my dog this morning through narrow, hilly neighborhood streets, I heard the brilliant "pyou pyou" of a cardinal standing on a tree limb twenty feet over my head. The bird was only about seven inches long, probably weighed less than two ounces, with a small pointed beak surrounded by a quarter inch of black, a tuft of feathers for a pointed crown, and a shockingly red breast and wings. "How does it do that," I thought, "this tiny thing making a noise that can be heard for blocks? A call louder than the loudest whistle you ever heard from that friend in high school who could put two fingers in his mouth and bring forth a shriek that made people cover their ears and would stop cabs in the street?"

After wishing the bird good luck in making a nest and finding a mate, I kept turning it over in my mind: "How does he do that?" I didn't really want the evolutionary history of bird sounds, or a structural account of his beak, throat, and lungs. I was way beyond such technical questions, and into the sheer wonder of it.

By analogy: Sometimes we look at the world's horrors (the Holocaust, slavery, sexual trafficking) and, despite all our sophisticated political *explanations*, still feel that we cannot *understand* how such things can be. Similarly, in moments of grace, we can feel the same lack of understanding, only this time with joy and boundless gratitude rather than despair.

How does the cardinal make that sound? Because the universe has been working for fourteen billion years to create just that bird at that time on that branch on that street. And it has also been working to create me—the person who can delight in the sound and marvel at the universe that made it possible.

Neither the bird nor I will be here—cosmically speaking—for very long. Death is just around the corner (how big a corner I cannot say) for both of us. And it is true, heartbreakingly true, that humans are wreaking havoc with so many other forms of life as well.

Is this a great tragedy? A loss to be hated and feared? In some ways of course. But there are other ways to think about it.

At least today I realize that condemning any reality always presupposes an alternative. If we ask "Is death—my own, or that of an entire species, or of earthly life itself— terrible?" We must first answer: "Compared to what?" Compared to there never having been a universe at all? Or a universe with no life in it? Compared to an evolutionary history so short that before we get much beyond the protozoa the whole thing stops short? What's the alternative to the reality of death? It is, perhaps, nothingness. If you want a world without loss, pain, and—sadly, so very sadly—injustice, try another universe.

Have we declined from a perfect Eden? Or miraculously appeared from nothing?

None of this means that nature is benign, or essentially sweet, or that the lion will ever lie down with the lamb (with both of them getting up afterwards, that is). I do not turn to Nature as the morally pure alternative to Human Culture—though surely it is not morally evil. Nature is not a video about cute animal babies and sweet-smelling orchids. For every species alive today five or ten didn't make it. Every life form lives by assimilating somebody else; parasitic wasps lay eggs in caterpillars, their young eating their way to life. The human engine of destruction is another creation of the cosmos, like the asteroid which destabilized the earth seventy million years ago and caused all those dinosaurs to fade into nothingness.

But nature with all its deaths and disappearances has given us everything we have: everything we love and care for and which cares for us. That gift, I feel (at the good times), is enough.

For me then, comfort comes in having been here at all. That the universe came into existence, and that the combined forces of particles, atoms, gravity, the strong force and the weak force, molecules, cells, DNA, evolution, weather patterns, and the like have enabled me—and the dolphin, the cardinal, the birch tree next to my house, marvels of rainforest and deer leaping through the forest and the sounds of a waterfall—to exist.

These are the forces so much more powerful, creative, and long-lived than my own little self. These are the forces to which I feel compelled and privileged to bow in gratitude.

That it ever was, and that I got to be a part of it. And that along with physical laws and countless species there have been millions of human beings in their own quiet or noisy ways inventing language, science, art, religion, human rights, poetry, chocolate cake, and peanut butter.

Could my life have been easier? You bet, but it also could have been much harder. Have I suffered? Give me a few hours and I'll tell you some details that would make your hair stand on end. Is there incalculable sorrow in the world? Yes.

But at least I got to be here, to love and be loved, listen to Beethoven and Bach, see Mount Everest close up, caress my wife's face, and hold my daughter when she was born. Did *I* make all that happen? Maybe one-tenth of one-tenth of one-tenth of one-tenth . . . (you get the idea). The rest was the product of all those other forces: impersonal laws, wonderfully chance evolutionary developments, the creative capacity of plants and animals and humans, and the support of air, earth, water, and fire.

And they all brought me to the cardinal this morning. Scared of death? Sure I am. I'm no hero and I'll probably fight against the dying of the light like anyone else.

But ultimately I'm just glad I got to be here. And grateful to *everyone* (and I mean that in absolutely the widest sense) who made it possible.

NOTE

1. Earlier versions of these ideas appeared as "Amour, Death, Song," Huffington Post Website: http://www.huffingtonpost.com/roger-s-gottlieb/amour-death-song_b_2880463.html; and "About Death II," Tikkun Daily Website: http://www.tikkun.org/tikkun daily/2013/03/21/about-death-ii/.

ACKNOWLEDGMENTS

My deepest gratitude to my teachers, students, and colleagues; to everyone who seeks to use intellectual gifts in the service of life; and to birds, fish, trees, and all the beings with whom we share this planet.

Sarah Stanton was an encouraging and supportive editor.

Jim Coccolla and John Sanbonmatsu made helpful comments on new material.

Miriam Greenspan—whose editing skills and love have blessed my life for forty years—helped me rethink the Introduction.

SOURCES OF PREVIOUSLY PUBLISHED ESSAYS

"The Transcendence of Justice and the Justice of Transcendence," *Journal of the American Academy of Religion*, Vol. 67, No. 1 (March 1999), pp. 149–166.
"Spiritual Deep Ecology and the Left: An Effort at Reconciliation," *Capitalism, Nature, Socialism*, Vol. 6. No. 3 (1995), pp. 1–20.
"Ethics and Trauma," *Crosscurrents: A Journal of Religion and Intellectual Life*, Summer 1994.
"Can We Talk (About Animal Rights)?" *Harvard Divinity Bulletin*, Vol. 42, Nos. 1 and 2 (Winter/Spring 2014), pp. 6–11. Copyright 2014 The President and Fellows of Harvard College. Reprinted with permission.
"Religious Environmentalism: What It Is, Where It's Heading, and Why We Should Be Going in the Same Direction," *Journal for the Society for the Study of Religion, Nature, and Culture*, Vol. 1, No. 1 (2007), pp. 81–91. © Equinox Publishing Ltd 2007.
"You Gonna Be Here Long? Religion and Sustainability," *Worldviews* 12 (2008).
"All in the Same Boat? Religious Diversity and Religious Environmentalism," Chad Meister, ed., *Oxford Handbook of Religious Diversity* (Oxford University Press, 2010). By permission of Oxford University Press, USA.
"Deep Ecology and World Religion: A Shared Fate, A Shared Task," in Roger S. Gottlieb and David Barnhill, eds., *Deep Ecology and World Religions* (Albany: SUNY Press, 2001).

"Earth 101," Worldviews: Environment, Culture, Religion, *Worldviews*, Volume 8, No. 2–3 (2004).

"Some Implications of the Holocaust for Ethics and Social Philosophy," *Philosophy and Social Criticism*, Vol. 8, No. 3 (1983).

"The Human Material Is Too Weak," in John Roth, ed., *Reflections on Genocide and Human Rights: A Philosophical Guide* (NY: Palgrave-Macmillan, 2005).

"Justice in a Time of Madness," *Zeek: A Journal of Jewish Thought and Culture* (January 2008), http://www.zeek.net/801justice/.

"What Difference Does it Make That We're Jewish? Global Climate Change and Transformations in Jewish Self-Understanding," *Sh'Ma: A Journal of Jewish Responsibility* (Spring 2008). Reprinted with permission from *Sh'ma* (http://www.shma.com) June 2008, as part of a larger conversation about the environment.

"The Occupation: A Fable with Three Commentaries," *Tikkun* (July–August 2007). All rights reserved. Reprinted by permission of the present publisher, Duke University Press. http://www.dukeupress.edu.

"The Tasks of Embodied Love: Ethics, Religion, Disability," in Michael Lerner, ed., *Best Jewish Writing 2002* (San Francisco: Jossey-Bass, 2002).

"Disability and Social Justice," Spotlight on Teaching, *Bulletin of the American Academy of Religion* (May 2005).

"One Truth Faith," coauthored with Bill J. Leonard, in Jennifer Howe Peace, ed., *My Neighbor's Faith: Stories of Interreligious Encounter, Growth, and Transformation* (Maryknoll, NY: Orbis Books, 2012).

INDEX

Abbey, Edward, 12, 39
Abram, David, 12
Adorno, Theodor, 185, 192n9
aesthetic, 7
African Americans, 74
afterlife, 258
Amour, 257
animal experimentation, 70
animals: suffering of, 67–68; uses of, 70.
    See also Animal Rights
animal rights, 67–74, 74n1, 75n4, 133;
    intuitions about, 68; and medical
    research, 72–73; and
    anthropocentrism, 69
anthropocentrism, 26–27, 32, 69
Auschwitz, 197

Barnhill, David, 131
Berry, Thomas, 80
Blake, William, 5
Bodhisattvas, ix
Buddhism, 126, 135; and mysticism, 4;
    Mahayana, 8; Therevada, 8
Bullit-Jonas, Margaret, 120, 122

capitalism, xii, 84, 170, 182–183; and
    environmental crisis, 182–183, 183;
    and the Holocaust, 169–170
Catch-22, 94
civic Environmentalism, 87

climate change, 89n11, 93, 205–206. *See
    also* environmental crisis
Coalition on the Environment and Jewish
    Life, 89n10, 201
Columbia River, Bishops of, 115–116
communication across difference, 69–70
consumerism, xiii, 18, 31, 31–32, 40, 98
cultural feminism, 51–52

Darkness at Noon, 140
Davidowicz, Lucy, 178n3
death, xvi, 100–101, 257–263
Deep Ecology. *See* spiritual deep ecology
desire, 6
despair, xvi
Dillard, Annie, 10
disability, xiv, xvi; and autonomy, 236; and
    caretaking, 221–233, 241–247; and
    community, 227–229; and democracy,
    220–221; and family life, 222–227,
    243–247; and gratitude, 224; and
    infinite worth, 223–224; and
    intelligence, 236; and justice, 237–238;
    and philosophy, 220–231; and
    teaching, 238–239; and technology,
    255; and virtue, 229–230; definitions
    of, 235–236; moral theory, 220
diversity (religious), xv, 83, 107–122;
    dissolving, 116–117; and religious
    environmentalism, 109–124; varieties
    of, 108

ABOUT THE AUTHOR

Roger S. Gottlieb is professor of philosophy at Worcester Polytechnic Institute and Nautilus Book Award–winning author or editor of eighteen books and more than a hundred articles. Internationally known for his work on religious environmentalism, he is contributing editor to *Tikkun Magazine* and writes for *Patheos.com* and the *Huffington Post*. His work has appeared in publications as varied as the *Washington Post*, *Boston Globe*, *Orion Outside*, and leading academic journals. His books include *A Spirituality of Resistance*, *Liberating Faith*, *Marxism: 1844–1990*, and the environmental fiction *Engaging Voices*.